CW01642334

After Modernist Painting

After Modernist Painting

The History of a Contemporary Practice

Craig Staff

BLOOMSBURY VISUAL ARTS
LONDON • NEW YORK • OXFORD • NEW DELHI • SYDNEY

BLOOMSBURY VISUAL ARTS
Bloomsbury Publishing Plc
50 Bedford Square, London, WC1B 3DP, UK
1385 Broadway, New York, NY 10018, USA
29 Earlsfort Terrace, Dublin 2, Ireland

BLOOMSBURY, BLOOMSBURY VISUAL ARTS and the Diana logo are trademarks of Bloomsbury Publishing Plc

First published in Great Britain 2013
Revised and updated edition published 2025

Copyright © Craig Staff, 2025

Craig Staff has asserted his right under the Copyright, Designs and Patents Act, 1988, to be identified as author of this work.

For legal purposes the acknowledgements on p. xiii constitute an extension of this copyright page.

Cover design: Elena Durey
Cover image: Dianna Molzan, *Untitled*, 2022. Oil on canvas on poplar. 81.3 × 61 × 3.8 cm. Courtesy of the artist and private collection and kaufmann repetto Milan/New York. Photo: Brica Wilcox

All rights reserved. No part of this publication may be reproduced or transmitted in any form or by any means, electronic or mechanical, including photocopying, recording, or any information storage or retrieval system, without prior permission in writing from the publishers.

Bloomsbury Publishing Plc does not have any control over, or responsibility for, any third-party websites referred to or in this book. All internet addresses given in this book were correct at the time of going to press. The author and publisher regret any inconvenience caused if addresses have changed or sites have ceased to exist, but can accept no responsibility for any such changes.

A catalogue record for this book is available from the British Library.

Library of Congress Cataloging-in-Publication Data
Names: Staff, Craig G., author.
Title: After modernist painting : the history of a contemporary practice / [Craig Staff].
Description: Revised and updated edition. | London : Bloomsbury Visual Arts, 2025. | Includes bibliographical references and index.
Identifiers: LCCN 2024026287 (print) | LCCN 2024026288 (ebook) | ISBN 9781350363823 (paperback) | ISBN 9781350363830 (hardback) | ISBN 9781350363847 (pdf) | ISBN 9781350363854 (ebook)
Subjects: LCSH: Painting, Modern–20th century. | Painting, Modern–21st century. | Conceptual art. | Minimal art. | Modernism (Art)
Classification: LCC ND196.2 .S73 2025 (print) | LCC ND196.2 (ebook) | DDC 759.06–dc23/eng/20240717
LC record available at https://lccn.loc.gov/2024026287
LC ebook record available at https://lccn.loc.gov/2024026288

ISBN: HB: 978-1-3503-6383-0
PB: 978-1-3503-6382-3
ePDF: 978-1-3503-6384-7
eBook: 978-1-3503-6385-4

Typeset by Integra Software Services Pvt. Ltd.
Printed and bound in India

To find out more about our authors and books visit www.bloomsbury.com and sign up for our newsletters.

CONTENTS

ILLUSTRATIONS

Color Plates

Figures

PREFACE TO THE SECOND EDITION

Approaching the tenth anniversary of when *After Modernist Painting* was first published, I was keen to explore the possibility of a second edition which would acknowledge the shifts and developments that had occurred during this ten-year period. In one sense, not only was I keen to articulate what I felt was the situation with painting in the present moment, but moreover how our understanding of those practices and debates over a period of some sixty odd years has also evolved.

The original impetus behind the first edition, namely to provide the interested reader with an inclusive account rather than a comprehensive survey of painting since the publication of "Modernist Painting" by Clement Greenberg, hasn't changed. That said, in addition to making a number of revisions, including taking the opportunity to further broaden the scope of the book's focus, this new edition also includes an additional chapter which, in effect, attempts to bring the book's principal focus up to date.

The original edition was borne out of the fact that in my estimation, an account of painting's evolution, if one can call it such, which emerged out of the practices and debates that worked to frame modernism had yet to be published. In seeking to address this particular omission, I envisaged its readership to be primarily those who were keen on learning more about what constituted a complex arena of artistic activity. Encouragingly, and in the months and indeed years following its publication I became aware of the breadth of its readership, from practicing artists to undergraduate students, from scholars working in a cognate field to researchers pursuing their Ph.D. It is my hope that the publication of the second edition will engender a readership of equivalent breadth and as such, will provide a further measure of insight, knowledge, and understanding into the manifold approaches to and interpretations of painting since the publication of Greenberg's text.

ACKNOWLEDGEMENTS

As I soon recognized whilst working on the original edition, a book of this nature is reliant upon the generosity and insight of those artists whose work it seeks to consider. This remains very much the case for the second edition. To this end, I would like to thank those artists who were obliging with regard to my requests. My gratitude extends to those galleries, museums and artists' estates who were equally accommodating and willing to support the project through the provision of images.

As with the first edition, what follows is dedicated to Judith, Céadach, Saoirse and Thora.

Introduction

Originally written for the United States Information Agency in the spring of 1960 and published as a pamphlet the following December by *The Voices of America* as part of their Forum Lectures Visual Arts Series, in many respects "Modernist Painting" can be understood as being emblematic of Clement Greenberg's criticism as a whole.[1] Certainly, reading the text as an elucidation of painting through the interpretive framework of modernism, albeit one that foregrounded the formal characterization of the artwork brings into focus the basic terms upon which Greenberg's criticism remains even today most directly associated with. However, whilst his claims did not go unnoticed—according to Thierry de Duve, the text stood as "a sort of aesthetic Organon for a whole generation of artists," neither did they go unchallenged.[2] Emerging out of a concurrent range of alternate practices that were all somehow antithetical to the critic's claims on behalf of modernism and for that matter, painting generally, amongst Greenberg's detractors were those who held a particular disdain for what was perceived to be his deeply entrenched formalist orthodoxy.

Nevertheless, within the historical milieu of the 1960s art scene, and for those today that are keen to understand the nature of the debates as they unfolded during this period in recent art history, "Modernist Painting" remains a significant benchmark.

Given Greenberg's stated ambitions for painting and their place within the discourses of modern art, it would seem appropriate then that an account of the medium that encompasses the practices, theories and debates of a period of approximately sixty years should use Greenberg's text as both a critical point of departure and as a historical backdrop. This is reflected in the title of the study that can be read in one of two ways. On one level, *After Modernist Painting* concerns a period of artistic practice and theoretical debate that emerged after the publication of Greenberg's text. Somewhat more speculatively, the title is also suggestive of a question that centers upon what constituted the terms of painting as a form of artistic practice *after* modernist painting, that is, when painting was no longer "modernist."

What then follows is a critical perspective upon painting during approximately the last half-century, rather than a definitive history thereof. In this respect, the book has sought to provide a measure of context to the ideas that informed the development of painting as a contemporary art during this period. Bringing critical shape allied with some form of rationale behind why certain painters painted what they painted and in turn, why certain critics conferred onto those self-same paintings certain values, opinions, or readings, the book equally doesn't lose sight of the particularity of the individual paintings themselves.

Interwoven within the argument that follows are two key strands that, to a certain extent work to bind together the argument as a whole. Firstly, at certain points the text seeks recourse to what were some of the more familiar, if not contentious claims Greenberg made on behalf of painting. Secondly, the question of abstract painting, its various histories, theorizations (including Greenberg's), and its development within a post-Greenbergian milieu remains a consistent point of focus. This is not to say that the argument deals exclusively with abstract painting but given the point at which the text works outwards, it remains a pertinent and ongoing question.

Although the material has been organized broadly chronologically, the attentive reader will soon note that this isn't strictly adhered to. This is partly to avoid the obvious pitfalls of an "a begets b" art historical chronology, an approach which Greenberg's criticism was arguably complicit with. Such an account of history which construes the development of art in terms of stylistic reaction, as Hal Foster points out, "is banal in the extreme; an ahistorical model, it cannot account adequately for any art."[3] Equally however, the discontinuity that attends, indeed underwrites the production and critical reception of painting during the period in question more truthfully represents and is indicative of the somewhat discursive and arguably disjointed nature of what were competing understandings of painting and more broadly the milieu within which it sought to stake some form of claim.[4]

As a means whereby an understanding of the critical and artistic terrain can, to a certain extent be mapped out, the first chapter seeks to establish the terms upon which painting was given, and indeed radicalized within an historical period that immediately followed the publication of "Modernist Painting". Rather than focus upon those artists whose respective practices Greenberg's criticism had become associated with, the first chapter is geared towards salient examples that presented either an adaptation or an alternative to Greenberg's account of abstraction.

Whilst for Greenberg the operation of self-reference within the context of modernist painting was geared towards rendering visible what were to be understood as the medium's "irreducible essences," the over-arching claim within the second chapter is that by adopting a more conceptual approach (albeit with the understanding that "conceptual" as a designation necessarily carries with it a certain degree of latitude), painting could be deconstructed rather than essentialized. For the artists who we will consider in this chapter, by aligning painting with a more analytical form of practice, the medium was understood not as a series or set of delimited essences, but rather as being contingent upon and given by a set of assumptions, be they cultural, perceptual, or ideological, that up until that point had worked to legitimize the work of art. As will become evident, by using, as it were, its epistemology against itself, the medium became organized around a form of auto-critique that was nevertheless able to avoid the reductivism implied by such a seemingly self-referential strategy.

Using Rosalind Krauss's example of an "expanded field" of artistic practice, a term that had originally been applied to the medium of sculpture, the third chapter seeks to explore the breadth of this field with respect to painting and the means by which it became characterized. Dealing with a period of artistic practice and debate that was protean, multivalent and contested, echoing on one level the broader milieu whereby a number of socio-political structures were being directly challenged, the chapter considers a range of different approaches to painting that were prevalent at the time. More specifically, and against the backdrop wherein a range of alternative practices that fell beyond the purview of discrete and firmly delimited disciplines worked, on one level, to challenge Greenberg's doctrinal and somewhat overly prescribed reading of painting, all of the examples that will be marshaled present a range of accounts of and responses to abstraction.

In 1976 the American painter R. B. Kitaj curated *The Human Clay*, an exhibition of figurative painting and drawing at the Hayward Gallery in London. The title of this exhibition was tendentious, referring to a line in W. H. Auden's poem *Letter to Lord Byron*. According to Kitaj: "[David] Hockney likes to quote the line from Auden's long poem *Letter to Lord Byron* which reads, 'To me Art's subject is the human clay.'" Betraying a somewhat unfashionable conviction towards the representation of the human form, Kitaj claimed that this was perhaps "the most basic art-idea, from which much great art has come." In many respects, *The Human Clay* anticipated what would subsequently become a renewed interest in painting and, moreover, one that became contingent upon particular understandings of "tradition." It was also during this time that the term Neo-Expressionism gained a degree of critical currency, working to emphasize those artists who worked in a direct, unabashed and expressive manner. Unlike the London School, Neo-Expressionism, originally a pan-European designation, also came to encompass certain painters working within America at that time. As well as seeking to examine this apparent resurgence of interest in the medium of painting, the aim of the fourth chapter is also to consider what other, arguably less hyperbolic models of painting, were being established contemporaneously.

Since the advent of photography during the latter half of the nineteenth century, painting has been subject to a succession of declarations regarding its alleged death. (Arguably the first such instance entails the apocryphal story of the French nineteenth-century painter Paul Delaroche's response upon seeing a daguerreotype, an early form of photography: "From now," he was reported to have exclaimed, "painting is dead!").[5] Locating the argument within a context during the 1980s when such declarations had almost reached fever pitch, the aim of chapter five is to consider the particular rationales that constituted this so-called "crisis" in painting. The theoretical impetus, if not the rhetoric informing certain key texts, including Douglas Crimp's *The End of Painting* and Thomas Lawson's *Last Exit Painting*, both published in 1981, will be examined along with the painting's that were made in response to this critical discourse.

Chapter Six will consider how painting was able to flourish during the 1990s. Although arguably the medium was no longer susceptible to the vicissitudes of some of the more exaggerated claims that had previously been made on its behalf, it was still required to locate itself against an artistic and theoretical backdrop that was pluralistic. In this respect, the central claim of this chapter is that painting responded to such a multifarious artistic climate by both atomizing and anatomizing abstraction, and in the process extending, consciously or otherwise, precepts derived from aesthetic formalism and Greenberg's pronouncements in particular. This was partly achieved by artists being increasingly at liberty to plunder, scavenge and select from what one commentator described was formalism's archive, and for that matter an archive that was no longer held in particularly reverent terms. If an artist like Jonathan Lasker could play fast and loose by appropriating and then short-circuiting particular tropes of modernist painting, then other painters sought to inhabit and explore what might be construed as disciplinary and thematic hinterlands, those interstitial spaces that were characterized by categorical slippage. Along with a consideration of what were the key debates pertaining to painting during this period, the proliferation of survey exhibitions of painting will also be considered. As one critic remarked, writing in a review of *Examining Pictures*, an exhibition held at the Whitechapel Art Gallery in 1999, unlike previous survey-type exhibitions on painting like *A New Spirit in Painting* that put forward an argument *for* painting, an exhibition like *Examining Pictures* ostensibly presented an argument *about* painting. Finally, within this culture of hybridity, plurality and historicism, the continued pursuit of an authentic abstract visual language by certain painters will also be considered.

Against a broader set of practices and debates, all of which were vying for position at the turn of the new century, the seventh chapter focuses upon how certain artists sought to, as it were, situate painting. As will become educed, and working in opposition to artistic modernism's understanding of painting as following a trajectory that was centripetal in direction, namely, that was towards its own irreducible essence or core, the "situational" within painting can be understood as denoting some form of orientation towards and consideration of context, however discursive, oblique or approximate that pertains to the painting either during its production, or in terms of how it is understood by its respective audience. Therefore, as well as considering those artists who have chosen to work directly onto the surface of the gallery wall, treating it, in effect, as the painting's support, other practices will be considered that attempt to situate painting within, for example, urban space. Moreover, rather than attempting to wrest any discernable context away *from* the work, as arguably Greenberg had attempted to do, these latter artists use the contexts within which their work is sited as the basis *for* the work.

Perhaps the most pressing questions for painters working today is how to respond to the rapid onset and proliferation of digital, image-based technologies. In an era when any image can be radically manipulated, infinitely reproduced and instantaneously disseminated to the four corners of the Earth, how does a medium that remains, for the most part analogue in scope and import position itself? By way of attempting to respond to the manifold ramifications this question carries, the main aim of the penultimate chapter is to consider those artists who on some level have chosen to respond to the cultural, social, artistic and ontological challenges presented by the digital either directly through the medium of painting or through digital technology itself. To this end, the selection of artists that populate the final section of the study all offer divergent responses to the digital and locate their work within a suitably eclectic range of contexts, both actual and theoretical. Whether it's Monique Prieto, Wade Guyton or Amy Sillman, how the digital becomes both imaged and imagined through the critical, material and historical purview of painting will be examined.

In addition to examining *The Forever Now: Contemporary Painting in an Atemporal World*, an exhibition staged at the Museum of Modern Art in New York in 2015, a key point of focus for the final chapter will be *Mixing It Up*, a major painting exhibition that was held at the Hayward Gallery in London in 2021 and which showcased work that "oscillate[d] between observation and invention, depiction and allegory, illusion and materiality."[6]

Indeed, this claim is equally applicable to the exhibition *Radical Figures: Painting in the New Millennium*, staged at the Whitechapel Gallery in 2020. Foregrounding modernism's pursuit of novelty, whilst seeking to reaffirm the role of the body within representational painting, the exhibition allied a so-called "new generation of artists" to the pursuit of figuration and its expressive potential.

Whilst *Bodying Back and Forth* examines key examples pertinent to this understanding, including the work of Lynette Yiadom-Boakye and Tschabalala Self, the chapter will also examine how the toing and froing, so to speak, of contemporary painting can be more broadly be applied to the multifariousness of genres, approaches, images, media and histories it seeks to engage with.

According to Peter Schjeldahl, writing in the catalogue that accompanied *Abstract Painting, Once Removed*, an exhibition that was held at the Contemporary Arts Museum in Houston in 1998, "the Renaissance until the 1960s, painting has symbolized the ultimate glory, the living end, of Western handiwork."[7] With regards to the question of what happened next, the following eight chapters is an attempt to provide, what is at the very least, the beginnings of an answer.

Notes

1 Following its public broadcast as the fourteenth lecture in the series on the February 6, 1961, the subsequent dissemination of "Modernist Painting" from this point on entailed its publication in *Arts Yearbook* 4 (1961): 101–108 after which it appeared in revised form in *Art and Literature: An International Review* 4 (1965): 193–201. In 1966 it was then published in Gregory Battcock's edited volume *The New Art: A Critical Anthology* (New York: E. P. Dutton, 1966), 100–110. However, as Francis Frascina points out, there has arisen a measure of confusion as regards the respective dates Greenberg's text was both broadcast and published. Citing John O' Brian's error of claiming that the lecture was first broadcast in the spring of 1960, Frascina points out that this confusion could well have arisen from Greenberg himself confusing the date it was recorded with the date it was actually broadcast. See Francis Frascina, "Institutions, Culture, and America's Cold War Years: the making of Greenberg's 'Modernist Painting,'" *Oxford Art Journal* 26, no.1 (2003): 72. For the reference of this mis-dating in O' Brian, see Greenberg, Clement. *The Collected Essays and Criticism*, edited by John O' Brian vol. 4, *Modernism With a Vengeance, 1957–1969* (Chicago: University of Chicago Press, 1993), 93.

2 Thierry de Duve, *Kant After Duchamp* (Cambridge, MA: MIT Press, 1998), 201.

3 Hal Foster, "Signs Taken for Wonders" (1986) in *Painting*, ed. Terry R. Myers (Cambridge, MA: MIT Press, 2011), 49.

4 As Ulrich Loock has succinctly observed: "I know it's always problematic to think in decades. Above all, thinking in decades can never do justice to the simultaneity of the unsimultaneous." Ulrich Loock, "The Beginning of the Eighties" in *The 80s A Topology*, ed. Ulrich Loock (Portugal: Museu de Arte Contemporânea de Serralves, 2007), 17.

5 Stephen Bann, *Paul Delaroche: History Painted* (London: Reaktion Books, 1997), 9.

6 Online at: https://www.southbankcentre.co.uk/whats-on/art-exhibitions/mixing-it-painting-today.

7 Peter Schjeldahl, "The Rise of Abstraction II" in Dana Friis-Hansen, *Abstract Painting, Once Removed* (Houston: Contemporary Arts Museum, 1998), 35.

1

Arbitrary Objects

The essential norms or conventions of painting are at the same time the limiting conditions with which a picture must comply in order to be experienced as a picture. Modernism has found that these limits can be pushed back indefinitely – before a picture stops being a picture and turns into an arbitrary object; but it has also found that the further back these limits are pushed the more explicitly they have to be observed and indicated.[1]

During the same year that "Modernist Painting" was first published in the Voice of America's *Forum Lectures*, the exhibition *Sixteen Americans* was held at the Museum of Modern Art in New York. Organized by the Curator of Museum Collections, Dorothy Miller, the show intended to survey the currency of American art and included the work of Ellsworth Kelly, Louise Nevelson and Jasper Johns. Miller also decided to exhibit the work of Frank Stella, after having visited his studio with the art dealer Leo Castelli. Stella's contribution were four large-scale paintings that had been systematically executed in black enamel paint on unprimed cotton duck canvas using a two-and-a-half-inch house painter's brush. Within the exhibition catalogue, alongside a photograph of the besuited 24-year-old was the following statement, penned by the artist Carl Andre:

> Art is the exclusion of the unnecessary. Frank Stella has found it necessary to paint stripes. There is nothing else in his paintings. He is not interested in sensitivity or personality, either his own or those of his audience. He is interested in the necessities of painting. Symbols are counters passed among people. Frank Stella's painting is not symbolic. His stripes are the paths of a brush on canvas. These paths lead only into painting.[2]

As de Duve points out, at this moment "Carl Andre's *Preface to Stripe Painting* appears utterly Greenbergian. It shares the same ontological assertion that painting is defined by its minimal, formal, and material 'necessities' or conditions, which exclude any symbolic subject matter."[3] But for all of what ostensibly appeared to be a shared agenda, Greenberg's "Modernist Painting" and Andre's statement were representative of two quite distinct impulses within the broader context of modernist painting. For whilst Greenberg's text and for that matter his criticism generally at that time was organized around a qualitative set of aesthetic judgments that were historical in their orientation and origin, Stella's practice sought to repudiate painting being critically framed this way and the essentially humanist reading it implied. After this point, Greenberg would direct his attention towards the "post-painterly abstractionists," the name he gave to those artists who he considered were the rightful heirs to formalism following Abstract Expressionism's demise.[4] In contrast, the austere, pared-down and obdurate materiality that characterized Stella's paintings at the time became understood, by some at least, as directly anticipating the subsequent development of Minimalism.

Despite Stella's paintings being seen in these terms, the movement itself was notable for the general paucity of painting that was directly produced in its name. This was partly due to the fact that many artists who were directly associated with it, and indeed, had begun their careers as painters, were trying to negotiate a critical position for their work that fell beyond the historically received understanding of art as being organized around a series of discrete disciplines or mediums, an understanding that underpinned Greenberg's approach to art criticism. Whereas Greenberg privileged medium specificity within his reading of the artwork, Donald Judd, an artist who would become Minimalism's unofficial spokesperson, wrote in 1965 that: "Half of the best new work in the last few years has been neither painting nor sculpture."[5]

However, whilst no painters became directly associated with Minimalism per se, there remained a number of artists who brought a similar attitude and set of ambitions towards painting. As Douglas Crimp notes, "it was precisely those moves made by Minimal sculpture and its dematerialized offshoots which invested painting with both a renewed aspiration for anti-illusionism and the strategies with which to pursue it."[6]

In marked contrast to the more overwrought tendencies that at least some of their Abstract Expressionist forebears had become associated with, the essentially monochromatic paintings of Jo Baer, Robert Ryman, Eleanore Mikus and Agnes Martin sought to present an account of painting that was notable for its apparent lack of incident and overt detail. Notwithstanding the subtle but important differences between their paintings, at the time all paid close scrutiny to the delimitation of what were considered to be, in effect, a number of painting's material givens. These included its actual or literal surface, its outermost edges and the facture that resulted from a particular application of paint.

Whilst the work that they were producing during the first half of the decade appeared to rehearse Greenberg's own assertions with regards to modernist painting, it would be erroneous to interpret stylistic affinities with conceptual ones. For example, although Eleanore Mikus's ostensibly blank paintings appeared to be very close to the white monochromes of Ryman, in terms of the rationales that were informing their respective practices, fundamental differences remained.

Mikus had moved from Rahway in New Jersey to New York in 1960, having an address first on Eighty-Eighth Street in New York City and then subsequently moving to a loft studio at 76 Jefferson. In 1962 two of her Tablet paintings, Tablets 2 and 6 were shown in a group exhibition at the Mortimer Brandt Gallery in New York.

The Tablet paintings were the result of an extended and iterative process that began with the artist bracing together a number of irregularly sized sections of wood. This formed the basis for the painting's support which was sanded and then applied with several layers of white gesso, a process which, according to the artist, took anything between "six weeks to a couple of years to complete."[7]

Whilst their pared down, physical appearance was broadly comparable with the unembellished and somewhat austere aesthetic of Minimalism (although the movement itself was very much in its infancy), the Tablet paintings remained somewhat out of step with both Minimalism and aesthetic formalism. Instead, they remained closer in sensibility to Robert Rauschenberg's white monochrome paintings that the artist began in 1951 and that were first exhibited two years later at the Stable Gallery in New York. Certainly, both sets of paintings eschewed any straightforward determination of authorial presence. Indeed, beyond being indicative of the fact that his ideas ran counter to those of the Bauhaus artist Joseph Albers, his teacher at Black Mountain College, Rauschenberg's claim that his practice was just an attitude about materials that was strong enough not to submit to Albers' dictum of "It's the *man* who does the painting"" verbally articulated what the white monochrome paintings visually espoused, namely the tendentious withdrawal of authorship.[8] Equally, rather than wanting to impose onto her work an individuated series of marks that would denote artistic identity as, arguably, certain Abstract Expressionists had attempted to do, Mikus spoke of wanting to capture a quality in her Tablet paintings that was akin to the worn surface of a turnstile.[9]

Whilst then, it could be argued that the somewhat anonymous appearance of both Rauschenberg's monochromes and Mikus's Tablets antedated Minimalism's own depersonalization of the artwork, where they arguably differed was with regards to the ideas that informed their respective practices. For example, whilst Rauschenberg along with John Cage were exploring ideas around Zen Buddhism, Mikus's predilection for worn surfaces was

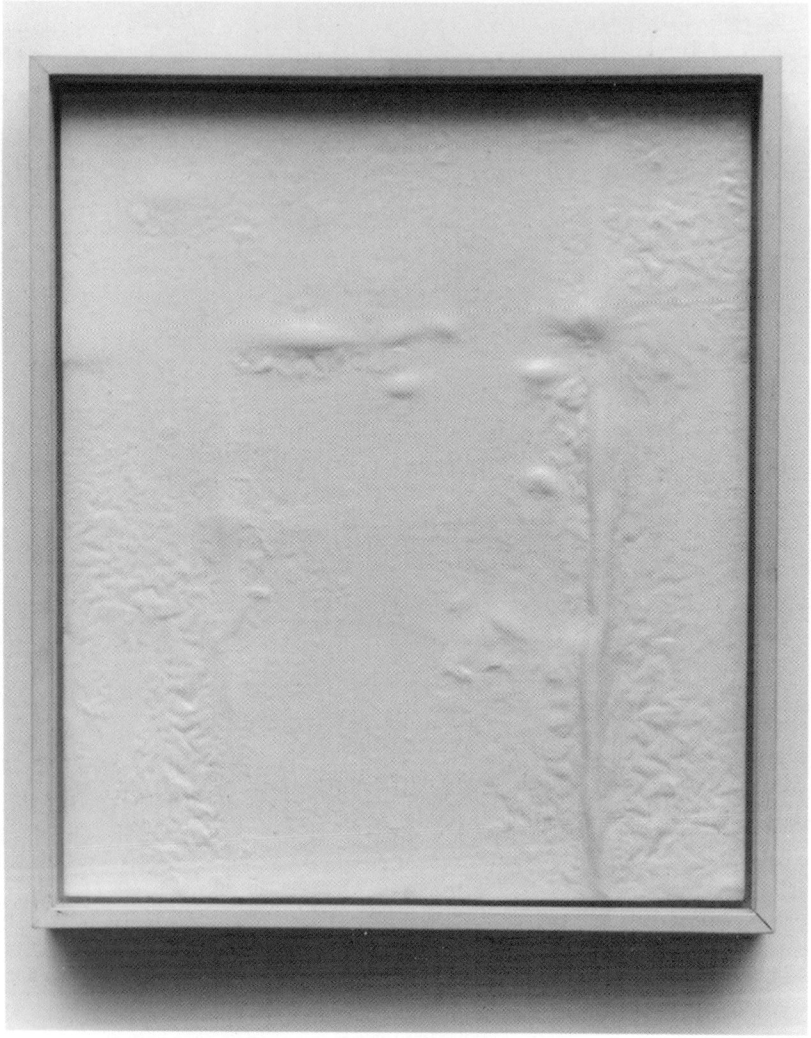

FIGURE 1.1 Eleanore Mikus, *Tablet 165*, 1968.

due to the particular resonances they could educe. Equally, whilst the approach to picture making by Mikus appeared to have a certain sympathy with Greenberg's own essentializing claims on behalf of the artwork, what worked against the Tablet paintings becoming assimilated within the more dominant discourses centering upon the status and condition of the modernist artwork was their somewhat equivocal status and willingness to open themselves up to a more associative, if not visually poetic set of readings.

For Greenberg, such essentializing claims centered upon the mobilization of painting towards that which was considered to be unique to itself. As the critic had claimed two years after "Modernist Painting" had been published, "the irreducible essence of pictorial art consists in but two constitutive conventions or norms: flatness and the delimitation of flatness."[10] However, whilst Greenberg was willing to valorize a purified form of abstraction, represented by the paintings of artists such as Kenneth Noland and Morris Louis, he appeared to stop short of wanting to critically engage with those artists, including Mikus, who were operating within the conceptual and technical parameters of the monochrome. What was it about the monochrome that meant it would have to be necessarily excluded from the formalist critic's canon?

Arguably, it was because within its *reductio ad absurdum* logic, the integrity of painting and specifically its characterization, for Greenberg at least, as a pictorial art was placed under considerable strain. The inherent danger of working with such an extreme position meant that, amongst other things, the artwork veered dangerously close to being understood as its obverse, that is, as a non-artwork, or, in Greenbergian parlance, as an "arbitrary object." However, whilst the monochrome forced abstraction's hand through the presupposition that there could be no (perceptible at least) difference between art and its quotidian counterpart, in actual terms it could never be seen *tout court*. Certainly, the theories and ideas that, up until that point, the monochrome had become bound up with and moreover, contingent upon attested to the fact that whilst it purported to be resistant to the strictures of language, it remained heavily reliant upon a developed level of critical discourse for its elucidation. For this reason, the monochrome, like its three-dimensional, Minimalist counterparts, "were never assumed to be *merely* objects, on a par with books and tables. They were always treated with the seriousness accorded to works of art."[11]

Greenberg for his part made very little direct mention of the monochrome in his writings; in fact, on the small number of occasions that he did, his observations were largely pejorative. For example, discussing the work of the sculptor Ann Truitt in 1968, he claimed that: "Had they been monochrome, the 'objects' in Truitt's 1963 show would have qualified as first examples of orthodox Minimal art. And with the help of monochrome the artist would have been able to dissemble her feminine sensibility behind a more aggressively far-out, non-art look, as so many masculine Minimalists have *their* rather feminine sensibilities."[12]

Both historically and geographically remote, the practice of monochrome painting in Europe, and specifically within Russia during the 1910s and 1920s became symptomatic of the mandate, rubber stamped by modernism, which foregrounded the monochrome as in one sense the *ne plus ultra* or logical end point of abstraction within painting. If Greenberg had expressed his dissatisfaction with the so-called "other tradition," a tradition whose span encompassed the sum of activities that fell under the rubric of Dada and extended to the provocations of Marcel Duchamp, then the legacy of modernism in Russia, and specifically its development of an avant-garde model of painting, was either casually dismissed or tendentiously ignored. Reviewing an exhibition in 1942 of MoMA's recent acquisitions at the Museum of Modern Art in New York, Greenberg would claim that the "works by [Kasimir] Malevich and his disciple [Alexander] Rodchenko, by [Michail] Larionov, the Russian 'rayonist' (he analyzed the visible in streaks of colored light), and by Umberto Boccioni, the Italian Futurist, all have documentary value but are meager in aesthetic results."[13]

It remains a point of debate with regards to the extent at which artists living and working in the U.S. during the period in question were aware of the Russian avant-garde that emerged during the 1910s. Certainly some artists would have read Camilla Gray's *The Great Experiment: Russian Art, 1863–1922* that was first published in 1962, but it remains understandably difficult to ascertain the exact extent at which this key text had been disseminated and was freely available. Clearly though, and notwithstanding what Lynn Zelevansky notes, was a discernable degree of prejudice that was directed against the legacy of European geometric abstraction and that Greenberg's statement was, to a certain extent, symptomatic of and complicit with those artists who became associated with both Minimalism and post-Minimalism conferred onto the developments of Russian modernism a particular significance.[14]

Beyond those artists who Greenberg perceived served as the next causal link within what had become the increasingly purified teleological chain of abstraction and equally, beyond those post-formalists who ostensibly attempted to proffer separate accounts of abstract painting without Greenberg's knowledge or, indeed, without his prior consent, other instances and approaches towards painting concurrently emerged. To this end, whilst the practice of abstract painting and the salient debates that attended modernist painting during this period in the U.S. remained foregrounded, to a certain extent by aesthetic formalism, the situation in Europe was in arguably marked contrast.

Unlike those figures, both artists and critics alike who perceived the practice of art making as being an essentially autonomous activity, the Nouveau Réalistes or New Realists movement which emerged in France towards the end of the 1950s appeared keen, following Rauschenberg's dictum, to act between the gap that separated art from life.[15]

Initially associated with the artists Arman, Daniel Spoerri, Yves Klein and Jean Tinguely, the movement was characterized by a number of unconventional practices that in one sense rehearsed Dada's own anarchic proclivities that had become played out some thirty years previously. Certainly, a salient aspect of Nouveau Réalisme was a tendency to appropriate and reconfigure various non-artistic and demotic forms that had previously shared a more utilitarian function. For example, Arman's *Accumulations* were in one sense just that; various containers, including in the case of *Bluebeard's Wife* (1969), a hollow female torso filled to the brim with manufactured and mass produced objects.

Spoerri for his part made a number of relief works, entitled *tableux-pièges*; picture-traps or snare pictures that attached various objects onto such surfaces as tabletops. These would then be displayed vertically, akin to how paintings would be conventionally hung.

Arguably the most prominent and certainly the most charismatic member of the Nouveau Réalistes was Klein, an artist who, like Piero Manzoni in Italy, also became associated with the "neo-avant-garde." This term, coined by Peter Bürger encompassed a broad swathe and to a certain extent heterogeneous range of practices that he claimed were in contrast to those movements, including Surrealism, that had formed part of the historical avant-garde.[16] In fact, Bürger had applied the term pejoratively, claiming that whilst the neo-avant-garde "proclaim the same goals as the representatives of the historic avant-garde movements to some extent, the demand that art be reintegrated in the praxis of life within the existing society can no longer be seriously made after the failure of avant-gardiste intentions."[17]

Nevertheless, and in spite of the conclusions Bürger subsequently drew, Klein assumed the guise of an agent provocateur who worked across art's categorical boundaries and produced in the process a series of theatrical gestures that were sometimes quasi-mystical in their orientation.

Nowhere was this more apparent than with his ultramarine blue monochrome paintings. Having patented IKB (International Klein Blue), the artist proceeded to use this color as the basis for both his more conventional paintings, those that consisted of a flat area of IKB consistently applied onto a support and, conversely, those paintings, again executed using his trademark blue that served as indexical registers for his "Anthropometry Performances." On one level, Klein's staging of painting in real time had been antedated by the live action paintings of Georges Mathieu who was arguably the first artist to directly conflate painting and performance. In 1954, and sporting historical garb, Mathieu had "performed" *La Bataille de Bouvines* (The Battle of Bouvines), his first entirely "live" painting.[18]

Along with both Mathieu and Klein, the possibility that painting could have some form of "live" dimension became somewhat more aggressively pursued through the so-called "shooting paintings" or *Tirs* of Niki de Saint Phalle. These entailed the artist embedding a series of small containers of liquid paint within plaster on a wooden support. The containers were then fired at either by the artist or by an invited participant. Having staged the first "shooting painting" on the twelfth of February, 1961 on what was a vacant lot directly behind the artist's studio at 11 Impasse Ronsin in Paris (Jean Tinguely owned the gun on this particular occasion), these proto performances would subsequently be staged in various cities across both mainland Europe and in the U.S.[19]

Inevitably, it's difficult not to interpret Saint Phalle's "shooting paintings" iconoclastically and within a set of terms that unequivocally sought to negate, if not entirely bring down the medium. Certainly, Saint Phalle's statements at the time would appear to corroborate such an interpretation. In 1960, the artist would proclaim that: "I shot because I was fascinated watching the painting bleed and die. I shot for that moment of magic ... Red, yellow, blue—the painting is crying the painting is dead. I have killed the painting."[20] Two year's later, she would locate the significance of what constituted her practice in direct relation to the perceived obsolescence of both the medium of painting and a tradition with which it was indelibly bound up: "Oil painting is finished, finished now because we are concerned with other problems ... The shooting is magic. The shooting is the moment. It's the only thing that lives because everything is dead afterwards. Nothing lives. Cézanne, Rembrandt, everything will be dead in the end."[21] Beyond the aggression that Saint Phalle directed towards those forces that were deemed to be culturally repressive, on a more personal level the *Tirs* appeared to offer the artist the basis by which a novel formulation of painting could emerge: "It was an amazing feeling shooting at a painting and watching it transform itself into a new being."[22] Seemingly then, the singularly destructive act that this series of paintings were borne out of was revelatory.

In terms of artistic precedent, whilst on one level the *Tirs* literally reimagined Jasper Johns' own target paintings, the work's destructive bent appeared perhaps closer in sensibility to Robert Rauschenberg's *Erased de Kooning Drawing* (1953), a piece that the artist had "authored" almost ten years prior to Saint Phalle's *Tirs*.

Understood as representing the oedipal-like struggle between, on the one hand, the hubristic fathers of Abstract Expressionism and, on the other, the recalcitrant artists who sought to challenge their forebears' ideological and artistic imperatives, the facts of this particular incident have been well rehearsed. Rauschenberg decided that he wanted to make an artwork through the wanton destruction, or in this particular case, "erasure," of someone else's artwork. As the story goes, the Abstract Expressionist painter Willem De Kooning willingly obliged and provided Rauschenberg with a drawing "important enough for him to miss, and one that was difficult to erase."[23] Because of which, it took the artist four weeks to obliterate what was almost the entirety of De Kooning's drawing.

Although their almost scatological painterly qualities further inscribed a particular relationship with Abstract Expressionism (though they remained neither "abstract" nor "expressionistic" in any received sense of the word), it was perhaps Performance Art that the *Tirs* were most directly comparable with. Indeed, Saint Phalle claimed that: "I used tear-gas for the grand finale of my shooting performances. Performance art did not yet exist but this was a performance."[24] Although her statement overlooked the fact that the development of modern art in Europe during the first two decades of the twentieth century had encompassed a broad range of performative practices, it nevertheless placed what she did within a particular context of artistic practice. Moreover, whilst along with Saint Phalle other artists including Klein and Mathieu were attempting to adopt a range of performative strategies as a means of generating novel responses to and formulations of painting in Europe, in America certain figures looked towards the legacy of Jackson Pollock as a means of reaching what were, in effect, a comparable set of ends. As Amelia Jones notes: "Within art discourse, reformulations of painting as act or performance in the 1950s and 1960s explicitly cite Pollock as the model for this new way of conceptualizing the work of art and the artistic subject."[25]

The provenance of this particular reading was the art critic Harold Rosenberg's 1959 text *The All American Action Painters*, wherein, as he would claim, "what matters always is the revelation contained in the act."[26] Moreover, further credence was given to this account of Pollock through the documentary footage of the artist at work in his studio in East Hampton that was taken by the young German émigré photographer Hans Namuth. A month after a series of Namuth's photographs had accompanied Robert Goodnough's article "Pollock Paints a Picture" in the May edition of *ArtNews* in 1951 and by way of further corroborating this reading of the artist, the Museum of Modern Art screened the color film of Pollock at work. From that point on, as Barbara Rose points out, "the images of Pollock in action attached themselves as additional meanings to his works to a degree that they began to color the perception of his paintings."[27]

In *The Legacy of Jackson Pollock*, published in 1958, Allan Kaprow, an artist who at the time would have been most readily associated with Fluxus, sought to review the significance of Pollock's career through his claim that whilst a number of characteristics the artist's name had become directly associated with and which included "the personal mark that builds its own form and meaning" had become outworn clichés, the performative dimension of his practice had anticipated a subsequent wave of proto-postmodern practices.[28] In this respect, and as Amelia Jones notes:

> In spite of its lingering romanticism in his characterization of the "grand … authoritative, and all encompassing … scale and daring" of Pollock's "ritual" statement (which aligns Pollock implicitly with modernist conceptions of the artist as heroic and individual), Kaprow's articulation of Pollock clearly aligns him with the kind of performative, open-ended, and processual conception of art-making that we now associate with practices critical of modernist formalism.[29]

Moreover, and like the example given by Saint Phalle, "Pollock's apotheosis as tragic genius of modernist painting opens out onto his destruction of the modernist conception of painting through performance."[30] Evidently then, this critique, if not destruction, of modernist painting, albeit in one particular sense of the term, shifted the ontological status of the medium from "idealism to a newfound realism" and, moreover, was not limited to one geographical locale.[31]

In her foreword to *Art Anti-Art Non-Art Experimentations in the Public Sphere in Postwar Japan 1950–1970*, Gail Feigenbaum observes that in Japan during the volatile period after the war, "artistic groups coalesced quickly, engaging in political, social, and artistic debates and protests, and, just as quickly, dissolved and were replaced by new collaborations."[32] One such artistic group was the Gutai Art Association. Founded by Yoshihara Jiro in 1952, Gutai, "was composed of two ideograms: *gu* (tool, or means) and *tai* (substance, or body) [which] could be understood as either *concrete* or *concreteness*."[33]

In 1964, Kazuo Shiraga (Plate 1), an artist who was a member of the Gutai Art Association, created *Tenkaisei Kohogi* by opting to paint it not with his hands but with his feet. As a counterpoint to Pollock's *Number 1, 1950 (Lavender Mist)* (1950), wherein Pollock marked the upper-right corner of the canvas with handprints, Shiraga's painting, whilst executed like Pollock's painting on a large area of canvas that had been laid directly onto the floor, indexed the artist's body through a print of the artist's right foot positioned in the bottom left-hand corner of the painting.

However, it remains an important point that rather than merely seeking to emulate Abstract Expressionism, the Japanese avant-garde at this time had a more ambivalent relationship with the developments of painting as they had been played out in America, and particularly with respect to certain factions of the so-called New York School during the 1940s and 1950s. Whilst the Gutai movement was perceived to have formulated its own variant of action painting, for certain artists working in Japan at the time someone like Pollock, or at least some of the readings that had been conferred directly onto Pollock's canvases, were held to be highly problematic.

For example, Shinohara Ushio, who in 1960 had created *Boxing Painting*, a piece produced by dipping his bound hands into paint and proceeding to "box" the surface of the support, deliberately assumed the role of a self-publicist so that he could challenge, as Merewether claims, "the lofty modern ideal of '*geijutsu* for the sake of *geijutsu*' making art the ultimate reward [believing] that the action itself was far more important than the resulting painting … an attitude that, in his opinion, separated his works from Jackson Pollock's."[34]

Whilst the Japanese avant-garde was representative of one trajectory that fell beyond an American-European axis, there were other examples, notably those artists who worked to develop an avant-garde within Latin America towards the latter half of the 1950s.

To this end, the Brazilian artists associated with Neo-Concretism, Hélio Oiticica, Lygia Clark and Lygia Pape, all sought to instigate a broadly non-representational, geometrical and modular approach to the production of the artwork that was often organized dialogically and, in this respect, ran counter to Greenberg's arguably more doctrinaire approach. Seen on one level as a recasting of European Constructivism, Neo-Concretism, as the name of the movement implied, sought to actualize the artwork partly through a phenomenological reorientation of the viewer in a way that was comparable to the experiential basis of the Minimalist object. Although, as Zelavansky points out, Neo-Concretism addressed the "interrelationship between the creation, experience, and meaning of the artwork," what members of the Brazilian avant-garde produced remained more overtly participatory than their American counterparts.[35] For his part, Oiticica believed that it was no longer possible to "accept development 'inside the picture,'" as Greenberg and his allies had chosen to do, indeed even fixated upon; instead, painting's salvation "would be to launch into space, so that it could become complete, not as surface or appearance, but as essence."[36]

Beginning in 1960, Oiticica devised a series of works that were organized around both ostensibly illusionistic and actual elements displayed in such a way that they enabled the viewer to become physically immersed within the artwork itself. For example, Oiticica's *Grand Nucleus, NC3, NC4, NC6* (Plate 2), produced during the first half of the 1960s "not only leave the wall, they cluster together to create enclosures that surround the 'participant' (Oiticica's word), emphatically engaging her physically."[37] In fact, Oiticica wasn't the only artist who at the time was seeking to develop the experiential basis of the viewer from one of merely being a passive spectator.

Whilst the creation of the *Nuclei* worked to create an immersive space that could be inhabited by the viewers that were directly contiguous with it, Yoko Ono's *Painting to Hammer a Nail* (1961) equally sought to instrumentalize the work through the audience's affective presence. Ono, an artist who like Kaprow was loosely associated with the trans-national and intermedial set of practices that fell under the rubric of Fluxus, devised a number of often ephemeral and often ad hoc "paintings" that sought to confer on the viewer a more participatory role.

Organized around an admixture of poetry, humor and critique, *Painting to Hammer a Nail* (1961), one of a series of dialogical works made under the auspices of what the artist described were "Instruction Paintings" invited willing members of the audience to hammer one of the nails that had been provided into what was a white monochrome painting. Rather than being, as Cage had somewhat lyrically described with regards to Rauschenberg's own white monochrome paintings "landing strips for dust motes, light and shadow," these works were designed to be the receptacles for a more deliberately aggressive, and in the part of the artwork's respective audience, participatory act.[38] Equally, *Painting to be Stepped On* (1960) was also premised on the idea that the activity of painting was dialogic rather than autonomous, an intersubjective process wherein the categorical boundaries that ordinarily worked to distinguish the production of the object from its reception became rendered, to a certain extent, porous. Moreover, and echoing a particular artistic strategy of Fluxus, these "paintings" were often presented not as concrete objects but as "event scores," that is, as solely written texts.

This was the case for *Painting for the Wind* that instructed its audience to "make a hole, leave it in the wind," a piece that was transcribed into Japanese characters by the artist Toshi Ishiyangai for the exhibition "Instructions for Painting" at the Sōgetsu Art Center in Japan in 1962.[39] Other instruction paintings were equally contingent upon the viewer's physical interaction. As Alexandra Munroe notes, "For *Smoke Painting*, the viewer was asked to burn the canvas with a cigarette and watch the smoke; the piece was completed when the canvas turned to ashes. *Time Painting* and *Painting to See in the Dark* required the viewer's imagination to complete, and *Painting in Three Stanzas*, which presented a vine growing out of a burned hole in the canvas, suggested concepts of organic growth, death, and eternity."[40]

As the example given by Shiraga illustrated, complicit within the actual production of the painting was the artist's body or corporeal presence. Within such an understanding was the idea, according to Darling, that the body's role could be that of either an "intermediary surface ... or implement."[41] Whilst, Günter Brus's *Selbstbemalung* (Self-Painting) (1964), wherein the artist's face became the support upon which was etched a thick black vertical line of paint was concomitant with the first of the two roles, Shigeko Kubota's *Vagina Painting* was arguably organized around the latter.

As part of the perpetual Fluxfest that was staged in New York in 1965, Kubota attached a brush to her underwear and then proceeded to apply red paint to an area of the floor that had been covered with paper. As it was, *Vagina Painting* "brought painting and menstruation, as well as sexual shock, together to mock the heroic gestures of the historically male-dominated tradition."[42] It also sought to inscribe the corporeal body within painting in a way that challenged a set of assumptions that previously had worked to privilege a particular understanding of authorship as somehow being enshrined within the sovereignty of the (usually male) artist's subjectivity. Indeed, one could arguably claim that this particular challenge that was brought to painting was not unique to Kubota's performance but in fact was a critical impulse that informed and helped steer a number of variant practices during the period in question—practices that ran directly counter to the account of artist practice as it was given by aesthetic formalism.

In one sense, all of the respective examples marshaled thus far can be seen as being symptomatic of, to a lesser or greater extent, a broadening of painting's modus operandi beyond the somewhat narrow prescriptions of Greenberg's text. Although these works were not necessarily either direct responses to either Greenberg's criticism in general or "Modernist Painting" in particular, collectively they nevertheless presented separate accounts of painting, albeit it with a competing set of possibilities that were in distinction to what was perceived by many to have become a deeply entrenched position and set of traditions, Greenbergian or otherwise. However, whilst Greenberg's position was perceived by many artists, including painters, to be problematic, an exploration of painting's physical means that didn't automatically equate to the type of formalism that

Greenberg was espousing remained, for some at least, a legitimate enquiry around which their respective practices could be organised.

During the second half of the 1960s, an artist who one could arguably claim sought to test out the limiting conditions not just of Minimalism's credo of truth to materials but also Greenberg's own aesthetic formalism was Sam Gilliam. Although Gilliam was initially associated with the so-called Washington Color School, a group of artists of whom both Greenberg and the art critic Michael Fried had significantly vested interests in, he sat somewhat awkwardly within this artistic milieu. Accordingly: "Mainstream scholarship considers him to be a part or descendant of the Washington Color School, the group of color-field painters led by Morris Louis and Kenneth Noland that emerged in the capital in the late 1950s and flourished in the 1960s ... In retrospect, it is clear that what has distinguished his aesthetic over the years is not its historical link to the Color School but how he upset the tradition of modernist art that Color School represents."[43]

Arguably, part of the reason why Gilliam remained somewhat out of step with the Washington Color School was because there were other points of reference beyond those that were being proffered by Greenberg's criticism that the artist was exposed to and chose to look towards. In this respect, one of the most influential figures at that time was the artist Thomas Downing. According to Binstock: "If Greenberg was a formalist, then Downing was a free-formalist, formalism having been just one among many tools in his store of analytical resources. For Downing, modernist art's implicit meanings were various, evolving, and derived from a much broader outlook than what Greenberg was proposing in the 1960s."[44] Indeed Gilliam claimed that "Tom was one of the first persons that ... let me know that Washington Color School painting wasn't about what was being written by Greenberg."[45] As it was then, Gilliam strove to negotiate a position for his practice at that time within a milieu whose parameters, with regards to abstraction at least, had become markedly exclusive and narrow. This was undertaken primarily through the artist's decision to explore the possibilities offered by painting's fabric support.

Gilliam's early canvases, his so-called free-form pictures that he began in 1966 were soon followed by his suspended paintings. Whereas the former still maintained, stylistically and procedurally at least, a link to Pollock and the painters that had emerged out of Abstract Expressionism and with which Gilliam had initially become associated the latter series seemed very much a rebuttal of Abstract Expressionism's heirs. Well perhaps, although Gilliam perhaps more truthfully was able to interpret the paintings of Helen Frankenthaler et al. within a set of terms that fell beyond the purview of Greenberg's formalist account of them. Recalling a visit the artist made to Noland in 1967, Gilliam provides us with this telling statement:

> It was curious when I was there how much [Noland] was playing with a sculpture that he had made with [Anthony] Caro, and how much he

> talked about his friend David Smith who had died, and how much he sort of suggested that there was no difference between painting and sculpture at all … the interesting thing is that, since that point … I haven't forgotten it. And that's what led to the draped paintings; I mean, trying to produce a work that was both about painting and sculpture.[46]

Taking this statement as the means wherein Gilliam's own response became mobilized, the suspended or draped paintings which sought to explore and extend the parameters of the medium rather than dispense with them, nevertheless repudiated a number of precepts that worked to underwrite, if not legitimize the formalist reading of painting.

Firstly, the paintings played fast and loose with modernism's articulation, both verbal and physical, of painting. Whilst they were, indeed, foregrounded by their materiality, their physical presence, their somewhat theatrical timbre eschewed the ostensibly reductivizing impulse of formalist aesthetics. Rather than engage in a discourse that was organized around a process of purification and repudiation of what was deemed to be unnecessary, extraneous detail, a painting such as *Light Depth* (1969) ratcheted up both the seemingly flamboyant and the playful within modernist abstraction—characteristics that formalist criticism had sought to avoid. Moreover, Gilliam's works at this time were some of the first to directly engage with notions of both interdisciplinarity and intermediality. Whilst these were very much rooted within the function and specificity of painting, they remained notable for their uniquely sculptural qualities. As a result, this would often entail the work's incursion into the real, as opposed to illusionistic space. According to the critic Douglas Davis, writing in the National Observer in the year that *Light Depth* was made, one "'enters' a Gilliam almost as if [one] would enter a room."[47] Equally, rather than merely being construed as simply yet another diluted response to Greenberg's formalist interpretation of painting, Gilliam's canvases at that time should be read as emerging out of an artistic and cultural climate within which a number of precepts that up until that point had organized art were either being dismantled or critically reimagined.

In this respect, and due to the fact that a work such as *Swing Sketch* (1968) eschewed the more essentializing aspects of Greenberg's stated claims on behalf of painting, the work can be understood as being more broadly symptomatic of a more open-ended enquiry that centered upon testing out the physical parameters of painting. As Binstock notes: "In the late 1960s the stretcher was something of a magnet for interrogations of the tradition of painting. From the prevalent fascination with the shaped stretcher to the spare, poetic, and flimsy ruinations of Richard Tuttle, artists were not taking for granted the parameters of the painting's support or its relationship to the wall."[48] According to Frances Colpitt, the "shaped canvas, although frequently described as a hybrid of painting and sculpture, grew out of the issues of abstract painting and was evidence of

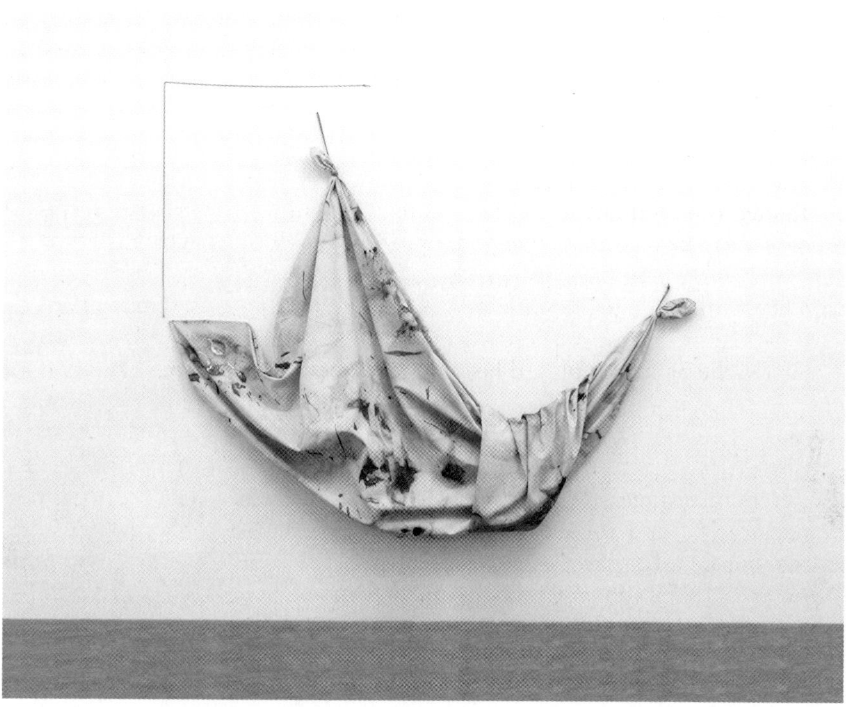

FIGURE 1.2 Sam Gilliam, *Swing Sketch*, 1968.

the desire of painters to move into real space by rejecting behind-the-frame illusionism."[49]

Arguably this particular preoccupation that was shared by certain artists and that became played out during the second half of the 1960s was preceded by the exhibition *The Shaped Canvas* at the Guggenheim Museum in New York in 1964 and interestingly, included the shaped canvases of Stella. Whilst the work of Sam Gilliam tendentiously played the two-dimensional off the three-dimensional in order to make a work that "was both about painting and sculpture," other artists adopted the same strategy as the means by which they could move painting into the realms of architectural space. To this end, two of the artists who showed in The Shaped Canvas, Sven Lukin and Will Insley, as Colpitt notes, had studied architecture before they had become painters.[50]

In one sense, the preoccupation with novel and sometimes eccentrically shaped supports was evidence that the essential norms of painting could indeed be pushed back indefinitely and, moreover, to paraphrase Greenberg, observed and indicated explicitly. However, by doing so, a different set of possibilities emerged than arguably those Greenberg had envisaged.

Along with Saint-Phalle, Ono and Gilliam whose respective practices were broadly indicative of a more open-ended approach to painting, an approach that was at times theatricalized, at other times dialogical, an additional impulse emerged. This impulse became configured against the critical and artistic backdrop of conceptualism and as such sought to stage painting as a form of reflexive critique, an approach and account that appropriated Greenberg's own reflexive account of modernist painting and used it not as the means by which the medium could be further shored up and entrenched within its own area of competence, but rather as a means of dismantling the various ideologies, histories and theories, including Greenberg's own, upon which painting had been constructed. It is towards this particular account of painting that we will now turn.

Notes

1 Clement Greenberg, "Modernist Painting" (1960), in *The Collected Essays and Criticism* vol. 4, *Modernism with a Vengeance, 1957–1969*, ed. John O' Brian (Chicago: University of Chicago Press, 1995), 89–90.

2 Carl Andre, "Preface to Stripe Painting (Frank Stella)," *16 Americans* (New York: MoMA, 1959), 76.

3 Thierry de Duve, *Kant After Duchamp* (Cambridge, MA: MIT Press, 1998), 202.

4 See "Post Painterly Abstraction" (1964), reproduced in Greenberg, *The Collected Essays and Criticism* vol. 4, *Modernism with a Vengeance, 1957–1969*. 192–197. This article accompanied an exhibition Greenberg curated at the Los Angeles County Museum of Art in 1964.

5 Donald Judd, "Specific Objects" (1965), in *Art in Theory 1900–2000 An Anthology of Changing Ideas*, 2nd ed. Charles Harrison and Paul Wood (Oxford: Blackwell, 2005), 824.

6 Douglas Crimp, "Opaque Surfaces" (1973), in *Minimalism*, ed. James Meyer (London: Phaidon, 2002), 257–58.

7 Robert Hobbs, *Eleanore Mikus: Shadows of the Real* (Seattle; London: University of Washington Press, 1991), 19.

8 John Gruen, "Robert Rauschenberg: An Audience of One," *Art News* 76, no. 2 (1977): 46, reproduced in Branden W. Joseph, *Random Order: Robert Rauschenberg and the Neo-Avant-Garde* (Cambridge, MA: MIT Press, 2003), 316.

9 Hobbs, *Eleanore Mikus: Shadows of the Real*, 19.

10 Clement Greenberg "After Abstract Expressionism" (1962), in Greenberg, *The Collected Essays and Criticism* vol. 4, *Modernism with a Vengeance, 1957–1969*, 131.

11 Francis Colpitt, *Minimal Art: The Critical Perspective* (Seattle, University of Washington Press, 1993), 112.

12 "Changer: Ann Truitt" (1968), in Greenberg, *The Collected Essays and Criticism: Modernism with a Vengeance, 1957–1969*, 290.

13 Clement Greenberg, "Review of Four Exhibitions of Abstract Art" (1942), in *The Collected Essays and Criticism* vol. 1, *Perceptions and Judgments, 1939–1944*, ed. John O' Brian (Chicago: The University of Chicago Press, 1988), 104.

14 Zelevansky, "Beyond Geometry: Objects, Systems, Concepts" 10. Zelevansky draws the reader's attention towards the abundance of evidence to this effect in Maurice Tuchman's essay "The Russian Avant-Garde and the Contemporary Artist." One such example is a quotation by Frank Stella regarding Kasmir Malevich's *White on White* that he saw as an "iceberg" that "kept us going, as a focus of ideas." See Frank Stella in Maurice Tuchman "The Russian Avant-Garde and the Contemporary Artist," in *The Avant-Garde in Russia, 1910–1930: New Perspectives* (Los Angeles: Los Angeles County Museum of Art, 1980), 120, reproduced in Zelevansky, "Beyond Geometry: Objects, Systems, Concepts," 30.

15 Robert Rauschenberg, "Untitled Statement" (1959) reproduced in *Theories and Documents of Contemporary Art: A Sourcebook of Artist's Writings*, ed. Kristine Stiles and Peter Selz (Berkeley, CA: University of California Press, 1996), 321.

16 Peter Bürger, from *Theory of the Avant-Garde* (1984), extract reproduced in *Art of the Twentieth Century: A Reader*, ed. Jason Gaiger and Paul Wood (New Haven, CT: Yale University Press, 2003), 61.

17 Ibid.

18 As Paul Schimmel wryly adds, although Mathieu remains "vested primarily in the formal attributes of his work, he was the forerunner of the self-promotional aesthetic of such artists as Andy Warhol and Jeff Koons, who expertly manipulated the mass media." Paul Schimmel, "Leap into the Void: Performance and the Object," in *Out of Actions: Between Performance and the Object, 1949–1979*, ed. Paul Schimmel (London: Thames & Hudson, 1998), 31.

19 Jill Carrick, "Phallic Victories? Niki de Saint Phalle's *Tirs*," *Art History* 26, no. 5 (2003): 705. According to Carrick, Saint Phalle presented her *Tir* performances in a number of different cities, including Paris, Amsterdam, Stockholm, Copenhagen, Figueras, Los Angeles and New York. Ibid.

20 Niki de Saint Phalle, "Artist's Statement" (1960), reproduced in Amelia Jones and Tracey Warr, *The Artist's Body* (London: Phaidon, 2000), 57.

21 Niki de Saint Phalle, in the film *[Niki de Saint Phalle Shooting a Tir]* (1962; color, sound, in English, 4.40 min.) (V 36 1962), Niki Charitable Art Foundation, in *Target Practice: Painting Under Attack 1949–78*, ed. Michael Darling (Seattle: Seattle Art Museum, 2009), 24.

22 Pontus Hulten, *Niki de Saint Phalle* (Bonn: Kunst- und Ausstellungshalle der Bundesrepublik Deutschland GmbH, 1995), 161.

23 Dario Gamboni, *The Destruction of Art: Iconoclasm and Vandalism since the French Revolution* (London: Reaktion Books, 1997), 268.

24 Hulten, *Niki de Saint Phalle*, 161.

25 Amelia Jones, *Body Art Performing the Subject* (Minneapolis: University of Minnesota Press, 1998), 55–56.

26 Harold Rosenberg, *The Tradition of the New* (New York: Horizon Press, 1959), 36.

27 Barbara Rose, "Hans Namuth's Photograph and the Jackson Pollock Myth: Part One: Media Impact and the Failure of Criticism," *Arts Magazine* 53, no. 7 (1979): 112.

28 Allan Kaprow, *Essays on the Blurring of Art and Life*, ed. Jeff Kelley, extended edition (Berkeley, CA: University of California Press, 2003), 2.

29 Jones, *Body Art/Performing the Subject*, 56.

30 Ibid.

31 Darling, *Target Practice: Painting Under Attack 1949–78*, 24.

32 Gail Feigenbaum, Foreword, in *Art Anti-Art Non-Art Experimentations in the Public Sphere in Postwar Japan 1950–1970*, ed. Charles Merewether (Los Angeles: Getty Research Institute, 2007), ix.

33 Charles Merewether, "Disjunctive Modernity: The Practice of Artistic Experimentation in Postwar Japan," in Merewether, *Art Anti-Art Non-Art Experimentations in the Public Sphere in Postwar Japan 1950–1970*, 7.

34 Reiko Tomii, "*Geijutsou* on Their Minds: Memorable Words on Anti Art" in Merewether, *Art Anti-Art Non-Art Experimentations in the Public Sphere in Postwar Japan 1950–1970*, 50.

35 Lynn Zelavansky, *Sense and Sensibility: Women Artists and Minimalism in the 1990s*, 2nd ed. (New York: MoMA, 1995), 22.

36 Zelevansky, "Beyond Geometry: Objects, Systems, Concepts," 19–20.

37 Ibid., 20–21.

38 Rebecca Roberts, *Robert Rauschenberg* (New York: MoMA, 2009), 6.

39 See Schimmel, *Out of Actions: Between Performance and the Object, 1949–1979*, 77.

40 Alexandra Munroe, *Japanese Art After 1945: Scream Against the Sky* (New York: Solomon Guggenheim Museum, 1977), 218.

41 Darling, *Target Practice: Painting Under Attack 1949–78*, 49.

42 Ibid.

43 Jonathan P. Binstock, *Sam Gilliam: A Retrospective* (Berkeley, CA: University of California Press, 2006), 2.

44 Ibid, 15

45 Ibid.

46 Ibid, 84.

47 Douglas Davis, "This is the Loose-Paint Generation," *National Observer*, 4 August 1969, 20. Reproduced in Binstock, *Sam Gilliam: A Retrospective*, 44.

48 Ibid., 51.

49 Frances Colpitt, "The Shape of Painting in the 1960s," *Art Journal* 50, no. 1 (1991): 52.

50 Ibid., 54.

2

Auto-Critique

The impersonal or anonymous nature of the work/product causes us to be presented with a fact (or idea) in its raw form; we can only observe it without reference to any metaphysical scheme, just as we observe that it is raining or snowing. Thus we can now say, for the first time, that "it is painting", as we say, "it is raining."[1]

If there were any discernable affinities between the broad range of approaches to painting we have thus far considered, then they arguably centered upon, albeit it in a loose sense, a respective set of attempts to outflank or circumvent the reductivizing impulse that marked the project of both Greenberg and Minimalism. This would have been no small undertaking primarily due, as Jonathan Binstock points out, to what was at the time a prevailing insistence on "defending the physical and conceptual integrity of each artistic discipline—painting, sculpture, and architecture—and the historically determined nature of their evolution."[2] As it was, and as Binstock points out, within "this critical milieu painting, in its guise of autonomy, was dominant over other forms, precisely because of its apparent physical and conceptual integrity and the ongoing resilience of its defining character."[3]

Whilst the artists that will be discussed within this chapter were unwilling to yield to Greenberg's edicts, they were equally reluctant to entirely relinquish Minimalism's emphasis upon the necessity to eschew illusionism in favor of a more theoretical form of practice.

This is not to say that if an artist sought to strategically orient their enquiry towards what was perceived to be fundamental to painting they would automatically be tarred with the formalist brush. Whilst Ad Reinhardt had claimed in 1962 that the "one subject of a hundred years of modern art is that awareness of art of itself, of art preoccupied with its own process and means, its own essence, its own reason," others sought to gravitate towards painting's elemental state or condition, rather than its essential one.[4] The difference was subtle but nevertheless significant. Whilst Greenberg tendentiously sought to reify what was, for him at least, the essence of painting, what in effect amounted to flatness and its delimitation, for other artists the construal of painting's elements, fundamental or otherwise, did not automatically entail a change in their ontological status. Although painting was still turned in on itself, this was in order not to eulogize it but to critique it. In this respect, the paintings of Giulio Paolini can be seen as adumbrating a subsequent set of critical strategies that were directed towards and, moreover, sought to theoretically unpack, painting's received status and condition.

A year after *Modernist Painting* was first published, Paolini made *Senza titolo* or *Untitled* (Plate 3), a "painting" that consisted of a used tin of paint that had been placed onto the lower horizontal bar of a wooden stretcher frame. Rather than stretch a more traditional support such as a length of canvas or linen onto the painting's frame, Paolini chose instead clear plastic, which contained, but didn't conceal, both the frame and the tin of paint. Notwithstanding the artist's visual pun that was organized around the Renaissance's proclivity to view painting as a form of "window" onto the world, Paolini appeared to have divested painting, or at least in this particular case, *this* painting (if we can indeed call it such), of any illusionistic attributes or characteristics. Instead, emphasis was accorded the fundamental means by which painting had traditionally pictured the world. Consequently, the tin of paint resting on the lower of the two horizontal stretcher bars existed within a nascent state, and painting was thus conceived as a hypothetical and hypothesizing object, functioning as a postulate that had yet to be proven, to be ascertained, to be *given*.[5] As it was then, *Senza titolo* functioned as a proto-conceptual statement *about* painting as much as it actually existed *as* one, deconstructing in the process both the conditions of production and by extension those of viewing as well.

Such a set of ambitions were equally in evidence in a piece made the same year, wherein the artist nestled one painting within the space behind another painting so that the two became coterminous and then proceeded to place these two within the space behind a third painting. Once these three paintings became amalgamated into a single structure, the piece was rotated one hundred and eighty degrees so that what would have conventionally functioned as the visible surface of the painting to be viewed was turned to face the wall. As well as exposing the three stretcher frames, by denying the viewer the opportunity to see the surface of any of the paintings meant that the act of viewing became deliberately obstructed and as a result, indefinitely postponed.

By adopting a more analytical and speculative approach to painting, Paolini's practice antedated those artists who collectively sought to critique and render explicable the cultural, historical and ideological structures that inhered within painting and worked to shore up its status. Whilst a work such as *Senza titolo* was oriented towards and foregrounded by the basic physical components that went to make up painting and that somehow enabled the world to become, as it were, pictured, the artists that we will consider in this chapter all sought, in their respective ways to examine the various discourses, including those that were bound up with ideas around vision, autonomy and authorship that attended such picturing and that were complicit in its legitimization.

Underscoring Greenberg's account of modernism was a certain privileging of the visual sense. To this end, as Yves-Alain Bois has pointed out, the "modernist interpretation of modern art ... rests on a certain number of postulates and exclusions: The first postulate is that visual art, especially painting, addresses itself uniquely to the sense of sight."[6] No doubt in part due to the development of Conceptual Art during the latter half of the 1960s, a number of conceptually oriented paintings sought to counter the perceived hegemony of the visual by way of strategically introducing the textual. This marked a shift in terms of both the operative conditions of painting and the protocols and procedures that governed its interpretation. By downgrading the visual, the inclusion of text meant that the conditions of possibility were such that painting could be read, as much as it could be seen. This further corroborated Conceptual Art's emphasis upon art as a theoretical form of practice that eschewed the elicitation of pleasures the visual sense was inextricably bound up with.

Arguably, Mel Bochner's "leading role in the inauguration of conceptualism."[7] was due in part to the fact that the artist's work amounted to the "analysis of how something is to be perceived and understood rather than in the construction of an object with a decidedly spatial presence."[8] Certainly, there was a degree of confluence between Conceptual Art demoting, if not repudiating modernism's privileging of the visual sense and Bochner's own attempts to disentangle the various historically received and culturally riven threads that had become entwined within the work of art. Moreover, what united both was an ambition to challenge the historically received understanding of the painter's subjectivity as being indelibly bound up with the "privacy of intention."[9] However, whilst Conceptual Art had no vested interest in painting per se, Bochner had claimed that "painting, as a way of thinking-about-the world, has always been the implicit horizon of my work."[10] Moreover:

> Without the history of the practice of painting as the background for all my work, it becomes a series of disparate gestures. I'm not interested in pronouncements like "painting is dead" or "painting is alive." Either way, what difference does it make when you're in your studio trying to think about something concrete? But once you recognize that my work is an analytical attempt to rethink painting's functions and meanings, you realize that it is all one continuous investigation.[11]

Such ambitions were evident within Bochner's *Theory of Painting* (1969–70). Originally installed in the Galleria Tosella in Milan in 1970, *Theory of Painting* was organized around four different permutations of the terms "cohere" and "disperse." Moreover, each of the four inter-related permutations—Cohere/Disperse; Cohere/Cohere; Disperse/Disperse and Disperse/Cohere, written in a plain sans serif font on the adjacent gallery wall, were accompanied by four areas of the floor covered with sheets of newspaper. (Due to space limitations, the first installation of *Theory of Painting* only presented three of the four different permutations.) Each configuration of newsprint sought to give concrete form to its respective permutation. So, for example, vinyl lettering spelling the words Cohere/ Disperse was inscribed on the gallery's wall directly adjacent to an area of the gallery floor that was covered with a number of seemingly randomly placed sheets of newspaper. On the surface of the middle section of these newspapers a rectangular area of blue paint had been sprayed. Equally, in the area representing the processes of dispersal and coherence, whilst all of the newspapers had been placed neatly so that one edge of the newspaper sheet directly abutted the neighboring one, covering the floor of the gallery space with a grid-like area of newsprint, various shaped areas of blue paint had been intermittently sprayed onto certain sections of it.

By proposing a "taxonomy of figure and ground" *Theory of Painting* provided a very concrete example of how the artist was attempting to unpick painting's condition, if not its status.[12] In its precision and economy the piece, according to Richard Field, vexed the viewer to consider the following: "Can the terms of painting, with all its visual illusion and literary allusion, be reduced to four arrangements of two set constants (area of paper and area of paint)? And if the answer must be a resounding 'no,' then what are we to make of *Theory of Painting*? Are they critiques or simply spoofs?"[13]

On one level, *Theory of Painting* was more broadly characteristic of a number of conceptually based artworks that were made during the same period that "shifted focus from a whole precious work of art to the material conditions and technical operations which underlie the making of walls, buildings and paintings."[14] In so doing, the work became self-reflexive or self-referential to the extent that coterminous with the work's meaning was also a form of meta-commentary centering upon the construction, be it aesthetic, cultural or ideological, of this self-same meaning. What amounted to, in other words, a form of auto-critique. Such a tendency can arguably be discerned within the context of Rosemarie Castoro's *Brushstroke* series of works.

Castoro's practice, according to Tanya Barson, "was formed in the 'crux' of the concurrence of Minimalism with an empowered female identity—a circumstance shared by other female Minimalist artists and practitioners including Agnes Martin, Anne Truitt, Eva Hesse, Simone Forti, Yvonne Rainer and [Lucy] Lippard."[15] To this end, the artist was one of eight women who were invited to respond to Linda Nochlin's essay "Why Have There Been No Great Women Artists?" At the time of the article's publication, Castoro was working on her *Brushstrokes* series of paintings.

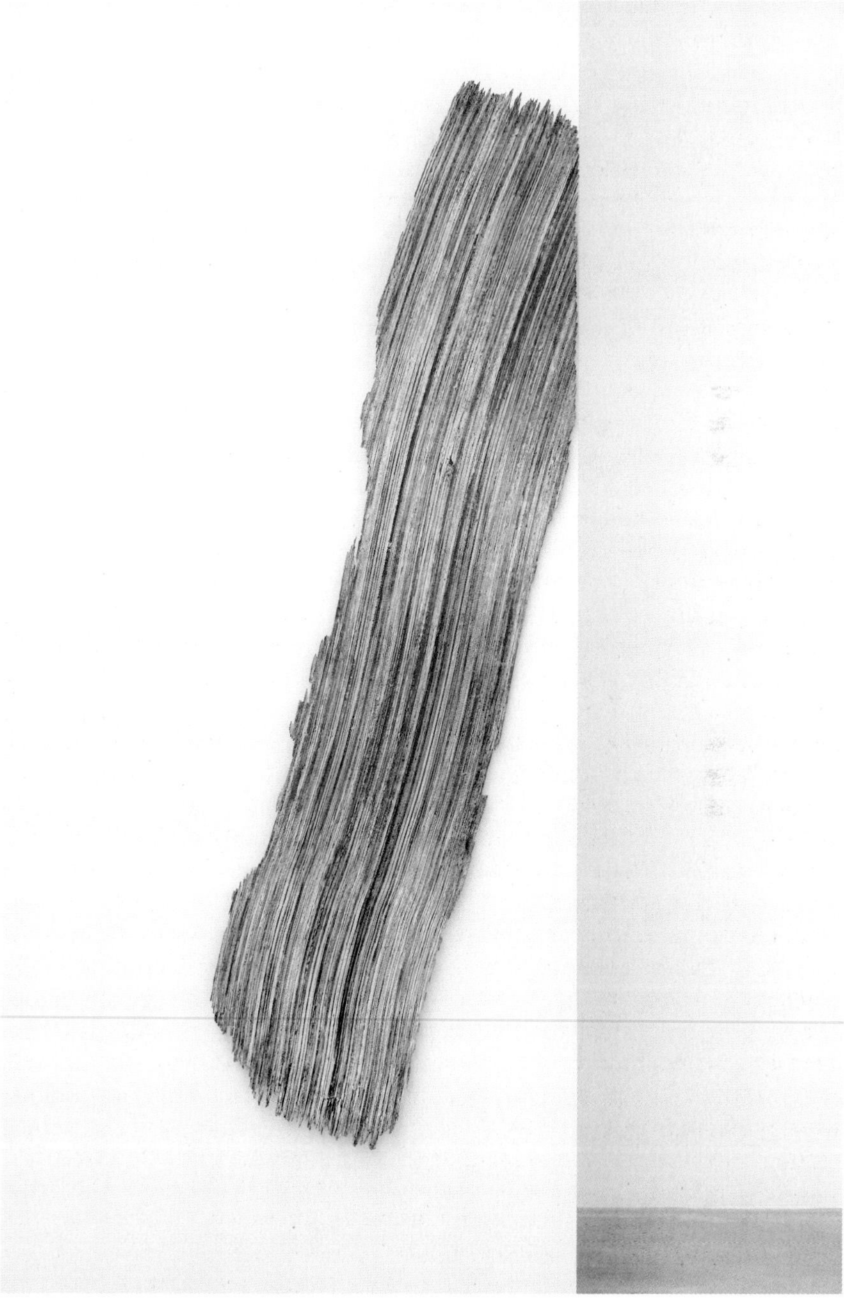

FIGURE 2.1 Rosemarie Castoro, *Corner Cut*, 1972.

They were made via a process wherein the artist, using a broom, "painted" an admixture of gesso and paste onto a sheet of masonite. The subsequent form that was arrived at on the surface of the masonite support was then cut out and then further worked on through a combination of sanding, a further application of the admixture on the artwork's edges and the surface being further worked in using a graphite stick and an eraser.[16]

On one level, deconstructing painting down to that which might be construed as being elemental to its status and condition, Castoro's *Brushstrokes* reimagines this most basic of units in sculptural terms.

Neither made in accordance with Abstract Expressionism's psychic generation of the brushstroke's élan, nor the more sardonic short-circuiting of this purportedly existential zeal as represented by Pop artist Roy Lichenstein's series of brushstroke paintings, made 1965–1966, Castoro's series define a new status and visibility for the brushstroke.

In addition to calling to mind Lichenstein's paintings, Kenneth Baker, writing in a review of an exhibition of her *Brushstrokes* for *Artforum* in 1972 claimed that Castoro's works "might also be seen as resembling curvilinear counterparts to some early Stella shaped canvases."[17] In the same year as Baker's review, Barbara Rose, writing in the *New York Magazine*, claimed that Castoro's brushstrokes were "ironically dripping with pseudo impasto."[18] Although the *Brushstroke* series were arguably at one remove from the subsequently more sardonic strategies associated with postmodernism, the works nevertheless worked to acknowledge a point that fell immediately *beyond* the assurances artistic modernism and specifically formalism had sought to proffer.

We may partly account for this imperative as being symptomatic of artists wanting to engage with the ideas of certain key twentieth-century thinkers. To this end, whilst Minimalism gravitated towards the phenomenology of Maurice Merleau-Ponty as a means of providing both a legitimizing rationale and a degree of critical purchase within the world of meaning, the philosophy of Ludwig Wittgenstein arguably provided an interpretive context within which the more cerebral and de-subjectivized approach to art making, an approach Conceptual Art, for the most part ushered in, could be understood. Although, as Stephen Melville remarks, the attraction that the ideas of Wittgenstein exercised remained suitably complex, broadly speaking, they stemmed from an "awareness that painting … could no longer assume its sensory availability without also assuming the linguistic mediation of that experience and so also the possibility that language and sensation might diverge or collide in any number of ways."[19] Moreover, "what Wittgenstein seemed to license was a certain practice of self-reference that could nonetheless count as rigorous, as measuring up to a certain (albeit obscure) standard of objectivity that would let art count as a mode of investigation more or less on par with—say, sharing a certain spirit with—modern science."[20]

Whilst the writings of Wittgenstein arguably provided an interpretive framework within which a piece like *Theory of Painting* could be read and made, to a certain extent explicable, the particularity of self-reference within this context, and specifically within the context of Bochner's work at the time emerged at a critical point at which it ostensibly became congruent with Greenberg's own ideas.

That Bochner's work could conceivably be compared to the criticism of Greenberg and in particular with respect to his edicts on painting arguably stemmed from what Melville has described was "the extraordinary epistemologism of the sixties—the general belief that art was a mode of knowledge and that its particularity as such lay in its self-reference."[21]

For the most part the interpretation of Greenberg's criticism as largely hinging upon a series of aesthetic judgments that were all, by and large, centripetal in their trajectory, hinges upon understanding Greenberg's account of modernist painting as that of entailing a seemingly inexorable descent towards what it perceived was its own essence. Moreover, Greenberg's ratification of what was claimed to be unique to painting and in particular the emphasis his writings gave to the idea of "self-criticism," have been on occasion interpreted within Kantian terms. However, whilst it is broadly conceivable to square Kant's enquiry with Greenberg's own, more localized ambitions, any estimation of their purported affinities would soon expose the limitations to reading Greenberg's criticism in this way. According to Jason Gaiger, and specifically with regards to the claims made in "Modernist Painting," "it would seem that all that Greenberg took up from Kant is the pivotal but highly generalized idea of self-criticism as the driving force of modernism and none of the actual content of Kant's own aesthetic theory."[22]

Evidently, whilst Greenberg adopted and, to a certain extent adapted, certain ideas that had initially been formulated by Kant, *Theory of Painting*, notwithstanding the claims made on its behalf with regards to its self-reference, to a significant extent remained resistant to being seen as the natural heir to Greenberg's formalism. In an interview with James Meyer, Bochner was asked whether his "reflection on painting and its physical and epistemological conditions" could somehow be read within a set of terms that were in concert with Greenberg and in particular with the art critic's "theory of modernist painting as an analysis of the conditions of the medium," a theory seemingly indebted to Kant's *Critique of Pure Reason*.[23] In his response Bochner remained at pains to distance himself from those critics associated with formalism:

> What I'm proposing is to examine every possible way in which the work can be thought about. To apply pressure on a variety of fronts, both conceptual and perceptual, and to permit discontinuities to surface. I think you have to set all this the context of the rhetoric of the sixties,

> which contended that all that counted existed *inside* the "framing edge." That, to me, was the repressive essence of formalism. I wondered what would change if you redrew the boundaries of the experience so that it didn't stop within the frame. How could a work reframe itself? ... All of those questions were a reaction *against* the position articulated by critics like Greenberg and Fried.[24]

In a sense, Bochner deconstructed the essentialist mythology and, equally, the mythologizing of essences that had been built up around modernist painting, with its rhetoric of "essential features" and "defining characteristics" (and what Greenberg had identified as specifically the medium's inexorable drive towards "flatness"). To this end, and as Field has observed, *Theory of Painting* undermined such "lofty philosophical criticism [by] substituting for it an almost childlike obviousness, a linguistic fundamentalism that seems to employ little than that which we have already known."[25]

Another artist who sought to disarticulate painting from formalism so as to challenge its underlying logic was the conceptual artist John Baldessari.

Directly before the *Cremation Project* of 1970, which saw Baldessari systematically burn all of his artworks from the period between 1953 and 1966, the artist produced a series of paintings that entailed particular statements being painted in black acrylic paint onto a white ground. Some of these paintings, like *Pure Beauty* (1966–1968), carried with them an ambiguity that appeared to both allude to painting's received role or function as being the vessel for an aesthetic that was both disinterested and distilled, whilst simultaneously short-circuiting that role. Others, for example *Examining Pictures* (1966–1968) (Plate 4), appeared less ambiguous and arguably more didactic in terms of how the painting, and for that matter, the text, became read. A small number also reproduced a statement from what would have been at the time of the painting's execution, a prominent art critic.

Clement Greenberg (1966–1968), was one such painting. Again, anonymously painted (Baldessari hired a professional sign painter), in a uniform layer of black acrylic painted directly onto a monochromatic ground, *Clement Greenberg* (the painting by Baldessari and not the formalist art critic), reproduced ad verbatim the following passage from Greenberg's text "Complaints of an Art Critic," first published in *Artforum* in 1967.

> Esthetic judgements are given and contained in the immediate experiences of art. They coincide with it; they are not arrived at afterwards through reflection or thought. Esthetic judgments are also involuntary; you can no more choose whether or not to like a work of art than you can choose to have sugar taste sweet or lemons taste sour. (Whether or not esthetic judgments are honestly reported is another matter.)[26]

Enmeshing the viewer within what was an iterative relay between the painted text and the text about painting, *Clement Greenberg*, like many works that fell within the purview of Conceptual Art "sought a kind of anarchy through rules and strategies that could verge on tautology."[27] Indeed, according to Rainer Fuchs, Baldessari's painted works "convey a veiling of painting that does not break categorically with its traditional material and technical presumptions but rather continues them, or places them under the rubric of conceptual art."[28]

However, this placing of painting under or within the auspices of Conceptual Art needs to be seen not as arbitrary but rather as being deliberately strategic to the extent that Baldessari "took the textual and theoretical focus of conceptual art literally ... and launched it in the enemy uniform of the traditional canvas painting."[29] The corollary of such a strategy, for the artist at least, was that painting simultaneously became both the means and the subject of a form of critique that sought to dismantle a set of discourses, both recent and historically given, that had worked to legitimize the medium.

Both *Theory of Painting* and *Clement Greenberg* then, became characteristic of a new analytical and, in the case of both artists, speculative mode of enquiry that entailed the production of paintings directly through the precepts, assumptions and ideologies by which the medium had been written and, if not, according to a number of its detractors, falsified.

Approaching the same broadly speculative approach that *Theory of Painting* had but fastening the work more readily onto the phenomenological co-ordinates of vision, *Project for an Artistic Attitude* (1970), by Antonio Dias diagrammatized the monochrome's transcendentalist ambitions. Ostensibly, by inverting the word "reality" and placing it centrally upon a monochrome ground, it appeared that the liminal threshold separating the actual realm of the viewer from the fictive realm of the painting, had been, in effect, breached. Having moved through the looking glass, that *Project for an Artistic Attitude's* text functioned on one level as the viewer now inhabited the hypothetical realm that certain accounts of the monochrome had implied. However, by being unable to relinquish painting's prior ontological condition (that is, the viewer continued to see "reality," continued to have "reality" in their sight, despite the fact that they now stood both somehow behind and indeed beyond it), *Project for an Artistic Attitude* worked to reveal their co-dependency, albeit in a way that as a project, it became reflexively stage-managed. Although in 1919 Kasimir Malevich, with reference to his white monochrome paintings had written "infinity is before you," the circuitry of Dias's painting meant that an equivalent mystical realm remained anterior or behind rather than before its respective audience.[30]

Whilst Dias's painting didn't necessarily negate painting per se but rather worked to explore, if not expose the operative conditions of the monochrome as it was conceived by an artist such as Malevich, Art & Language's *Secret Painting* (1967–1968) approached the monochrome with an arguably more deflationary set of ambitions.

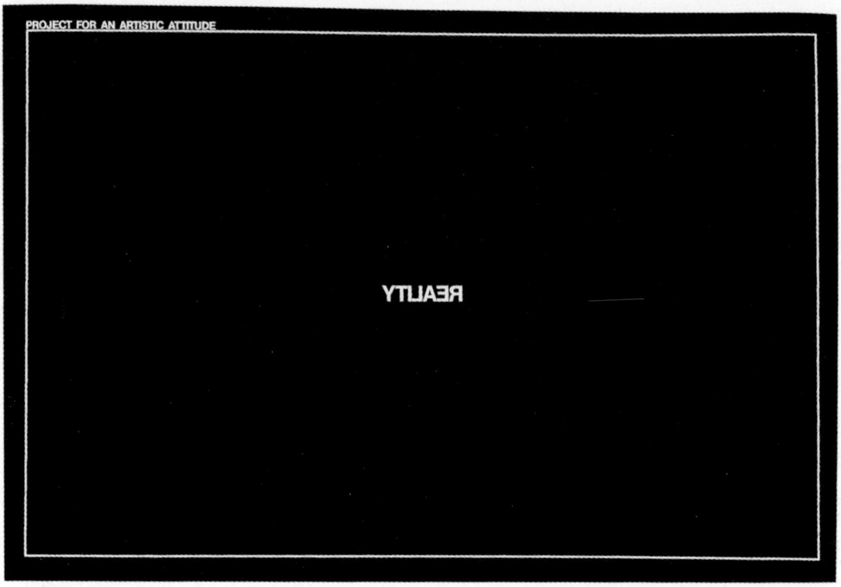

FIGURE 2.2 Antonio Dias, *Project for an Artistic Attitude*, 1970.

Consisting of a black monochrome, which hung directly alongside a framed statement reading "The content of this painting is invisible; the character and dimension of content are to be kept permanently secret, known only to the artist," *Secret Painting* worked to expose the monochrome's reliance upon language in terms of its explication whilst simultaneously and paradoxically, the text served only to negate the conditions of possibility for any such explication. In one sense the work demonstrated the fact of the visual and the verbal's interdependence. To this end, the more "abstract" a painting became, that is, the more it appeared to eschew recognizable content, the greater was its reliance upon a form of critical discourse for its explication. Indeed, the danger appeared to be one of the textual usurping the visual. As Charles Harrison, noted, "the more theoretically sophisticated the supporting structure of criticism by which abstract painting and sculpture was upheld in the 1960s, the more the art in question was reduced to the status of mere demonstration, leaving the writing looking more and more like the effective representational medium."[31] If, as Harrison claimed, the verbal carried with it greater interpretive cogency than the visual, could an artist simply marshal these qualities that abstract painting was purportedly foregrounded by? In the case of Marcel Broodthaer's *Paintings/Peintures (serie l'art les mots)*, 1973, with its inscriptions, written in French, of particular terms that pertained to what was ostensibly fundamental to painting and which included "coleur" (color), "pinceau" (brushwork) and "dessin" (drawing), evidently the answer was yes, they arguably could.

Other paintings by Art & Language during this period sought to debunk the ontological claims that had been made on behalf of abstraction through countering its proclivity to imply the fictive by simply stating the factual. To this end *100% Abstract* (1968) (Plate 5) merely detailed, or rather deadpanned the four percentages that collectively went to make up its physical constitution. Again, whilst the title implied verification, the four percentages, totaling 100%, short-circuited those ambitions and in the process short-changed the viewer by merely stating how the artwork had been constituted physically, rather than metaphysically.

On one level, *100% Abstract's* paradoxical basis reflected a similar attitude that On Kawara had adopted with regards to his so-called date paintings.

Begun in January 1966, this ongoing series has involved the artist inscribing upon a prepared monochrome surface the date the painting was made using the language of the country that the painting was executed in. Whilst certain limitations were imposed with regards to the format, for example the hand painted sans serif font was white, other aspects, including the canvases' size and color, remained variable. As in the case of *100% Abstract*, On Kawara eschewed any overt, painterly detail in favor of a more straightforward and unembellished presentation of a certain number of key facts relating to its actual construction. However, unlike a work such as *100% Abstract*, the presence of the artist was at least implied in the sense that by reading the painting in relation to the factual information it denoted, its execution necessarily encompassed, however obliquely, an autobiographical dimension. Indeed, On Kawara's practice incorporated other facets of "self-documentation" that were equally congruent with such an autobiographical reading.[32] During this period the artist produced maps that traced particular routes he had taken and sent telegrams to various friends that carried the message "I am still alive." Given the existential dimension of On Kawara's work at this time, his practice remained conceptually closer to the Polish artist Roman Opalka's own process of self-documentation.

In 1965, Opalka began *Opalka 1965/1–∞*, a lifelong project that in effect entailed the artist counting from 1 towards infinity. Each canvas or *Detail*, measuring 196 × 135 cm, the same dimensions as his studio door became the receptacle for the accumulation of numbers that were hand painted in white using a no. 0 paintbrush. In 1972, having counted/painted up to 1,000,000, the artist made the decision that the gray background of each successive *Detail* would be lightened by 1 percent using white paint. Along with the *Details*, Opalka also incorporated other means by which he documented his existence, including having his voice recorded as he counted and having his portrait taken photographically once a particular canvas had been completed. As Desa Philippi points out, "the recording of his voice will also serve a practical purpose once the written numbers can no longer be read on the canvas. As the background of the paintings becomes lighter, the moment will be reached when the artist paints white on white and has to rely on his recorded voice to guarantee the accuracy of the inscription."[33]

On one level, the paintings of both On Kawara and Opalka were rooted within a broader, more discursive set of practices that nevertheless were all broadly somehow conceptual in orientation and execution. To this end, the adoption of working with numerical sequences allowed artists "to defer to the driving force of a work's internal logic. Exempt from the necessity of material embodiment, the integers forming part of numerical progressions and permutations participate as the primary visual elements of a work rather than in preparatory studies or drawings."[34] Moreover, the adoption of such working methods enabled artists to engage with the medium of painting whilst at the same time sidestep considerations around formalism's conflation of painting with the primacy of the aesthetic.

In an attempt to return painting to its ostensibly elemental state, the statements and actions of the BMPT group, consisting of Daniel Buren, Olivier Mosset, Michel Parmentier, and Niele Toroni began on January 3, 1967 at the 18e Salon de la Jeune Peinture or so-called Salon of Young Painting at the Musée d'Art Moderne in Paris. During this event, the four artists made work according to the method of production they all had recently adopted. For Buren, this was the vertical stripe, for Mosset, it was a black circle painted on a square white ground. Parmentier, having folded his primed canvas into a series of pleats 38 cm wide and then spray painted the concertinaed surface, subsequently unfolded it, exposing in the process the concealed and unpainted areas. Finally, Toroni's application of paint was via a series of regularly placed brushstrokes using a no. 50 brush.

Along with producing artworks in their respectively adopted "styles," disseminated during their demonstration was a flyer gnomically proclaiming:

> Because painting is a game,
> Because painting is the application (consciously or otherwise) of the rules of composition,
> Because painting is the freezing of movement,
> Because painting is the representation (or interpretation or appropriation or disputation or presentation) of objects,
> Because painting is a springboard for the imagination,
> Because painting is spiritual illustration,
> Because painting is justification,
> Because painting serves an end,
> Because to paint is to give aesthetic value to flowers, women, eroticism, the daily environment, art, Dadaism, psychoanalysis and the war in Vietnam,
> *We are not painters.*[35]

A total of four BMPT events occurred during that year, after which Parmentier defected from the group, having expressed his objection to the suggestion made by the other artists that each of the four member's respective techniques should be transferable.[36]

The recurring motif in Buren's work, namely the vertical, colored band or stripe, which was usually 8.7 cm in width, stemmed from his decision in 1965 to purchase striped awning cloth at the Marché St Pierre in Paris. Having initially used this material in the more conventional means as a support, by 1968 Buren was placing these stripes, newly liberated from functioning in their received sense as receptacles for paint, within and indeed beyond the confines of the museum and the gallery space. According to Buren, from the outset the artist considered it necessary "to rid the object of its 'painting' I very quickly noticed that it was equally necessary to get rid of the object."[37]

Subsequently allied to a broader set of practices that were collectively premised upon an "examination of the framework that determines the reading conventions of artistic signs, as well as an analysis of the structuring principles of the sign itself," the significance of Buren's decision to work entirely with the pre-existent motif of the stripe was twofold.[38] Firstly, by working with what was in effect a "readymade" material, the artist could avoid the surface of the artwork carrying any discernable trace of the artist's hand. This conferred onto the status of the pieces a certain level of anonymity which in turn negated Buren being perceived, in any straightforward way at least, as the work's artist-producer. Secondly, having ostensibly divested painting of any of its illusionistic attributes, Buren was able to demonstrate the contingent nature of art. If indeed the artist was correct in his estimation that "a thing never exists in itself," then the latent contingencies of which his practice spoke, indeed, worked to expose were those organized around both the production and subsequent reception of the work of art.[39] This was achieved, on one level, by siting his striped pieces within particular public spaces. For example, during one particular night in March in 1968, Buren pasted approximately 200 sheets of green and white striped paper onto 200 billboards in and around Paris. These seemingly random incursions onto the architectural and often, importantly, commercial facades of the everyday became enigmatic yet ambiguous statements, anonymous contributions towards the pre-existent urban palimpsest.

By developing this approach, which Buren described as that of being "in situ," the artist was in a position to directly challenge the assumption, both generally with regards to the history of western art and specifically in relation to the theories of Greenberg, that the work of art was necessarily autonomous.[40] However, that is not to say that Buren's practice at the time remained entirely impervious to Greenberg's annexation of painting through what he claimed was the medium's "self-criticism" or self-reflexivity. However, rather than use self-criticism or auto-critique as the means by which the work could be hermetically sealed off from the world, Buren's self-critical investigation sought to do the very opposite; that is, to open the work up and out onto the world. In this sense, Buren's stripes became a

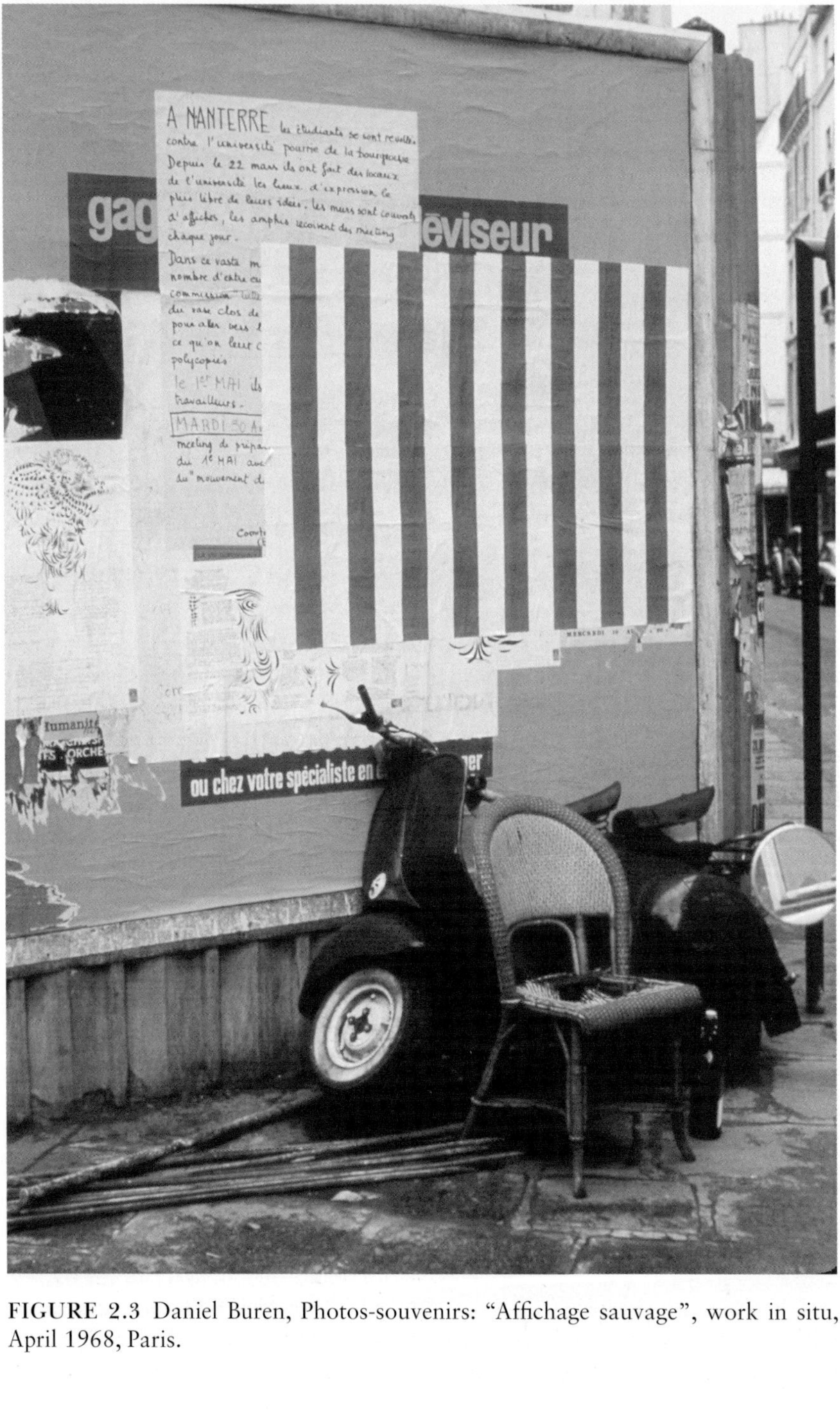

FIGURE 2.3 Daniel Buren, Photos-souvenirs: “Affichage sauvage”, work in situ, April 1968, Paris.

tactical investigation into the world it inhabited, rather than a withdrawal from it.

Along with his strategically placed stripes repudiating the conditions of possibility for painting to operate within an entirely autonomous field of operation, Buren's practice equally worked to negate the tache or "touch" of the expressive mark. Whilst the inherently expressive dimension of painting, even up until Abstract Expressionism had been read in terms of the individuated brush stroke being synonymous with the expressive identity of the author-artist, for many painters, such an understanding had become moribund, if not entirely obsolete.

Whilst in Buren's case the negation of the personal became mobilized through the ostensibly anonymous nature of the stripe, along with the photographic image Gerhard Richter's choice of depersonalized subject matter included working with a set of color charts.

Non-hierarchical and, at least in any received sense, non-expressive, Richter's eighteen color chart paintings of 1966 were banal, almost deadpan in the way that Andy Warhol's silk-screens of Campbell's soup cans were.

Richter had acquired the commercial color charts from a number of trade shops around Dusseldorf. All but one from the series was painted using enamel and for the most part Richter devised his own configurations with regards to the placement of each individual swatch of color. Whilst they appeared, stylistically at least to engage with the history of geometric abstraction and in particular the latter grid-like paintings of Piet Mondrian, what first attracted Richter to making paintings in this way was, conversely, the fact that "the beautiful effect of these color patterns was that they were so opposed to the efforts of the Neo-Constructivists, such as [Joseph] Albers, etc."[41]

Working within a similar vein, Richter's Gray paintings provided the conditions of possibility for the artist to make a related body of work that was equally borne out of artistic indifference. According to the artist, "gray is the welcome and only possible equivalent for indifference, noncommitment, absence of opinion, absence of shape."[42]

Begun a year after the artist had commenced working upon his color chart paintings, the gray paintings would form part of the artist's practice until 1976. In what were in effect monochrome paintings, the works appeared to inhabit some form of ontological hinterland with regards to their purpose or the role that had been conferred on them. Certainly, they attested and gave concrete form to Richter's observation that their color "makes no statement whatsoever; it evokes neither feelings not associations: it is really neither visible nor invisible."[43]

An interesting counterpoint to Richter's Gray paintings were the British artist Alan Charlton's own ongoing series of paintings which since the early 1970s have consistently remained one color, namely gray. Although, as with Richter's Gray series of paintings and indeed his practice generally Charlton's enquiry was keyed into the selfhood of the artwork rather than as a conduit wherein the selfhood of the artist could be made manifest, the terms upon which each respective series of paintings were given remained, to a certain extent, distinct. For whilst, by Richter's own admission, in addition to indifference gray became the ideal color for "fence-sitting, keeping quiet, despair," for Charlton such apparent neutrality could nevertheless be put towards more positive and positivistic ends.[44] Claiming that he wanted his paintings to be "abstract, direct, urban, basic, modest, pure, simple, silent, honest, absolute," Charlton's practice appeared to be, at the very least adumbrated by painters such as Stella and Ryman, both of whom had sought to deal directly and unequivocally with painting's concreteness.[45]

In one sense this was given through both Stella and subsequently Ryman invoking the law of identity. Expressed in mathematics as =, 2+5=7 is read as 2+5 is identical to 7. Within the realm of language, when someone states that the capital of France is Paris, the "is" functions on the same terms as the = sign to the extent wherein "is" can be taken to mean "is the same as."

In 1964 in a radio interview Stella claimed that "My painting is based on the fact that what is there *is* there. It really is an object. Any painting is an object and anyone who gets involved enough in this finally has to face up to the objectness of whatever he is doing."[46] Three years later, Ryman would invoke the law of identity in order to make, broadly speaking, the same claims on behalf of his own practice: "What the painting is, is exactly what [you] see: the paint on the corrugated and the color of the corrugated and the way its done and the way it feels. That's what's there."[47] Indeed, critics weren't necessarily immune from this tendency of summoning the law of identity as a means of legitimizing the ostensibly plainspoken matter-of-factness of painting. Writing in "The Silent Art" in 1969, Lucy Lippard would claim that the paintings of "Ralph Humphrey, Robert Ryman and Brice Marden ... emphasize the fact of painting as painting, surface as surface, paint as paint in an inactive, unequivocal manner."[48]

In addition, and as with Stella's canvases that would become increasingly architectonic and Ryman's own claims on behalf of what centered upon an "outward" rather than an "inward" aesthetic, Charlton's canvases by their very nature worked to activate their immediate surroundings due to having the appearance of being almost physically embedded within the spaces that they were exhibited in.[49] In this respect, and as John Slyce points out, painting for Charlton is "not a self-contained vehicle to be looked at, but a work to be seen in relation and aspect to the space it exists in."[50]

Along with Charlton's adoption of the color gray, Marcia Hafif's *An Extended Gray Scale* (Figure 2.4) equally approached painting within what could be argued were an empirico-positivist set of terms.

Consisting of 106 22 × 22 inch oil paintings, the first being white, the last being black, Hafif's series of paintings were organized around a series of almost imperceptible shifts in tone. Whilst the works repetitive, serial nature was reminiscent of Conceptual Art's proclivity to sequentialize and diagrammatize information, be it visual or textual, the enquiry remained

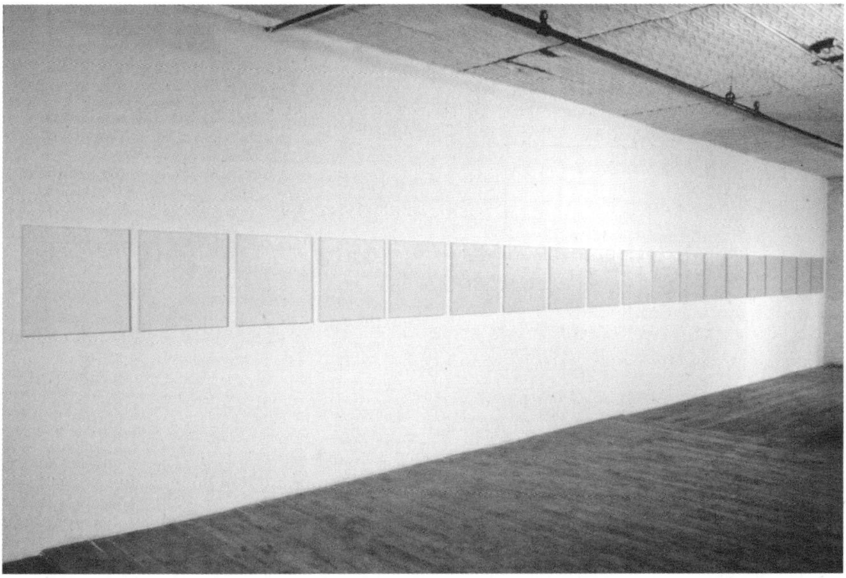

FIGURE 2.4 Marcia Hafif, *An Extended Gray Scale*, 1973.

bound up with the particular positivistic co-ordinates painting was believed, by Hafif, to occupy. Hafif described the piece thus:

> Each gray would be painted on a separate small canvas. Each painting would be of the same size and manufacture, differences being only in the shade of gray and in unavoidable variations in the paint and its application. Each shade would be barely distinguishable from the next. The number of paintings would be unknown until all the possibilities were exhausted. The project would end when distinguishing another intermediate shade became impossible.[51]

Whilst on one level Richter's own gray paintings countered the teleological progression of painting Greenberg had promulgated by adopting an attitude of indifference, it appeared that by the early 1970s other artists were attempting to key their respective enquiries into what was ostensibly fundamental to painting.[52]

Charlton's practice during the period in question had centered on a relationship to a very particular category of abstract painting that emerged concurrently with the advent of artistic modernism during the first two decades of the twentieth century. Indeed, one might argue that the monochrome represented the *ne plus ultra* of modernism's quest for technical radicalism. Be that as it may, and perhaps suggestive, somewhat paradoxically, of its pliability, an interest in the monochrome wasn't the sole preserve of artists working either in Europe or North America. As the 1970s played out, a number of Korean artists also looked towards the monochrome as the basis within which to develop their own respective artistic enquiries.

Dansaekhwa or Tansaekhwa, which means "monochrome painting" or "one color painting" bracketed a loose grouping of Korean artists who were active during the 1970s and who explored materiality, spirituality and for many, produced works that foregrounded process and painting's physicality. According to Simon Morley, "Dansaekhwa became a significant part of South Korea's quest for a modern cultural identity in a period marked by slow economic development and repressive politics."[53] As such, it suggested "a context within which Korean artists encountered the liberating example of Western modernism and sought to break with their own heritage and to assimilate and emulate Western modernism's styles."[54] However, alongside this emulation, and as Morley contends, "the monochrome painters felt compelled to re-examine their own indigenous cultural traditions without abandoning the knowledge they had acquired of progressive Western art, and thereby the native cultural and historical context within which they self-consciously emerged establishes criteria that both intersect with and differ from those customarily employed in relation to Western abstract art."[55]

Despite Joan Kee's admission that "Tansaekhwa was never an official movement; there was no consolidated group of artists who consciously worked together toward actualizing a particular set of ideas," what the artists who were associated with Dansaekhwa shared "was a commitment to thinking more intensively about the constituent elements of mark, line, frame, surface and space around which they understood the medium of painting."[56] For example, Ha Chong-Hyun utilized the so-called bae-ap-bub painting technique as the basis for an ongoing series of paintings entitled *Conjunction* (Plate 6), which he began in 1974. Reversing the traditional means by which a painting is made, according to the artist:

> Bae-ap-bub is a method that is the opposite of traditional painting, or applying paint on the front surface of the canvas. I push paint from the back to the front of hemp cloth. I was interested in creating a whole new method of creating that involved both the back and front of the surface. Although it sounds simple, there are many variations when paint is pushed through the holes of a hemp cloth. Depending on the piece, some holes are big while some are small, and this affects the paint that seeps through. For instance, when the holes are small, meaning that the cloth is more tightly woven with thinner threads, the paint that comes out onto the surface is thinner and longer, creating a totally different effect from that applied to the more loosely woven cloth. On the other hand, the pressure that I apply gives countless variations to the paint that seeps through.[57]

Whilst Ryman, Charlton, Chong-Hyun and Hafif continued to key their respective enquiries, to a lesser or greater extent into a set of concerns that first emerged during the period under question, the account of abstract painting as it developed during the 1970s and that will be discussed in the next chapter sought to look beyond what up until that point had been principal points of artistic reference, namely Conceptual Art and Minimalism.

If, as many had claimed, the implications that were held by Greenberg's theories had been systematically worked through, the paintings of Blinky Palermo were, certainly with respect to abstraction, emblematic of a newfound attitude artists were adopting and bringing to painting. Associated with but not beholden to artistic formalism, the work referenced and became connected with an additional set of contexts that tendentiously fell beyond the purview of Greenberg's theories.

Born Peter Schwarze, the artist adopted the pseudonym Blinky Palermo at the suggestion of Joseph Beuys, his teacher at the Academy in Dusseldorf. Beuys had previously likened his appearance to that of Blinky Palermo, a small-time mobster and boxing promoter, after which the name stuck. He began to make his *Stoffbilder* or cloth paintings in 1966. Comprised of sections of commercially produced fabric, their surfaces were *sui generis* to the extent wherein having stretched these sections of fabric, no paint was then subsequently applied. Instead, their final design derived from small number of these sections of colored fabric being mechanically sewn together.

Conceived to occupy a space where "painting, object and architecture intersect," Palermo's decision to work with commercially derived and mass-produced source material echoed what was more broadly indicative of a number of artists who oriented their respective practices towards a more mass-produced and depersonalized choice of subject matter.[58] Beyond Pop Art's fascination with the banal but nevertheless seductive veneers of mass culture, including advertising, Hollywood cinema and commercial design, 1966 was also the year that Richter began working directly from color charts that, like Palermo's sections of fabric, were derived from commercial outlets in the German city of Dusseldorf. Indeed, the artists were friends if not allies, having both enrolled at the Dusseldorf Academy in 1962.

Whilst the *Stoffbilders* abjured Greenberg's claims with respect to painting operating within a purely autonomous realm, they appeared unwilling to entirely relinquish their kinship with both the paintings of certain post-painterly abstractionists such as Kenneth Noland and a more discursive range of object-paintings which amongst others, included works by Ellsworth Kelly, Richard Tuttle and Karen Carson. Indeed, Palermo's cloth paintings inhabited an interstitial space between those artists, including Ellsworth Kelly and Richard Tuttle whose activities arguably remained modernist in both scope and import and Carson's own canvases, specifically her "Zipper" paintings that offered a less reverential approach towards abstraction.

Comprising her Masters exhibition in 1971 at the University of California in Los Angeles, the zipper pieces were canvases that consisted of sections that could be both zipped and unzipped by the viewer as a means of configuring different compositional designs. Beyond their obvious affinities with other participative forms of painting such as those already considered by Yoko

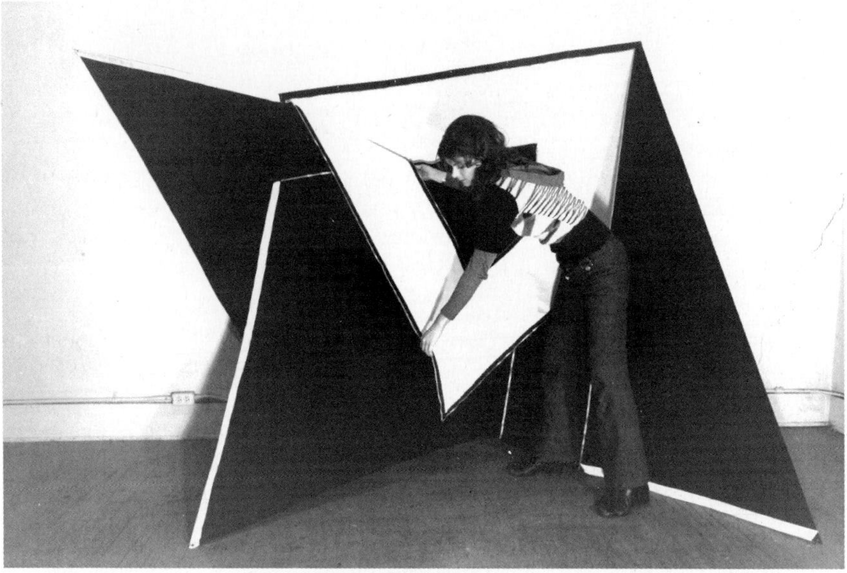

FIGURE 2.5 Karen Carson with *Untitled*, 1972.

Ono and, equally, particular moments within the history of abstraction—stylistically Carson's literal zips were reminiscent of the visual "zips" that punctuated the canvases of Barnett Newman, the series nevertheless lacked any clear or straightforward affinities with the strategies that either artistic formalism or its detractors had developed. It was possibly for this reason that the paintings of both Palermo and Carson represented a watershed moment in terms of presenting an account of abstraction derived not from the rarefied realm of art, but from a more demotic horizon that appeared more at ease with itself and less anxious to militate against Greenberg's formalism. However, and as Laura Meyer notes, it was arguably the democratizing effects of this series, directed towards artistic creativity and including a willingness to incorporate downgraded so-called "feminine" elements that became suggestive of how artists, and in particular those that were women, might engage with abstract painting after the perceived exhaustion of both Greenberg's criticism and those movements, including Minimalism and Conceptual Art, that ran directly counter to artistic formalism.[59]

Notes

1 Daniel Buren, "It Rains, It Snows, It Paints," in Lawrence Weiner, Daniel Buren, Mel Bochner and Sol LeWitt, "Documentation Conceptual Art," *Arts* Magazine 44, no. 6 (1970): 43.

2 Binstock, *Sam Gilliam: A Retrospective*, 85.

3 Ibid.

4 Ad Reinhardt, "Art-as-Art," *Art International* (Lugano) (1962), in *Art-as-Art: The Selected Writings of Ad Reinhardt*, ed. Barbara Rose (Berkeley: University of California Press, 1991), 53.

5 Echoing the artist's speculative approach to painting, Paolini claimed that his first work, Geometrical Drawing (*Disegno Geometrico*) (1960), should be described as a "proposition" rather than as a painting. Carolyn Christov Bakargiev, *Arte Povera* (London: Phaidon, 1999), 132.

6 Yve Alain Bois, *Formless: A User's Guide* (New York: Zone Books, 1995), 25.

7 Zelevansky, "Beyond Geometry: Objects, Systems, Concepts," 26.

8 Anne Rorimer, *New Art in the 60s and 70s: Redefining Reality* (London: Thames & Hudson, 2004), 182.

9 Rosalind E. Krauss, "Sense and Sensibility: Reflections on Post '60s Sculpture," *Artforum* 12, no. 3 (1973): 47.

10 "Artist's Statement Mel Bochner," in *High Times Hard Times New York Painting 1967–1975*, ed. Katy Siegel (New York: Independent Curators International, 2007), 58.

11 "How Can You Defend Making Paintings Now? A Conversation between Mel Bochner and James Meyer," in Philip Armstrong et al., *As Painting: Division and Displacement* (Cambridge, MA: MIT Press, 2001), 199.

12 Richard S. Field, "Mel Bochner: Thought Made Visible," in Richard S. Field, *Mel Bochner: Thought Made Visible 1966–1973* (New Haven, CT: Yale University Art Gallery, 1995), 45.

13 Ibid., 46.

14 William S. Wilson, "Dan Flavin: Fia Lux," *Art News* 68 (1970): 48.

15 Tanya Barson, "Rosemarie Castoro 1964–79: An Obstacle Course for a Dancer?" https://img.macba.cat/public/uploads/20180606/Tania_Barson_Rosemarie_Castoro_eng.0.pdf.

16 Rachel Stella, "Metamorphosis and Transmigration," *Rosemarie Castoro Working Out*, Thaddaeus Ropac London, 2022, https://ropac.net/usr/library/documents/main/rc_london_booklet_final.pdf.

17 Kenneth Baker, "Rosemarie Castoro. Tiber de Nagy Gallery," *Artforum* 10 no. 9 (1972): 87.

18 Barbara Rose, "Recommended," *New York Magazine*, 28 (February 1972): 69.

19 Stephen Melville, "Aspects," in Ann Goldstein and Anne Rorimer, *Reconsidering the Object of Art: 1965–1975* (Cambridge, MA: MIT Press, 1996), 234.

20 Ibid.

21 Ibid.

22 Jason Gaiger, "Constraints and Conventions: Kant and Greenberg on Aesthetic Judgment," *British Journal of Aesthetics* 39, no. 4 (1999): 379.

23 "How Can You Defend Making Paintings Now? A Conversation between Mel Bochner and James Meyer," in Armstrong et al., 200.

24 Ibid.

25 Field, "Mel Bochner: Thought Made Visible," 46.

26 See Greenberg, "Complaints of an Art Critic" (1967), in Greenberg, *The Collected Essays and Criticism Vol. 4 Modernism with a Vengeance, 1957–1969*, 265.

27 Friederich Meschede, "Wunderkammer Images," in Jessica Morgan, *John Baldessari: Pure Beauty* (Los Angeles, CA: Los Angeles County Museum of Art, 2009), 266.

28 Rainer Fuchs, "Uncovering the Hidden," in Morgan, *John Baldessari: Pure Beauty*, 242.

29 Ibid.

30 Kasimir Malevich, "Non-Objective Art and Suprematism" (1919), in Harrison and Wood, *Art in Theory 1900–2000 An Anthology of Changing Ideas*, 293.

31 Charles Harrison, *Conceptual Art and Painting: Further Essays on Art & Language* (Cambridge, MA: MIT Press, 2001), 24.

32 Peter Wollen, "Mappings: Situationists and/or Conceptualists," in *Rewriting Conceptual Art*, ed. Michael Newman and Jon Bird (London: Reaktion Books, 1999), 36.

33 Desa Philippi, "Matter of Words: Translations in East European Conceptualism," in Newman and Bird, *Rewriting Conceptual Art*, 154.

34 Rorimer, *New Art in the 60s and 70s: Redefining Reality*, 164.

35 Daniel Buren, Olivier Mosset, Michel Parmentier and Niele Toroni, "Statement" (1967) reproduced in Harrison and Wood, *Art in Theory 1900–2000 An Anthology of Changing Ideas*, 861.

36 See Laura Lisbon, "Michel Parmentier" in Armstrong et al., *As Painting: Division and Displacement*, 139.

37 "Interview with Jérôme Sans: Daniel Buren on the Subject of…" in *Daniel Buren: Intervention II Works in Situ* (Oxford: Modern Art Oxford, 2007), unpaginated.

38 Benjamin H. D. Buchloh, "Allegorical Procedures: Appropriation and Montage in Contemporary Art," in *Art After Conceptual Art*, ed. Alexander Albero and Sabeth Buchman (Cambridge. MA: MIT Press, 2006), 33.

39 Daniel Buren, "On the Autonomy of the Work of Art," in *Daniel Buren: Around "Punctuations"* (Lyon: Le Nouveau Musée, 1980), unpaginated, reproduced in Ann Goldstein and Anne Rorimer, *Reconsidering the Object of Art: 1965–1975* (Cambridge, MA: MIT Press, 1996), 90.

40 According to Buren, "in situ" describes a situation wherein the work of art "not only has a relationship with the place in which it finds itself, but also which has been made entirely in its place." "Interview with Jérôme Sans: Daniel Buren on the Subject of…" in *Daniel Buren: Intervention II Works in Situ*, unpaginated.

41 Gerhard Richter quoted in Benjamin H. D. Buchloh, "Interview with Gerhard Richter," in *Gerhard Richer Paintings* (Chicago: Museum of Contemporary Art and Toronto Art Gallery of Toronto, 1988), 19.

42 From a letter to Edy de Wilde, February 23, 1975 in *Gerhard Richter: Text, Writings, Interviews and Letters, 1961–2007* (London: Thames & Hudson, 2009), 97.

43 Ibid.

44 "Interview with Jan Thorn-Prikker, 2004" in *Gerhard Richter: Text, Writings, Interviews and Letters 1961–2007* (London: Thames & Hudson, 2009), 478.

45 See "Alan Charlton," *Annely Juda Fine Art*, https://www.annelyjudafineart.co.uk/artists/39-alan-charlton/overview.

46 Bruce Glasner, "Questions to Stella and Judd," in *Minimal Art: A Critical Anthology*, ed. Gregory Battcock (London: Studio Vista, 1968), 58.

47 Phyllis Tuchman, "Interview with Robert Ryman," *Artforum* 9 (1971): 53. As if to reassert this reading, Ryman reiterates this sentiment by claiming in 1992 that the "painting is exactly what you see." Thomas McEvilley, "Absence Made Visible," *Artforum* 30 (1992): 92.

48 Lucy R. Lippard, "The Silent Art," quoted in *Abstract Art in the Twentieth Century*, ed. Frances Colpitt (Cambridge: Cambridge University Press, 2002), 58.

49 David Bachelor, "On Paintings and Pictures: An Interview with Robert Ryman," *Frieze* 10 (1993), 45.

50 John Slyce, "Alan Charlton: Vertical Integration," *Contemporary* 82, https://www.galerie-tschudi.ch/media/pages/press/vertical-integration/359e1c466a-1682427492/gt_2006_alan-charlton_contemporarymagazin.pdf. Although as Slyce adds, Charlton's canvases are not usually made with a specific gallery space in mind. Ibid.

51 Jean-Charles Massera in *Marcia Hafif, From the Inventory*, catalog for the exhibition in 1994 at the Kunsthall Barmen in Wuppertal-Barmen, 53–9.

52 Fundamental Painting was the title of an exhibition that was staged at the Stedelijk Museum in Amsterdam in 1975 and included a selection of gray paintings by Richter.

53 Simon Morley, "Dansaekhwa Korean Monochrome Painting," *Third Text* 27, no. 2 (2013): 189–207.

54 Ibid., 192.

55 Ibid., 195.

56 Joan Kee, "Skin & Surface: What is Dansaekhwa and what is its legacy today?" *Frieze* 169. https://www.frieze.com/article/skin-surface.

57 Ines Min, "A Conversation with Ha Chong-Hyun," *Ocula* July 13, 2017, https://ocula.com/magazine/conversations/ha-chong-hyun.

58 Dietmar Elgar, *Gerhard Richter: A Life in Painting*, trans. Elizabeth M. Solaro (Chicago: The University of Chicago Press, 2009), 182.

59 Laura Meyer, "Constructing a New Paradigm: European American Women Artists in California. 1950–2000," in *Art, Women, California, Parallels and Intersections, 1950–2000*, eds. Diane Burgess Fuller and Daniela Salvion (Berkeley, CA: University of California Press, 2003), 110.

3

Painting in the Expanded Field

Almost everyone is agreed about '70s art. It is diversified, split, factionalized. Unlike the art of the last several decades, its energy does not flow through a single channel for which a synthetic term, like Abstract Expressionism, or Minimalism, might be found ... We are asked to contemplate a great plethora of possibilities in the list that must now be used to draw a line around the art of the present: video; performance; body art; conceptual art; photo-realism in painting and an associated hyper-realism in sculpture; story art; monumental abstract sculpture (earthworks); and abstract painting, characterized, now, not by rigor but by a willful eclecticism.[1]

First published in the journal *October* in 1979, "Sculpture in the Expanded Field" sought to map out, as the title of the article suggested, an expanded field of practice generally and sculpture's place within this field in particular. Adopting the diagrammatic structure of a Klein group, the author, Rosalind Krauss, posited within it two pairs of key binary terms, namely "architecture," "not-architecture," "landscape" and "not-landscape."

As a survey of what had been the prevailing artistic milieu over a period of approximately ten years, "Sculpture in the Expanded Field" was characterized by an attempt to rationalize what had become by the time the text was written an intrinsically discursive set of practices into a coherent matrix of categories and proper names. Moreover, according to Krauss, the critical discourses that such work had engendered were complicit in the purported "manipulation" of a received set of terms that included sculpture:

> The critical operations that had accompanied postwar American art have largely worked in the service of this manipulation. In the hands of this

> criticism categories like sculpture and painting have been kneaded and stretched and twisted in an extraordinary demonstration of elasticity, a display of the way a cultural term can be extended to include just about everything.[2]

Although for Krauss, and for several commentators who have subsequently reflected on her text sculpture was understood "not as a medium, but as a term that operates semiotically in opposition to both 'architecture' and 'landscape,'" arguably the question of the medium's place within an expanded field of practice was what Krauss remained, on one level, preoccupied with.[3] However, although by her own admission painting as a form of cultural practice had equally been read in terms of its "elasticity," what this meant in real terms remained, in Krauss's text at least, an intriguing but nevertheless untested claim. Rather than attempt to graft the medium of painting onto Krauss's schema, this chapter will explore the text's more salient claims apropos certain approaches to painting that emerged during the 1970s. As the universal category of sculpture had "been forced to cover such a heterogeneity that it [was] itself, in danger of collapsing," the aim of this chapter will entail an attempt to map out an equivalent heterogeneity that marked the practice of painting during the period in question. In one respect, the multifarious currents, trajectories, allegiances and contestations that worked to define painting as a whole at that time remains unfortunately beyond the scope of what this chapter could suitably accommodate. Rather, and notwithstanding the climate wherein Greenberg's writings for many had become deeply problematic, if not anathematic, my aim is to consider how particular instances of abstraction, if one can still legitimately apply that term, were nevertheless still able to proliferate and, moreover, negotiate a legitimate position for itself.

With its drive towards the rationalization of sculpture by seeking to ascertain its epistemological as much as its ontological construction (according to Krauss, during the early sixties sculpture had entered a "categorical no-man's land"), "Sculpture in the Expanded Field" in effect book-ended a period of approximately fifteen years of artistic production that had begun with Minimalism. Indeed, arguably sculpture had been able to "expand" due to Minimalism opening up the possibilities of what constituted sculpture as a form of three-dimensional practice and the implications this held for the experiential basis of the artworks that fell within its critical purview. Certainly, it was Minimalism that challenged the historically received illusionistic basis of sculpture in order to present a very separate set of possibilities with regards to both the artwork's production and its reception. To this end, the dialectic of Minimalism entailed an expansion into a separate set of contingencies that were governed by a separate set of operations and contexts. Indeed, the tendentious enveloping of the embodied spectator's presence by the Minimalist object was partly why Fried sought to challenge its position within the late American avant-garde in his essay, "Art & Objecthood," published in *Artforum* in 1967. However, whilst sculpture as an artistic idiom underwent profound changes, the development of painting into separate categorical modes was arguably less pronounced. Nevertheless, numerous accounts of artistic production within the context of the late 1960s and the early 1970s worked to emphasize the fact that painting had become increasingly marginalized by a series of object and performance-based practices that fell beyond the purview of discrete disciplines and "essential conditions." Whilst this reading of late modernist practice remains credible, if not somewhat commonplace, inevitably it tends to give credence to a somewhat polarized account of artistic production, one that, in its "definitiveness [and] in the certainty of their positions—one must paint, or one cannot paint [formulates an historiography] based on either/or propositions and sudden historical breaks."[4]

Nevertheless, for various reasons a number of artists appeared to have outgrown the medium. As well those artists who subsequently became labelled "Minimalist," several prominent conceptual artists who had begun their careers through an engagement with painting quite rapidly moved beyond the medium. For example, between 1963 and 1965 Lawrence Weiner produced a series of what were called Propeller Paintings. These took as their central motif the television test patterns that would be broadcast through the night. However, like those other artists that had first sought recourse to the world of ideas through painting, Weiner quickly positioned his practice beyond its seemingly narrow and ideologically riven confines.

Notwithstanding what Krauss had claimed was painting's "elasticity" as a cultural term, along with its arguably more novel counterparts, the question remained as to what extent painting could still be considered, as it had been during the 1950s, as a progressive mode of practice. For certain commentators what stood in painting's way, what indeed would always stand in painting's way, was its inability to relinquish its complicity with illusionism and, by extension, tradition. As Douglas Crimp, writing in 1973 had observed:

> The problem for painting's survival in the mid 1960s was the perennial problem of illusionism. In fact, a major impetus to Minimal sculpture was the feeling among its practitioners (some of whom had previously been painters) that painting could never be successfully anti-illusionistic … In a sense, the very success of Minimal sculpture depended on its ability to define itself specifically as a mute object, i.e., as an object which bespeaks only itself. This, it was thought, was something which painting as an inherently opposed medium could not do; a painting will always evoke, if nothing else, a virtual space from that real space which it actually inhabits.[5]

The Minimalist sculptor Donald Judd had highlighted this problem that was ostensibly unique to painting eight years previously when he remarked

"Almost all paintings are spatial in one way or another."[6] Arguably then, painting was a conflicted medium—unwilling or indeed unable to relinquish its ties to the past yet, at the same time, wanting to ensure currency by way of establishing a legitimate position for itself within this so-called "expanded field" without such an ambition merely being construed as a form of either tokenism or appeasement. As David Reed notes:

> Painting was under attack as an outmoded medium in the late 1960s and early 1970s, and the experimental painting that interested me was caught in the middle. It was condemned by the conservative defenders of tradition, who used outmoded definitions and old-fashioned criteria to make judgments against it. At the same time, it was dismissed by those who did not see how painting could be connected to other forms of experimental art. For these critics, no kind of painting was possible.[7]

Although for many painting had fallen out of critical favor, the very fact that it was perceived as a peripheral form of practice afforded artists a certain degree of latitude and, equally, provided a mandate by which painting could be investigated, interrogated and potentially reimagined. As the artist Alan Shield noted: "Everybody in that time was thinking about change anyway. We were thinking about changing the social structure, thinking about changing the legal system ... [It was] fairly evident for me to say, 'well, I'd like to change the format of painting.'"[8] In short, whilst a certain number of painters who had emerged out of a set of precedents that had first been espoused by Greenberg continued to develop, if not further entrench their work according to what remained, for the most part, a formalist orthodoxy, others were more willing to open up, as it were, their respective practices to the currents that were emerging both within the discourses and the milieus of art and, for that matter, within society at large. Certainly, what characterized the work of Joan Snyder at this time was a preoccupation not only with the legitimacy of painting within a critical terrain of post-Minimalism, but equally whether the medium could engage with "content" in a more direct and unabashed manner.

Having moved to New York in 1967, the paintings that she produced during this time were characterized by the recurrence of a box-like motif. Although this provided Snyder with the impetus by which to generate imagery and, albeit it in a somewhat oblique way, explore subject matter, there was another motivation behind adopting this trope. Having worked under the Minimalist Robert Morris at Rutgers University in New Jersey, Snyder was keen to distance herself from the pared down aesthetic that Minimalism had become synonymous with. As the artist recounted: "I took Morris's minimal boxes and made them as crazy and decorative as I could. I put a breast in them, things hanging off them, boxes in landscapes, trees and grass in boxes, pieces of bodies in a box under the ground."[9]

At this point within the artist's practice, Snyder became perhaps most well known for her "Stroke Paintings" which she had begun in 1969 with *Lines and Strokes* (1969), a painting that is now considered to be the first in this series. Comprised initially of a number of horizontal stokes of irregular lengths, as the series developed the paintings subsequently encompassed both a richer vocabulary of marks organized within a more elaborate and at times ornate series of designs and patterns. Arguably what remained consistent throughout the series though was its emphasis upon the singularity of the individual brush mark or stroke as a fundamental component of the image. However, whilst the proclivity to focus upon the technical means of painting was characteristic of formalism's rationale (and moreover, the Stroke Paintings echo Maurice Merleau-Ponty's description of Paul Cézanne's canvases as comprising a series of "patient hatchings"), Snyder also understood the strokes' function as autobiographical ciphers, albeit suitably ambiguous ones: "The strokes in my paintings speak of my life and experiences. They are sometimes soft ... they sometimes bleed and cry and struggle to tell my story with marks and colors and lines and shapes. I speak of love and anguish, of fear and mostly of hope."[10]

In the paintings that immediately followed after the stroke paintings, whilst they remained autobiographical, they became more explicitly oriented towards an engagement with a more overtly political subject matter. This stemmed from her engagement with feminism, and specifically the types of questions that were being directed towards painting by women artists during the 1970s. For Snyder, the issue was one of whether "there was a female esthetic or wasn't there? And I was one of those who was out to prove that there was, that our work comes out of our lives, and that women's experiences are somehow different from men's experiences, so our work is going to be different."[11] Arguably it was with *Small Symphony for Women*, painted in 1974 (Plate 7), that Snyder was able to articulate and work through at least some of these far-ranging questions.

Adopting the historically received convention of the triptych format, *Small Symphony for Women* sought, as the title suggested, to be a symphony "of women, about women, for women ... a symphony with words and marks, colors and squares."[12]

Reading the painting from left to right, the first panel is comprised of what is in effect a series of speculative statements that worked to set out the painting's political agenda. Posing questions such as "Can symphonies be made out of this subject?" in the artist's own handwriting, the canvas, stylistically at least, was reminiscent of certain paintings by Cy Twombly, with their often semi-legible graffiti-like scrawls and scribbles. However, whilst Twombly was drawn to a classical and arguably idealized past, *Small Symphony for Women* attempted to confront a very real and lived present. With Snyder's proclivity towards the inclusion of ciphers and symbols within her earlier canvases, the second panel can be seen as both a visual elaboration and exploration of at least some of the words and phrases within the first panel. For example, in the upper left-hand corner of the second panel a square of cadmium red directly corresponds to the abbreviation "CAD RED MED" that forms the first listed color, placed in a column in the middle of the first panel and under the heading "COLORS." Equally, a rudimentary image of a house that stands directly adjacent to what we take to be the sun and a tree within the second panel provides the viewer with, at the very least a visual approximation of what is written in the first panel, "LANDSCAPE SPACE." Finally, the third panel, an irregularly shaped and colored grid arguably should be seen as a distillation, if not resolution of the first two panels.[13]

Another artist who approached the dominant discourses that shaped both the production and critical reception of modernism in America during the 1960s with a certain degree of suspicion and ambivalence was Mary Heilmann.

Having undertaken graduate studies in sculpture at the University of California in Berkeley, Heilmann moved to New York in 1968. Becoming a painter for Heilmann was an "antagonistic move."[14] Indeed, such a combative approach was evident when the artist claimed that,

> I had seen the work of Christensen and Young, and also Al Held, and had started doing some painting while at school, but I had little in common with the painting students. In fact, they were adversaries. The same was true in New York. I didn't fit with the group informed by the Greenberg-influenced discourse. So even though I looked askance at the culture of painting, I chose it as a practice in order to have arguments with people like Robert Smithson.[15]

The challenge then, as Elizabeth Armstrong notes, "was to find a way to paint while rejecting the history of painting."[16]

Whilst to a certain extent *Little* 9 × 9 (1973) (Plate 8) is organized around the modernist trope of the grid, it remains characterized by a somewhat nonchalant series of vertical and horizontal lines that have been etched into the painted surface of the canvas and its edges apparently by the artist's finger or another blunt instrument. Unlike, for example, one of Mondrian's linear abstractions that imbued its geometry with a quasi-spiritual austerity, Heilmann's painting by comparison appears lackadaisical, reminiscent of a child using their finger or a fork to make some form of repeated pattern on their dinner plate. In both cases whilst there is intent, there is also a distracted playfulness.

Whilst Heilmann used the dominant "Greenberg-influenced discourse" as a critical point of departure by which she could begin to formulate her own painterly language, like many artists of her generation, the initial orientation of Lynda Benglis's practice was towards Abstract Expressionism.

Having received a BFA in painting from The H. Sophie Newcomb Memorial College for Women in 1964, the same year in which she moved to New York, it was Abstract Expressionism that "served as a kind of patrimony that gave permission to assert emotionalism and spontaneity, and to be passionately involved with one's materials."[17]

A preoccupation such as this was all the more remarkable for the fact that by 1965 both Minimalism and Conceptual Art had made a clean and decisive break with both the perceived hegemony of aesthetic formalism generally and Abstract Expressionism in particular. Unlike Abstract Expressionism, or at least those artists who adopted an animated painterly style and drew upon a range of iconographic and symbolic motifs, Minimalism and Conceptual Art tendentiously eschewed both psychological depth and abstraction's proclivity towards a particular identification of the artist-author through an overtly expressionistic and subjectivized form of mark-making. Broadly speaking, what their efforts resulted in were objects, rather than specifically paintings, that appeared to be devoid of both conventional meaning and the effects of having been handcrafted. However, whilst Benglis sought to emulate certain salient characteristics of Abstract Expressionism, including its emphasis on material process and individual artistic agency that foregrounded the maker's body, there remained the need to keep its more verbose tendencies in check.

A relatively early work such as *Embryo II* (1967) anticipated the subsequent development of Benglis' practice that often encompassed a direct, physical engagement with the materials she had chosen to work with which, with regards to the experiential basis it engendered on the part of its respective audience, was often embodied. To this end, in *Embryo II* form was found as much as it became consciously made through the gradual, layered application of hot colored wax onto an elliptical support whose length, at thirty-six inches, was roughly comparable to the length of the artist's arm.[18] Moreover, and as Nora Lawrence discerns: "Installed, it occupies the space of an adult head and torso, and its bright tentacles reach out to engage its viewer directly."[19]

Beginning in 1969, Benglis then made a series of works that entailed pouring pigmented polyurethane foam onto the gallery floor. The comparison with Pollock's own technique of flinging paint directly onto a horizontally placed support was inevitable and in an article that was published in *Life* magazine in 1970 this connection was made explicit through the juxtaposition of Benglis making a poured work alongside images of Pollock in his studio at East Hampton.[20] Indeed, beyond the way these polyurethane poured pieces functioned as the means by which Benglis could establish a performative material practice, arguably the development of Benglis's career during the latter half of the 1960s sought to re-engage, as Abstract Expressionism had done, with Romanticism. However, such an ambition, at least for Benglis, required eschewing the tendency for solipsism that it invariably became complicit with. As a result, Benglis's poured works often became conflated with a somewhat indeterminate understanding of nature. According to Thomas Hess, a critic who had written extensively on the paintings of Willem de Kooning:

> Benglis's concern with making soft things hard while preserving their insouciant memories of softness may or may not have something to do with feminism, phallicism, and other politico-sensualities. She is more concerned, I think, with the Romantic concept of the artist as a force of Nature. Nature can change states—freezes water, melt rocks; Benglis, too, can congeal or liquefy matter—and in the process make sculpture as calculated, precise and refined as icicles.[21]

Whilst some of the more overtly theatrical and imposing polyurethane foam installations that Benglis made during the period in question appeared to present the viewer with an account of nature that existed within an elemental and nascent state, with lava-like organic forms appearing to emerge out of the wall and spill directly into the gallery space, these installed pieces were nevertheless resistant to the problematic conflation of nature with the "feminine." As Susan Krane points out:

> Whereas many women artists of the period identified with landscape from a universal, nurturant viewpoint (as personified by the mythological "mother earth"), Benglis associated with the more volatile and capricious side of nature's titanic forces, with the sublime and *terribilità*. She refused, however, to dichotomize nature and culture, body and mind; she was involved simultaneously with the realm of primal sensations and with cultural critique and art-historical revisionism.[22]

As Krane's statement suggests, Benglis, like many other women artists working at this time strategically adopted a critical position in relation to a set of male dominated art historical and cultural precedents wherein "the conceit of the canvas as surrogate for the female body, and of the act of painting as phallic [had] long been endemic to art discourse."[23]

Although, and as has already been observed, Benglis was initially sympathetic to certain strategies that had previously been adopted by Abstract Expressionism, there remained a certain resistance to allowing her own work to be entirely assimilated within it. This was partly achieved through the production of a set of objects that were, in effect, hybrid. For Benglis this wasn't so much a rejection of painting per se but rather entailed "trying to redefine what it was."[24]

Part of the critical discourse that had prefaced Benglis's own practice had centered upon the idea of medium specificity. Although the term itself has been applied retrospectively, what it sought to articulate was an impulse within formalism's account of modernism that worked to ensure that the traditional mediums of art, in this case painting and sculpture respectively, remained categorically discrete and mutually exclusive. To this end, even a cursory glance directed towards the formalist art criticism during the 1960s, in effect, from "Modernist Painting" on, would very soon establish the fact that for the likes of Greenberg and Fried (although there were others), what made modernist painting modernist was its ability to firmly entrench itself within its own unique area of competence. This drive to safeguard the discreteness of a particular medium and, equally, the fear of painting becoming contaminated by particular attributes which characterized other mediums is evident in the following statement by Fried, made in 1967:

> For example, a failure to register the enormous difference in quality between, say, the music of Elliott Carter and that of John Cage or between the paintings of [Morris] Louis and those of Robert Rauschenberg means that the real distinctions—between music and theater in the first instance and between painting and theater in the second—are displaced by the illusion that the barriers between the arts are in the process of crumbling ... and that the arts themselves are at least sliding towards some kind of final, implosive, highly desirable synthesis. Whereas in fact the individual arts have never been more explicitly concerned with the conventions that constitute their respective essences.[25]

In a sense, Fried's claims ran counter to a period wherein there was much discussion, albeit beyond the purview of those debates that were being played out within the somewhat narrow confines of formalist art criticism, that centered upon notions of hybridity and intermediality within the visual arts.

The year before Fried had sought to challenge Minimalism's own claims on behalf of late modernist practice, Dick Higgins, an artist associated with Fluxus, had published a text entitled "Intermedia" in the first edition of *Something Else*. In contradistinction to Fried's own claims on behalf of the artwork, Higgins made the following observation: "Much of the best work being produced today seems to fall beyond media."[26] Indeed, Higgins detected a more sinister agenda behind those who still sought to give credence to medium specificity: "The idea that a painting is made of paint on canvas or that a sculpture should not be painted seems characteristic of the kind of social thought—categorizing and dividing society into nobility with its various subdivisions, untitled gentry, artisans, serfs and landless workers—which we call the feudal conception of the Great Chain of being."[27]

Given the currency of such a term during the period within which Benglis was attempting to critically locate and define the nature of her own practice, inevitably other artists would equally want to somehow extend the remit of abstract painting beyond the narrow parameters that had been imposed upon it by the dialectic of formalism.

As we have seen, Benglis's poured paintings worked outwards, in one sense, from a reading of Jackson Pollock's so-called "all-over" canvases. In so doing, the work acknowledged the performative dimensions of painting. The emphasis given to both material process and the maker's body through this performative approach also characterized the work of Helen Almeida. Although her practice had what Maria Luísa Coelhohas has described as a "communality of aesthetic vocabulary linking her work with conceptual and minimalist art, as well as with performance and body-art," during the 1970s Almeida consistently sought to engage with the visual language and historical conventions of painting. [28]

During this period she produced three inter-related series, *Canvas(es) for wearing* (1969–1970), *Inhabited Painting(s)* (1975–1976) and *Studies for Inner Improvement* (1977).

According to Delfim Sardo, it was the slashed canvases of Lucio Fontana, which Almeida had occasion to see in Paris in 1964 that "promoted her to start seeing the physical support used for painting—the canvas and the stretcher—as a vehicle for a spatial, conceptual approach to painting that takes the body as its principal point of reference."[29]

Dialectically engaging with Leon Battista Alberti's foundational claim that one is to construe painting as an "open window through which the subject to be painted is seen," in *Tela Habitada (Inhabited Canvas)*, 1976, we see the artist initially positioned directly behind what is in this instance a transparent support, revealing what is usually concealed, namely the stretcher frame of the painting.[30] As we read the sixteen images from left to right and from top to bottom, we see Almeida press against and then subsequently penetrate the surface of the painting, allowing her hand and her face to appear. The visual coda, as it were, to these actions consists of three images. In the first we see the aftermath of Almeida's actions, namely the two points wherein the substrate has been perforated. The second of the two images is comprised of the artist seemingly "veiled" by the substrate. The final image, by being a duplicate of the first brings the process full circle. In so doing, Almeida acts out her "desire to conquer an aesthetic space."[31] Here Almeida "directs" the production of how she is represented rather than simply being an object of representation. In so doing, the artist's body becomes "an active producer of meaning and art objects" rather than a static, and essentially passive image.[32]

In one respect, a work such as *Tela Habitada (Inhabited Canvas)* demonstrated the artist's intention of wanting to become one with painting. As she asserted in 1999: "I was my work. There was no distinction between the canvas, the dimension of the canvas, and me. There was no distinction between the inside or the outside. My inner self was my outer self and my outer self was my inner self."[33] Indeed, although it was Fontana and not Pollock that, in one respect prefaced her enquiry during the period in question, this statement nevertheless is reminiscent of Pollock's claim of wanting to be, as it were, "in the painting."[34]

Geta Brătescu, an artist who significantly contributed to Conceptual Art in Romania during the 1970s, also produced work that was process-oriented and which sought to collapse the categorical boundaries that separated the body of the painting from the body of the artist. For example, in her performance *Towards White* (1975), and taking Pollock's aforementioned statement at face value, we witness the artist's studio and then the artist gradually being visually collapsed into each other through the various surfaces of the studio and of the artist's body being covered with white paper and paint.

What, on one level united the work of Benglis, Almeida and Brătescu was the fact that their respective practices all entailed an acknowledgement of, if not direct incursion into the realm of three-dimensional space. Rather than produce anything that might have been construed as sculpture *per se*, the conflation of painting with sculpture meant that artists could not

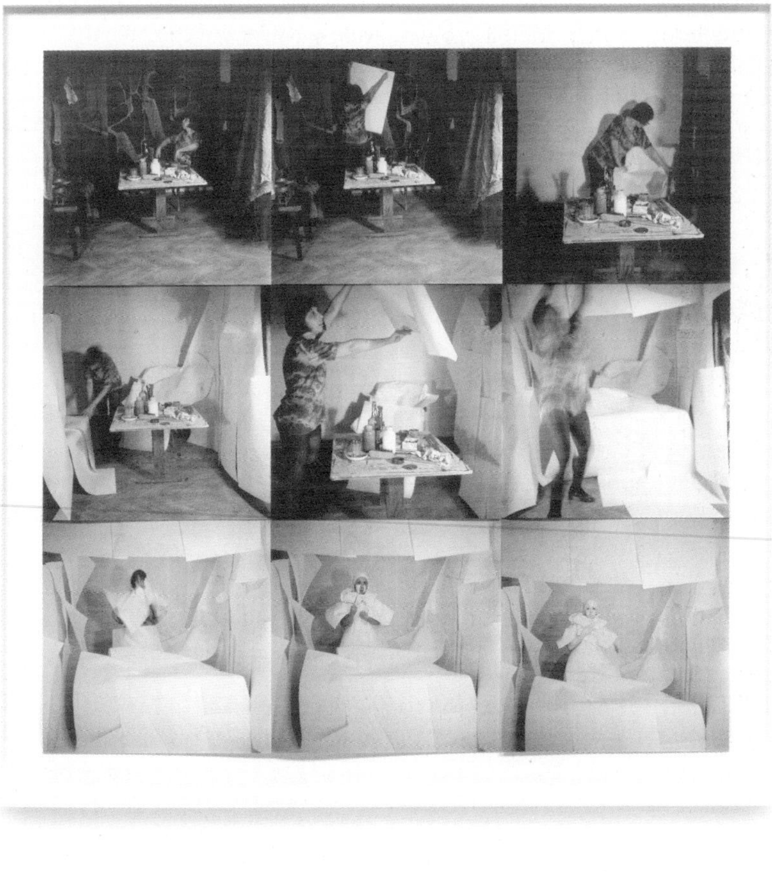

FIGURE 3.1 Geta Brătescu, *Către alb (Towards White)*, 1975.

only circumvent painting's historical basis within illusionism, it could also develop a post-Greenbergian account of abstract painting to the extent that it was now no longer reducible down to a set of essential characteristics or clearly defined limiting conditions.

On one level, Benglis's poured pieces placed under question the role or ascribed function of painting's support. In her case, by eschewing the medium's conventional means of support meant that the studio or gallery floor fulfilled this role instead. Whilst Benglis's work appeared in this respect to echo Greenberg's own assertion wherein within the context of modernism and its testing conditions "more and more conventions of the art of painting have shown themselves to be dispensable, unessential," her work drew a very separate set of conclusions to this premise.[35] Moreover, what was nascent within Greenberg's admission that a "tacked up canvas already exists as a picture," by the mid-1970s had become an actuality.[36] This can be seen in what Edward Lucie-Smith described as "off-stretcher" painting, that is, paintings that had "no wooden framework to support it."[37]

For his part, Lucie-Smith, writing in his study *Art of the Seventies* marshaled the work of the British artist Stephen Buckley and that of Claude Viallet, an artist associated with the Supports/Surfaces group, which coalesced in the south of France around 1970. The American artist Joe Overstreet, who had adopted the same approach to painting claimed that "by 1970 I had broken free from notions that paintings had to be on the wall in rectangular shapes."[38]

As Chave has noted, this particular form of artistic promiscuity that allowed painting to open out and become receptive to separate disciplinary fields including, for example both sculpture and video was "against Greenberg's edicts as to the necessary 'purity' of the medium."[39] And so, whilst artists felt at liberty to, as it were, extend the categorical boundaries of painting, other artists, including Marcel Broodthaers, sought to reposition painting entirely within a separate medium, raising a set of questions in the process with respect to the operational conditions of intermediality. Such questions centered upon whether it implied an aggregative process wherein the medium of painting was positioned so that it directly abutted other mediums or, conversely, whether as a term it denoted a form of synthesis which resulted in an object that was characterized by an admixture of different facets from different mediums.

Arguably the second of these two possibilities was represented by the Belgian artist Broodthaers's work of 1973 entitled *Tableau Bateau*, which entailed the transposition of painting, or more specifically one instance of painting, into a separate context and within a mutually exclusive form of media.

Tableau Bateau or Boat Painting was comprised of eighty 35 mm color transparencies that were placed in a carousel and shown on an adjacent wall using a slide projector. All of the images were derived from a nautical painting that the artist had sourced from an antique shop. With a scene depicting a ship nestling within somewhat choppy waters, Broodthaers deconstructed the *object tableau* or found painting into a series of visually discrete, incidental details including, amongst other things, the actual grain of the canvas and the facture of the paint as it had been used to describe, for example, the tricolor blowing in the wind at the top of the mast. In so doing, the medium of painting was presented only in a highly mediated and truncated form. However, through its transposition and, arguably, its partial dematerialization into another medium, the possibility became presented, according to one commentator at least, for painting's essentially static nature to be countered by the artist's "jump cuts and strategic editing of the images."[40]

This wasn't the only instance wherein Broodthaers approached the medium of painting from without, rather, as had been the case with modernist painters, from within. In this sense, Broodthaers's motivation wasn't merely one of attempting to overhaul the material basis of painting, but rather could arguably be construed as a playful reenactment of a number of conventions that pertained to the medium and that could somehow become transposed into a separate context, either, in the case of *Tableau Bateau*, in photography, or in the case of *Paintings/Peintures (serie l'art et les mots)* (1973), through language. As we have already seen, this piece entailed the artist covering a total of nine canvases with a series of terms, written in cursive script that related to the activity and cultural presence of painting. Either way, what underscored both pieces was the impulse to deconstruct painting so that it might possibly be thought anew.

Evidently then, artists who were working with, if not necessarily committed to the conventions and particularities of painting did so as a means by which a more inclusive and expansive account of the medium could be proffered. To this end, whilst certain artists sought to confer an "increased dimensionality" on painting by adopting strategies which included repositioning the medium so that it appeared almost quasi-sculptural in appearance, the period in question was also notable for its renewed interest in ideas around the "decorative."[41]

Whilst the production of modernist painting, according to Greenberg had involved orienting one's practice to a specific agenda, an agenda which was usually bound up with ideas around medium specificity, the plastic expression of universal truths and the eradication of all that was deemed superfluous or superficial, there appeared to be equally much that was to be avoided. This included the "decorative," which, according to one critic writing in the journal *Art in America* in 1975, carried with it a "pejorative implication," no doubt because on one level it carried with it connotations of the superficial and indeed the trivial.[42] Greenberg's complicity with this interpretation was evidenced relatively early on in his career when in 1948 he claimed that the "all-over picture" (no doubt he had Pollock's canvases in mind at the time the article was penned), as the "sort of painting [that] comes closest of all to decoration—to wallpaper patterns capable of being extended indefinitely."[43]

Nine years later, he expressed his feelings towards the decorative within what were a less qualified set of terms. Reviewing the paintings of the American artist Milton Avery, he admonished decoration by claiming that it was "the specter that haunts modernist painting, and part of the latter's formal mission is to find ways of using the decorative against itself."[44]

As well as being associated with the trivial and the superficial, within the context of the post-war American avant-garde there was a tendency to construe the decorative within a set of terms that were gendered. Certainly, this appears to be the assumption informing the Abstract Expressionist Barnett Newman's text of 1946 wherein the production of "primitive decorative art" is beholden only to women. Whilst by his own admission this constituted a form of "heightened design," it remained "a separate function carried on by women and took the form of geometric, non-objective pattern."[45]

In one sense this issue was brought to a head when the British photographer Cecil Beaton was commissioned by *Vogue* in 1950 to do a photoshoot at the Betty Parsons Gallery in New York. At the time the gallery was showing a recent body of work by Pollock so three paintings by the artist, *Autumn Rhythm* (1950), *Lavender Mist* (1950) and *Number 27* (1950) became the inadvertent backdrop against which models sported the latest designs in evening attire by Irene and Henri Bendel. As Marcia Brennan points out, the Beaton photographs "relegat[ed] the drip paintings to a subsidiary role as backdrops for the fashionable presence of the female models. As a result, the metaphorical masculinity of the drip paintings became displaced by the literal presence of the *Vogue* fashion models."[46]

Whilst this particular moment within the history of modernist painting and, for that matter, Greenberg's own deep-seated reservations with regards to the "decorative" was pervasive, it was not inviolable and it was during the first half of the 1970s that such a mindset became directly challenged.

Between 1974 and 1975, and consisting of eleven artists with respective bases in New York, Los Angeles and San Diego, the Pattern and Decoration movement coalesced due to their shared interest in and affinity with pattern, decoration and the propensity for art to orient itself towards beauty.[47] Their first representative exhibition, *Ten Approaches to the Decorative* was held at the Alessandra Gallery in Soho, New York in the autumn of 1976 and included work by Joyce Kozloff, Valerie Jaudon, and Miriam Schapiro. As a means of further establishing what for the movement constituted the terms of their practice, the exhibition was accompanied by a statement, penned by Kozloff, that consisted of 112 antimodernist words, including "anti-reductivist," "anti-formalist" and "anti male dominated." These were then countered by an antonymical set of terms that sought to demarcate the artistic, contextual and historical terrain within which the movement tendentiously operated. Moreover, "decorative," "narrative," "vulgar" and "ornamented" all appeared, in the first instance at least, to be antithetical to the "limiting conditions" of painting as they had been discussed by Greenberg.[48]

As Kozloff's statement suggested, part of what defined the movement and gave it a degree of critical purchase was its inherently oppositional character. On one level, this was directed towards the legacy of formalism and the way in which it sought to characterize the work of art through its exclusivity, separateness from society at large and purity. With regards the latter, Jaudon and Kozloff, in a text published in 1977 entitled "Art Hysterical Notions of Progress and Culture" directed the following question towards Greenberg's text of 1976, "Detached Observations": "In the polemics of Modern Art, "purity" represents the highest good. The more the elements of the work of art are pared down, reduced, the more visible the "purity." Here Greenberg equates reductivism with rationality and function. But it is never explained why or for whom art has to be functional, nor why reductivism is rational."[49]

In addition to Pattern and Decoration's outspokenness being directed towards the criticism of Greenberg, part of the impetus informing its trajectory was wanting to recover denigrated or marginalized forms of cultural practice, forms that traditionally had fallen outside of the purview of so-called "high-art."

Three years after Painting and Decoration had become established, Schapiro, working collaboratively with the painter Melissa Meyer coined the term "femmage," a term that sought to recast the modernist technique of collage so as to encompass a range of "traditional women's techniques … sewing, piecing, hooking, cutting, appliquéing, cooking and the like—activities also engaged in by men but assigned in history to women."[50]

Such orientation towards what were construed as activities that collectively fell under the auspices of what historically had become construed as "women's work," "vernacular forms, such as quilts, embroidery, and beading—and the domestic in ways that [had] been previously verboten in the art world" occurred at a time when a broader set of debates were placing the continued legitimacy of painting into question.[51] According to Majorie Kramer, writing in 1971 in an article entitled "Some Thoughts on Feminist Art," the

> most controversial conclusion I came to seems to be whether a feminist painting can be abstract or not. I feel that abstract can communicate, but only abstract ideas such as power, violence, a sense of flux (Gorky), or a moving sense of order (some oriental carpets). Feminism is not a quality like that. I think the images in a feminist painting have to be socially legible, that is, recognizable. Figurative. [52]

However, and notwithstanding the prohibitions that were being directed towards the practice of art making, and painting in particular, the permissive artistic climate of the late and early 1970s meant that the movement would have had a mandate to orient its practice towards decoration, seeing as by that point it "had become the common wisdom that anything could be art."[53]

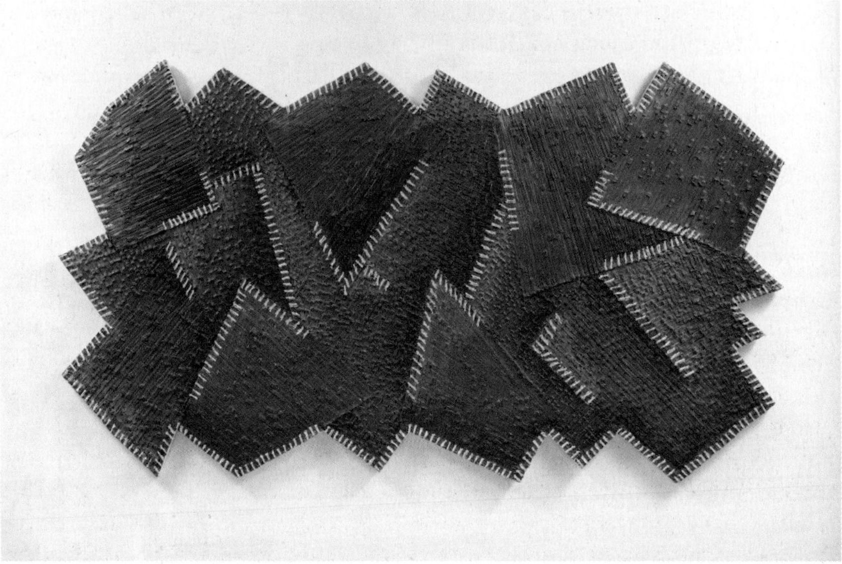

FIGURE 3.2 Cynthia Carlson, *Cascading Crystal Kaleidoscope*, 1976.

The paintings themselves utilized a range of designs, encompassing geometric patterns, as in the case of Cynthia Carlson's *Cascading Crystal Kaleidoscope* (1976) to a preoccupation with a more floral and arguably florid style of painting.

Along with encompassing marginalized forms of cultural production that historically had been understood as only functioning within the sphere of the "feminine," several artists associated with the Pattern and Decoration movement were equally keen to key their respective enquiries into those forms of visual culture that fell beyond the purview of the "West." To this end, if Schapiro was drawn to certain practices of western material culture, then other Pattern and Decoration artists were drawn to aspects of material culture derived from the Middle East.

Robert Kushner was one artist who, having visited Iran, Turkey and Afghanistan during the spring of 1974 with the art critic Amy Goldin, utilized his own deep-rooted fascination with the visual culture of this geographical region as a means to expand the categorical boundaries of painting beyond the confines of both the stretcher frame and the picture plane.

In 1975, the same year that the Metropolitan Museum of Art in New York had completed its renovation of its Islamic galleries, this ambition manifested itself in *Persian Line II, Leonard Street*, which, like previous performances the artist had staged, displayed the artist's preoccupation with the world of fashion. As the artist explained:

> Back in New York, painting on more fabric, trying new colors and designs, I found a piece of green jersey and decided to make a chador

> [the full-length veil traditionally worn by Muslim women in Iran] ... After cutting the shape, I thought it would be an interesting format for a painting. Relatively soon, many old paintings became chadors; the shapes were more satisfying than rectangles[54]

As it was then, and as Swartz notes, "P&D represented an energetic alternative to the then-dominant formalism espoused by Clement Greenberg, among others."[55] Moreover, by wanting to "go beyond the discourse of modernism," the movement spoke of and equally spoke to notions, however inchoate, of the postmodern.[56] Indeed, according to Schwartz, Pattern and Decoration became the first postmodern art movement by virtue of the fact that the artists utilized a broad array of source material and embraced "the impermanent, the common, and the excluded in their content."[57] It could also be said to have been postmodern in scope and import due to the fact that not only was one of its operative methods that of appropriation, a strategy that became virtually ubiquitous during the 1980s, but also because that which it appropriated, that is, putatively downgraded cultural forms, fell beyond the purview of canonically received practices of artistic production.

As this chapter has demonstrated, rather than the 1970s witnessing an unequivocal rejection of painting on the grounds that it was an obsolete mode of artistic practice, a significant number of artists evidently oriented themselves towards the medium, continuing to conceive it both as a viable form of cultural practice and as a contemporary form of art.[58] This is not to deny the fact that for many women artists, abstract painting carried with it a highly problematic set of issues and assumptions, evident in the artist Monica Sjoo's pamphlet "Towards a Revolutionary Feminist Art," which was published on the occasion of the exhibition "Women Power" in London's Swiss Cottage Library in 1973 wherein she questioned "the abstract researches, playful gimmicks characteristic of contented and successful male artists."[59] Nevertheless, the broadening of abstraction's parameters during the period in question was more widely symptomatic of the fact that by this point modernism, such as it now was, was characterized by a range of contrasting, if not antithetical approaches to the production of the artwork. Moreover, such approaches eschewed, if not directly challenged the hegemonic, exclusionary and arguably patriarchal account of the work of art that Greenberg had espoused. As the art critic Lucy Lippard observed: "The 1970s might not have been pluralist at all if women had not emerged during the decade to introduce the multi-colored threads of female experience into the male fabric of modern art."[60]

Notes

1 Rosalind Krauss, "Notes on the Index: Seventies Art in America," *October*, Vol. 3 (1977): 68.

2 Rosalind Krauss, "Sculpture in the Expanded Field," *October* 8, no. 9 (1979): 30.

3 Mark Linder, *Nothing Less than Literal: Architecture after Minimalism* (Cambridge, MA: MIT Press, 2004), 4.

4 Siegel, *High Times Hard Times New York Painting 1967–1975* (New York: Independent Curators International, 2006), 29.

5 Douglas Crimp, "Opaque Painting," in Meyer, *Minimalism*, 257.

6 Donald Judd, "Specific Objects" (1965), reproduced in Harrison and Wood, *Art in Theory 1900–2000 An Anthology of Changing Ideas*, 827.

7 Siegel, *High Times Hard Times New York Painting 1967–1975*, 22.

8 Ibid., 29.

9 Hayden Herrera, "Joan Snyder: Speaking with Paint," in Hayden Herrera, *Joan Snyder* (New York: Harry N. Abrams, Inc., 2005), 22.

10 Joan Snyder, artist's statement, Joan Snyder's personal archive, reproduced in "Joan Snyder: Speaking with Paint," Herrera, *Joan Snyder*, 33. In a lecture at Yale Summer School in 1973 Snyder had claimed that: "The painting always has to do with my life." Joan Snyder, lecture delivered at Yale University at Norfolk, 1973, ibid., 41. Maurice Merleau-Ponty's description of Cézanne can be found in Maurice Merleau-Ponty, "Cézanne's Doubt" in *Sense and Non-Sense* (Evanston, IL: Northwestern University Press, 1964), 11

11 Herrera, *Joan Snyder*, 37.

12 Ibid, 39. This statement of the artist's intent was written on a sketch that Snyder produced in the same year as *Small Symphony for Women.*

13 Herrera, in his essay claims the latter, although I would be inclined to interpret the final panel as being somewhat more inconclusive and for this reason enigmatic.

14 Mary Heilmann, "Biography," in *Mary Heilmann: A Survey* (Boston: ICA, 1990), unpaginated.

15 "Mary Heilmann," in Siegel, *High Times Hard Times New York Painting 1967–1975*, 45.

16 Elizabeth Armstrong, "To Be Someone" in *Mary Heilmann: To Be Someone*, Elizabeth Armstrong et al. (Newport Beach, CA: Orange County Museum of Art, 2009), 20.

17 Susan Krane, *Lynda Benglis: Dual Natures* (Seattle: The University of Washington Press, 1991), 12.

18 Nora Lawrence, "Lynda Benglis," in *Modern Women: Women Artists at the Museum of Modern Art*, eds. Cornelia Butler and Alexandra Schwartz (New York: Museum of Modern Art, 2010), 337.

19 Ibid.

20 See David Bourdon, "Fling, Dribble and Drip," *Life* 68, February 27, 1970. 62–6.

21 Thomas Hess, "Review," *New York Magazine*, 8, no. 49 (1975): 114.

22 Susan Krane, "Forces of Nature" in Krane, *Lynda Benglis: Dual Natures*, 32–33.

23 Anna Chave, "Outlaws: Women, Abstraction, and Painting in New York, 1967–1975" in Siegel, *High Times Hard Times New York Painting 1967–1975*, 127.

24 Lynda Benglis, "Artist's Statement" in Siegel, *High Times Hard Times New York Painting 1967–1975*, 131.

25 Michael Fried, "Art and Objecthood" (1967) reproduced in Michael Fried, *Art and Objecthood* (Chicago: The University of Chicago Press, 1998), 164.

26 Dick Higgins, "Intermedia" (1966) reproduced in Johanna Burton et al., *Open Systems: Rethinking Art c. 1970*, ed. Donna De Salvo (London: Tate, 2005), 170.

27 Ibid.

28 Maria Luísa Coelho, "Woman-Body-Paint: Helena Almeida and the Visual Inscription of Sexual Difference." *Luso-Brazilian Review* 54, no. 1 (2017): 59.

29 Delfim Sardo, "Helena Almeida," *Aperture* (Winter 2015), https://aperture.org/editorial/magazine-helena-almeida.

30 Leon Battista Alberti, *On Painting*, ed. and trans Rocco Sinisgalli (Cambridge: Cambridge University Press, 2011), 39.

31 Coelho, "Woman-Body-Paint: Helena Almeida and the Visual Inscription of Sexual Difference," 56.

32 Ibid., 61.

33 "Conversation between Helena Almeida and Maria de Corral," 1999. *Helena Almeida* (Centro Galego de Arte Contemporánea (cGac), Galicia 2000), 172.

34 Jackson Pollock, "My Painting." *Possibilities*. New York (Winter 1947–1948). Reproduced in *Jackson Pollock: Interviews, Articles, and Reviews*, ed. Pepe Karmel (New York: Harry N. Abrams, Inc., 1998), 17.

35 Clement Greenberg, "After Abstract Expressionism" (1962), in Greenberg, *The Collected Essays and Criticism* vol. 4, *Modernism with a Vengeance, 1957–1969*, 131–132.

36 Ibid.

37 Edward Lucie-Smith, *Art in the Seventies* (Phaidon: Oxford, 1980), 40.

38 Siegel, *High Times Hard Times New York Painting 1967–1975*, 42.

39 Ibid., 133.

40 Darling, *Target Practice: Painting Under Attack 1949–78*, 64–5.

41 Carole Schneeman, "Artist's Statement," in Siegel, *High Times Hard Times New York Painting 1967–1975*, 137.

42 Amy Goldin, "Matisse and Decoration: The Late Cut Outs" (1975) reproduced in *Amy Goldin, Art in a Hairshirt: Art Criticism 1964–1978*, ed. Robert Kushner (Stockbridge, MA: Hard Press Editions, 2011), 144.

43 Clement Greenberg, "The Crisis of the Easel Picture" (1948), in *The Collected Essays and Criticism*, vol. 2, *Arrogant Purpose, 1945–1949*, ed. John O' Brian (Chicago: University of Chicago Press, 1986), 223.

44 Clement Greenberg, "Milton Avery" (1957), in Greenberg, *The Collected Essays and Criticism* vol. 4, *Modernism with a Vengeance, 1957–1969,* 43.

45 Barnett Newman, "Northwest Coast Indian Painting" (1946), in *Barnett Newman, Selected Writings and Interviews*, ed. John P. O'Neill (Berkeley; CA: University of California Press, 1992), 106.

46 Marcia Brennan, *Modernism's Masculine Subjects: Matisse, the New York School, and Post-Painterly Abstraction* (Cambridge, MA: MIT Press, 2004), 107.

47 As Arthur C. Danto notes, "'Pattern and Decoration' or 'P&D,' as its members and supporters called it, declared itself a movement in the late 1970s when the very idea of movements seemed to belong to an earlier era." Arthur C. Danto, "Pattern and Decoration as a Late Modernist Movement" in *Pattern and Decoration: An Ideal Vision in American Art, 1975–1985*, ed. Anne Swartz (New York: Hudson River Museum, 2008), 7–8.

48 Ibid., 114–15.

49 Valerie Jaudon and Joyce Kozloff, "Art Hysterical Notions of Progress and Culture" (1977–1978), reproduced in Stiles and Selz, *Theories and Documents of Contemporary Art: A Sourcebook of Artist's Writings*, 156. "Detached Observations" was published in *Arts Magazine*, Vol. 51, no. 4, December 1976.

50 Miriam Schapiro and Melissa Meyer, "Waste Not Want Not: An Inquiry into What Women Saved and Assembled—FEMMAGE" (1977–1978), originally published in *Heresies* 1, no. 4, Winter 1977–1978, pp. 66–9, reproduced in *Stiles and Selz, Theories and Documents of Contemporary Art: A Sourcebook of Artist's Writings*, 151–2.

51 Swartz, *Pattern and Decoration: An Ideal Vision in American Art, 1975–1985*, 31.

52 Marjorie Kramer, "Some Thoughts on Feminist Art" (1971) in *Feminism-Art-Theory: An Anthology 1968–2000*, ed. Hilary Robinson (Oxford: Blackwell, 2001): 293.

53 Danto, "Pattern and Decoration as a Late Modernist Movement," 10.

54 Robert Kushner, "The Persian Line," Eddy magazine (1978): 58–65, reproduced in Holland Cotter, *Robert Kushner*: *Garden of Earthly Delights* (New York: Hudson Hills Press, 1997), 26.

55 Swartz, *Pattern and Decoration: An Ideal Vision in American Art, 1975–1985*, 25.

56 Ibid., 29. As Swartz notes, this approach "is the inverse of modern artists' use of non-Western art as a way toward formalism, like Matisse with Islamic art or Picasso with African art, used to fragment and geometicize forms as the basis for his cubist innovations." Ibid.

57 Ibid., 23.

58 Arguably a historiography of painting that claims, in effect, that artists stopped painting ca. 1965 still persists. In their introduction in the catalogue

that accompanied the exhibition *Reconsidering the Object of Art: 1965–1975*, Ann Goldstein and Anne Rorimer write that the "most salient characteristic of this exhibition is the absence of painting on canvas." Goldstein and Rorimer, *Reconsidering the Object of Art: 1965–1975*, 13.

59 Monica Sjoo, "Images of Women Power," Arts Manifesto in *Towards a Revolutionary Feminist Art* 1 (1972): 4.

60 Lucy Lippard, "Sweeping Exchanges: The Contribution of Feminism to the Art of the Seventies," *Art Journal* 41, no. 1/2 (1980): 36.

4

A Costume of Rags

Like Orestes, the hero who peeped around corners in his return from exile, painting was wily and cautious. To salvage what it could of the wreckage of modernism, it incorporated elements of Conceptualism as if a redeeming ichor. As if to demonstrate its awareness of its past sins, it returned from exile with a self-critical manner. As if to redress its former arrogance, it returned with self-mockery. As if to offset its former elitism and puritanism, it returned in a costume of rags collected from everywhere.[1]

Teleologically, Greenberg's historicism amounted to him imputing modernist painting's purity to its revision of painting's "cardinal norms." Accordingly, this began with Edouard Manet, from which point on other artists subsequently oriented their practice, self-critically, towards what Greenberg, writing in *Modernist Painting* identified were the "limitations that constitute the medium of painting—the flat surface, the shape of the support, the properties of the pigment."[2]

Elsewhere in the text and by Greenberg's own admission, this process was understood as being continually unfolding, monolinear and without historical rupture:

> And I cannot insist enough that Modernism has never meant, and does not mean now, anything like a break with the past. It may mean a devolution, an unravelling, of tradition, but it also means its further evolution. Modernist art continues the past without gap or break, and wherever it may end up it will never cease being intelligible in terms of the past.[3]

Evidently, Greenberg's historicism, which largely centered upon the medium of painting moving increasingly towards an essentialized state or condition, seemed no longer possible, nor, for that matter, desirable. Indeed, both Greenberg's ambitions on the part of the artwork and the subsequent wave of late modernist practices that were performatively and conceptually oriented were now viewed from some quarters with a degree of suspicion. According to Christos M. Joachimides, writing in the exhibition catalogue that accompanied the Royal Academy's exhibition *A New Spirit in Painting* in London in 1981, the "overemphasis on the idea of autonomy in art which brought about Minimalism and its extreme appendix conceptual art, was bound to be self-defeating. Soon the avant-garde of [the] 1970s, with its narrow, puritan approach devoid of all joy in the senses, lost its creative impetus and began to stagnate."[4]

On one level, the alleged puritanism of much photo and conceptually based art became the implicit horizon against which painting could now attempt to define, once again, a legitimate position for itself. Along with seeking, as Joachimides' statement implied, to argue its difference through its reliance upon the senses, be they visual or tactile, what was particular to painting as an expressive medium was the fact that it had recourse to content, which, in contrast to the prohibitions conferred on the artwork by formalism, was seemingly unexpurgated and often entailed artists readily borrowing from a range of traditions. However, and despite the proliferation of these historical forms, this didn't in itself signal a return to tradition per se. For whilst certain paintings borrowed directly from artistic, mythological and cultural precedent, the palpable disquiet which the paintings often betrayed was on one level symptomatic of a broader anxiety with regards their relationship to history: As McEvilley notes:

> In the last decade the subject of history has dominated much art, not just art history, or our own history, but the question of the whole nature of history: is it a force? a presence? a projection? a fantasy? a myth? a con game? What shape does it have (if any)? Where is it going (if anywhere)? What kind of hold does it have on us really?[5]

Certainly, these questions would prove to be far reaching and against the critical backdrop of Greenberg's own historicism, the aim of this chapter is to explore the resurgence of painting through its annexation and appropriation of historical forms. If painting was indeed beholden to historical precedent, then what was within its reach and what, perhaps more importantly, did it choose to hold on to?

One factor that precipitated the resurgence of figurative painting towards the end of the 1970s and through into the following decade were several group exhibitions, both in Europe and in the United States, that were all somehow united in their over-arching ambition to reposition painting within what had become an increasingly heterogeneous milieu. Whilst the exhibitions did not entirely eschew those artists who were continuing to work within an abstract idiom, *The Human Clay*, *New Image*, *Zeitgeist* and *A New Spirit in Painting* were all characterized by a gravitation towards a set of traditions and historical moments within the broad sweep of twentieth-century art history and, moreover, a deliberately overt choice of subject matter.

The Human Clay was the result of the painter R. B. Kitaj being invited in 1976 by the British Arts Council to purchase works for their collection and to present what he had selected in the form of a group exhibition at the Hayward Gallery in London. Appearing as a somewhat defiant, if not anachronistic, venture it sought to elucidate upon what Kitaj stressed was the fundamental importance of pictures that "represent[ed] people, and more specifically, the single human form."[6]

The provenance of the exhibition's title had originated from a line in W. H. Auden's poem "Letter to Lord Byron," although the actual impetus behind Kitaj's borrowing of Auden was via one of the selected artists in the exhibition, David Hockney. As Kitaj claimed in the exhibition catalogue, "Hockney likes to quote the line from Auden's long poem *Letter to Lord Byron* which reads, 'To me Art's subject is the human clay.'"[7]

To this end, and notwithstanding the somewhat anomalous presence of Stephen Buckley's abstract painting *Three Figures Dancing* (1976), the work selected by Kitaj appeared to reassert the importance of a traditional set of artistic skills, including drawing, which served to embody what the artist, and in this guise the curator, described was the "earthed human image."[8]

So, for example, *Portrait of George Thompson* (1975), a work painted by Leon Kossoff that was included in the exhibition is comprised of thick, impasto-like brush strokes that delineate the sitter's head and torso. Whilst the figure itself is somewhat crudely rendered, the roughly hewn physicality of the paint on one level becomes consonant with and analogous to the physicality of the sitter's body to the extent whereby Kitaj's adoption of Auden's term appeared particularly resonant.

Along with the valorization of those artists who sought to make paintings and drawings by maintaining some form of fidelity with the human form, Kitaj's exhibition was also notable for the fact that it gave a name to what up until that point had been a loose grouping of artists, all of whom understood art as a historically bound and solemn undertaking and that were united by their geographical location (which often became not only their artistic milieu but their subject matter as well). So, to this end, along with Leon Kossoff, artists such as Francis Bacon, Lucien Freud and Frank Auerbach all had studios in London and their respective practices were united by what was a certain preoccupation with the human form.

However, in 1976 "The School of London" remained a label that, by Kitaj's own admission, was partly his own invention: "If some of the strange and fascinating personalities you may encounter here were given a fraction of the internationalist attention and encouragement reserved in this barren time for their provincial and orthodox vangardism, a School of London might become even more real than the one I have construed in my head."[9]

Along with *The Human Clay*, other exhibitions equally sought, if not to proffer an account of painting that was largely figurative in both scope and import, then stage a public defense of painting more broadly as a form of contemporary art that nevertheless, and somewhat paradoxically, remained indebted to certain understandings around "tradition."

In a sense we can take what the group exhibition *A New Spirit in Painting* included as being more broadly indicative of the various currents that went to make up painting at that time. Whilst there was a strong German contingent, something that didn't escape the notice of Edward Lucie-Smith, who, writing in the introduction to *Art of the Eighties* noted that "there were no fewer than eleven Germans," the exhibition remained notable for its inclusivity and historical breadth.[10] To this end, whilst one salient approach, represented by the German artists' respective contributions was broadly figurative, other artists appeared to be continuing to work within an abstract idiom that equally entailed a continuation with and within a set of traditions, albeit ones whose provenance differed from that of the so-called Neo-Expressionists. For whilst Karl Horst Hödicke's *Appelschimmel (Dapple Grays)* of 1980 arguably borrowed both its equine imagery and its facture from the German Expressionist Franz Marc, visually and conceptually Brice Marden's *Grove Group II* (1972–1973) presented a very different proposition that was organized around a very different set of historical reference points.

Based on Marden's experiences of the Mediterranean and specifically associations around the idea of the olive grove, whilst visually they were somewhat pared down, consisting of either two or three bands of muted color, the artist's intentions for the work were such that it was hoped that they would nevertheless be redolent of a particular time and place.

Although it would be a mistake to interpret the paintings that Marden contributed, along with those that were shown by Robert Ryman, Alan Charlton and Gotthard Graubner as all somehow being the continuation of Greenbergian formalism (to this end Marden's canvases arguably should be seen as distillations of the Mediterranean landscape, whereas Graubner's over-arching concern centered upon the instrumental presence of color), the monochrome or near-monochrome paintings of all four artists, at the very least provided some form of visual counterpoint to the more vigorous Neo-Expressionist offerings. However, and notwithstanding their formal differences, the paintings of Ryman, Marden, Charlton and Graubner were not, for all intents and purposes representative of some new vanguard seeking to move painting towards some projected logical end point, as Greenberg's historicism with respect to modernist painting had dialectically advanced some twenty years previously. Instead, their canvases appeared as one, and only one option amongst many, all of which, in some respect and on some level were conditioned by and indebted to a particular conception of tradition. Indeed, as Joachimides claimed, the "exhibition presents a position in art which conspicuously asserts traditional values."[11] In what was almost the same breath, he would also claim that "consciously or instinctively, then, painters are turning back to traditional concerns."[12] In this respect, the currents of painting that had gained a certain foothold during the period in question remained, for Joachimides at least, incontrovertibly tied to historical precedent, whether it was Willem de Kooning's anticipation of Koberling or Graubner's indebtedness to, albeit obliquely, nineteenth-century German Romanticism.[13]

Although Kitaj personally chose to rebut artistic developments that were concurrently occurring over the other side of the Atlantic, evidently what constituted at least part of the historical backdrop to painting's renaissance at this time was the United States during the period when Abstract Expressionism was the pre-eminent mode of painting. Even if artists and, for their part critics were not entirely beholden to this epoch in painting's recent history, there remained, at the very least, a series of instances whereby the discourses of painting during the 1980s sought recourse to a reading of painting, its status and condition through what had occurred some three decades previously. Equally, when artists or critics sought to play down the significance of Abstract Expressionism, it nevertheless appeared to remain one of the salient historical backdrops against which the new figurative idiom of painting could be developed. According to Joachimides:

> The current orthodoxies about painting were defined as long ago as the nineteen fifties by American critics and achieved almost universal acceptance during the following decades. These orthodoxies, which had some but by no means complete validity, aggressively proclaimed the work that was produced in and around New York to be virtually the only universally acceptable art—anything else was at best provincial.[14]

Such as it was, the New York School of painters, if not the criticism of Greenberg, still appeared to have some form of cachet within the discourses that were working to critically frame the development of painting during the start of the 1980s. Joachimides's sentiment was echoed by Robert Rosenblum, writing a year later in the catalogue that accompanied *Zeitgeist*, another major survey exhibition of painting that was held at the Berlinische Galerie in Berlin in 1982 wherein he claimed that "the points of closest affinity in the long dynasty of twentieth century art lies with certain expressionist currents of the 1940s and '50s, both American and European."[15] Moreover, the painters of the 1980s carried a particular and deep-rooted kinship with the New York School through their shared "attraction to a willfully primitive style, where turbulent emotions churn in fluid spaces and where primordial symbols—eyes, winged creatures, male and female archetypes—are depicted with a deliberate crudeness that evokes the dawn of feeling and of image-making."[16]

More specifically, in an essay for the same catalogue written by Hilton Kramer, one can also discern the tacit persistence, if not concurrence with Greenberg's ideas, and the fact that a historically received formalist orthodoxy still continued to color discussions of painting approximately twenty-five years after *Modernist Painting* had first been published. "For a hundred years or more, the vitality of painting had seemed to depend on stripping it of its conventions and resources in order to isolate some irreducible core or essence."[17]

Susan Rothenberg, an artist who had been the only female painter selected to show in *Zeitgeist*, had also expressed an interest in essences, which for her became characteristic of a working method whereby one took "things from the particular rather than the general."[18]

However, whilst Rothenberg's statement, to a certain extent was characteristic of Greenberg's own approach to painting, for his part he gave short shrift to Rothenberg and her associates. Speaking in a public debate in 1987, he dismissed those areas of practice which he felt were over reliant upon the "idea" and that were, moreover, quite simply "boring," professing that he couldn't "otherwise explain the success of the likes of painters like Julian Schnabel and David Salle, or Susan Rothenberg, or Jennifer Bartlett, or Frank Stella's relief constructions with their awful color."[19]

Repetitive, feathered brush marks where the opalescent suggestion of form, often in the guise of a silhouette or an outline appeared to have been conjured as much as made more broadly educed the fact that Rothenberg worked intuitively. Whilst she was initially associated with paintings that proffered painterly, linear approximations that collectively delineated the shape of a horse, a recurrent image within her practice at the time that

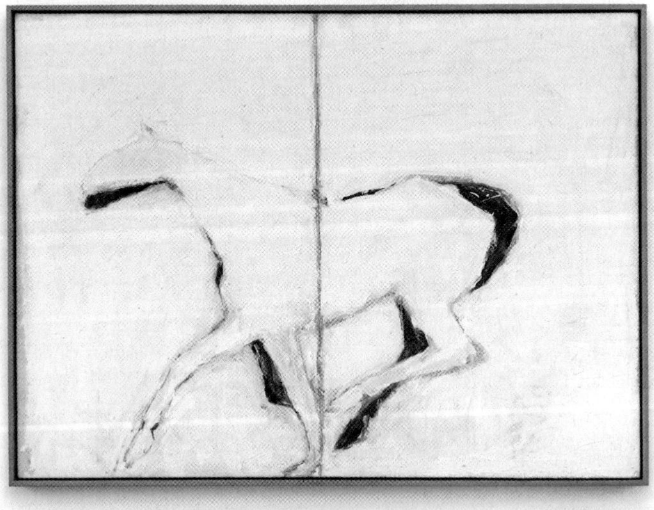

FIGURE 4.1 Susan Rothenberg, *August*, 1976.

functioned as much as a formal motif as a heraldic symbol, subsequent works expanded the breadth of the artist's iconography to encompass the figure.[20] However, and as Rothenberg's statement from 1982 suggests, what remained consistent within what she did was the precedence she gave to working instinctively: "The way the horse image appeared in my paintings was not an intellectual procedure. Most of my work is not run through a rational part of my brain. It comes from a place in me that I don't choose to examine. I just let it come."[21]

It was with these paintings that Rothenberg's practice, whether rightly or wrongly, became construed as "expressionist" and as such, became conflated with Neo-Expressionism. With respect to whether this was an entirely appropriate reading of Rothenberg's paintings, the artist had claimed that: "When asked if I'm an Expressionist, I've always said, "I suppose so." To me "Expressionism" means expressing a personal viewpoint about reality, but the word also means "juicy." I guess I'm a semi-Expressionist in terms of the visuals and surfaces of my paintings."[22]

As an attempt to engender a critical discourse that would be able to account for the novelty of such preoccupations, various terms emerged, most of which invariably contained the prefix "neo" or a variation thereof. Along with *Neue Wilde*, neo-geo and "neo-realism," it was Neo-Expressionism that arguably gained the greatest degree of critical purchase as a designation during the 1980s. Moreover, it was the paintings of artists working in Germany, including Jörg Immendorf, Georg Baselitz, Anselm Kiefer and A. R. Penck who, given the qualities that were claimed characterized the term, became initially and, for that matter, most readily identified with this particular style of painting.

Beyond their engagement with, if not fidelity to painting, and more specifically a figurative or semi-figurative idiom of painting, in their respective ways, and as the term suggested, much of what they produced harkened back to and was reminiscent of the Expressionist style of painting that emerged prior to the First World War. To this end, their canvases were characterized by a distinct lack of finish, dissonant or often muddied palettes and frantic, often erratic brushwork that served only to approximate or hazard the appearance of a thing rather than proffer a more straightforward, and in representational terms, conventionally legible description. Gone was even a cursory form of modelling to be replaced by a vigorous, expressive and often idiosyncratic approach to mark-making.

Beyond the works' frank acknowledgement of German Expressionism and its apparent valorization of a period in the history of early European modernism, for Baselitz at least formalism, or at least what amounted to a putative interpretation of formalism, retained some form of legitimacy. To this end, and according to McEvilley, "Baselitz is generally described by his critics as an unreconstructed formalist and seems, by his own account, to invite or even demand such a description. One critic, for example, describes Baselitz's work as 'painting for its own sake,' and speaks of Baselitz's 'liberation from the classical idea of subject matter.'"[23] Citing Baselitz's claim that the object expresses nothing, Edward Lucie-Smith equally claimed that what differentiated Baselitz from that of his Neo-Expressionist peers was "his insistence upon the formal qualities of the work—on its identity as paint"[24] However Baselitz's own perceived attempts at fencing off the work from the world, an ambition that was partly achieved by the artist turning his figures 180 degrees so they were depicted upside down and thus somewhat estranged from the received conventions of representational picture-making, proved to be the exception rather than the rule. Whilst Baselitz appeared to orient his practice towards the primacy of the materials and to that of the act, others evidently viewed such preoccupations as the means by which the drive towards and the pursuit of content, content rooted in, as Michael Compton claimed, the "moral, political, existential," could be expedited.[25] In other words, and to what would have been to Greenberg's chagrin, a significant number of painters during the 1980s remained deeply committed to what the critic had labelled, vis-à-vis Surrealism, "outside subject matter."[26]

This is evident in the work of Anselm Kiefer, a German artist whose practice somewhat erroneously became associated with Neo-Expressionism.

A provocative early work by Kiefer, the *Besetzungen* or *Occupations* (1969) consisted of the artist visiting various sites that, given the themes that he was seeking to address, were imbued with historical resonance. Whilst there the artist had himself photographed in the throes of giving, what was, in effect, a Nazi salute. On one level the *Occupations* would anticipate what would prove to be an overriding preoccupation in Kiefer's practice, namely the attempt to disinter specific facets of recent German history that, following the Second World War, had been repressed by a certain collective amnesia. However, whilst the *Occupations*, by way of parody, sought to directly confront what Germany had attempted to dissemble (a Nazi salute to this day remains a criminal offence), subsequent works offered a more nuanced and introspective reflection upon the deeds that had been committed in the name of nationhood.

Starting in 1980, Kiefer produced a series of paintings based on architectural plans and photographs pertaining to a number of structures and spaces of the Third Reich. Using as its visual and thematic starting point a photograph of Hitler's Reich Chancellery that was designed by his architect Albert Speer, *Interior* (1981) rendered what was once a very literal embodiment of fascist ideology into a more equivocal and ambiguous architectural space.

On one level, given the artist's ongoing consideration of the actions of his country's recent history, Kiefer's early "Occupations" and his subsequent paintings based on architecture both evidenced the artist's proclivity in his work to revisit historical sites of trauma, an aspect of the work that was also evident in his paintings which were organized around the image of a receding train track.

Consisting of three such tracks that converge under a somewhat leaden, apocalyptical-looking sky, the landscape that the tracks in *Lot's Wife* (1989) inhabit is scorched, barren and devoid of vegetation. Unlike the lower half of the composition wherein its respective audience can at least begin to orient themselves within the picture, the upper half of the painting generally remains more spatially indeterminate. With its diverse range of media that encompasses oil paint, ash, salt and applied elements, *Lot's Wife* is characteristic of the artist's innovative and highly individuated approach to painting. But whilst there is an emphasis given to materiality, the work's meaning rests upon a very particular conflation of the theological with the historical. In other words, and as Lisa Saltzman has claimed, "Kiefer's work resolutely, if not at times repetitively, puts forth subject matter."[27]

The title of the painting derives from the biblical story in the Old Testament of Lot's wife who was turned into a pillar of salt as punishment for ignoring God's warning not to look back at the devastation, at God's hand, which was being meted out onto Sodom and Gomorrah. With respect to the complicity of Kiefer's practice with Germany's Nazi past, inevitably one associates the railroad tracks in *Lot's Wife* with those that ferried the unsuspecting victims to numerous concentration camps as part of Hitler's Final Solution. Given the actions of Lot's wife, Kiefer's inclusion of such discomforting imagery means that both the biblical story and the painting's narrative become organized around the act of looking, or, perhaps more specifically, of deliberately choosing not to avert one's gaze from what was for both, a deliberate act of destruction. By implication, looking, or more specifically looking back, is as much a moral as it is a physiological act. This dimension the painting, and arguably Kiefer's practice generally carries is echoed in the following statement made by the artist in 1987: "There is too much *ars gratia artis*, which does not give much food for thought. Art is very incestuous: it is reacting to other art, not thinking about the world. It is at its best when it responds to things outside of art, and when it comes from a deep [inner] need."[28]

Whilst Kiefer's attempts to come to terms with his country's recent past was frequently given through Nazi-derived imagery, he wasn't unique in this endeavor.

Appropriating the visual traits of geometric abstraction, in 1984 the artist Martin Kippenberger made *With the Best Will in the World, I Can't See a Swastika*, a painting that conflated abstraction's proclivity to obfuscate recognizable form with what was a broader, collective amnesia in a way that was arch, if not somewhat ironic. Equally, Jörg Immendorf frequently sought recourse to both the heraldic eagle and swastika-shaped imagery during a five-year period of activity, beginning in 1977 wherein his "Cafe Deutschland" series were made. However, unlike the paintings of Kiefer, both Kippenberger and Immendorf's adoption of such historically loaded imagery arguably lacked a comparable gravitas. Certainly, there was an inherent playfulness to the work that ran counter to the more muted and somber tenor of Kiefer's work. This is evident within the work of Sigmar Polke's *Paganini* (1981–1983), which, like the aforementioned other examples of German painting considered, also included the image of the swastika. However, its immediate connotations, as with both Immendorf and Kippenberger, became muddled, if not entirely shorn by the artist's collaged style that fused together an eclectic, heterogeneous range of other types of imagery. Be that as it may, and as their respective practices educed, painting sought to address the collective trauma of the past, if not the political exigencies of the present. This concern also characterized the work of Peter Mulindwa, an artist who produced a series of paintings in response to the rule of the military dictator Idi Amin in Uganda during the 1970s.

It is perhaps worth acknowledging that from the 1940s, a number of art schools and centers became established across Africa.[29] As Everlyn Nicodemus contends:

> Art was crucial in the political-cultural process. In the same way as the African nations aspired as a matter of course to an equal position among nations in a modern world, African artists took up a modernist course. Major institutions of art education and professional training were established throughout Africa, schools that became focal points for creative growth and innovation around individual artists and teachers.[30]

Within the context of Uganda, Margaret Trowell, a graduate of the Slade School of Fine Art in London established the School of Art at Makerere University in Kampala in 1937. Rather than look towards the pictorial conventions of the Renaissance or those of modernism, Trowell's pedagogy encouraged her students to "visualize East African rural life, or poems and stories she narrated to them."[31] Because of which, and because, in one respect, Trowell's teaching methods appeared to be consonant with the British policy of indirect rule in its African colonies, there remains a question, albeit an open one, as to whether Trowell challenged or further rehearsed colonialism's proclivity to recognize indigenous communities as subaltern.[32]

Trowell's replacement, following her resignation in 1958 was Cecil Todd. According to Katrin Peters-Klaphake: "Todd shifted the art school's curriculum towards establishing academic disciplines according to the Western model of university education. He emphasized the teaching of high technical skills and scientific aspects of art education as well as world art history. He clearly deflected from the anti-modernist Africa centered model that Trowell had promoted."[33]

In one respect, the tensions between "nationalist claims and Eurocentric training" that arose through Todd's teaching threw into sharp relief a much larger set of questions that concerned the visibility of Ugandan art within a global setting.[34]

As Wanjiku Nyachae contends: "External categorizations of art from Uganda and Kenya center on discussions about their 'inability' … to stand up to European academic structures, thus intimating a center–periphery relationship, with Western art in the center and all else revolving like satellites in constellations of ever-decreasing importance."[35]

In an attempt to move beyond the binary of center/periphery, Stuart Hall has sought instead to define the world in relation to "a set of interesting centers, which are both different from and related to one another."[36] Moreover: "If you think about where important movements are being made, sometimes they happen in the center, but the most exciting artists are those who live simultaneously in the center and at the periphery. We are embarking on a hundred different ideas of 'the modern,' not one, and therefore, of a thousand practicing modern artists."[37] In other words, and as Chika Okeke-Agulu argues:

> There has been in recent scholarship the now-fashionable tendency to theorize non-European modernist art—or actually those modernist practices that fell outside the concerns of Paris–New York's will-to abstraction—as alternative, vernacular, parallel, or cosmopolitan modernism. The problem with these propositions, however, is that they invariably insinuate Paris–New York as the site of modernism, while the others represent, at best, the other, and in some sense not-quite-the-real modernism. Rather than propose modernist art from outside of Paris–New York as alternative or parallel modernism, it is more meaningful to see modernism not as a closed, historically and geographically situated phenomenon, but as a constellation of formal and conceptual strategies adopted by artists everywhere who, exploiting ideas and expressive forms from within and outside of their cultural contexts, fashioned new ways of seeing and experiencing the modern through art.[38]

According to George Kyeyune, Mulindwa, Elimo Njau, Theresa Musoke, and Jak Katarikawe

> are in one way or the other, products of the Makerere Art School in the '50s and '60s … Makerere functioned as a space for discussing and exploring matters of identity and inclusion, especially in the run up to independence and during the independence decade. The School of Fine Art, where these artists were nurtured, was itself a space of intellectual contestations as Uganda's political and economic climate changed, which encouraged tensions to emerge and be sustained.[39]

Mulindwa graduated from Makerere Art School in 1971, the same year, as George Kyeyune points out, that Idi Amin seized power in Uganda in a military coup.[40] Like many students and staff at Makerere during the time of Amin's presidency, Mulindwa produced various forms of propaganda for the military dictator, including portraits, medals and insignias.[41] However, during this period the artist also produced a body of work that was critical of Amin's regime. According to George Kyeyune, for fear of being accused of espionage, "Mulindwa shrouded his compositions ... in mythical subjects. Myths and legends from Bunyoro, his home region, were the key resources and references for his imagery."[42]

For example, *Untitled* (1981) is comprised of a cramped, cacophonous space wherein a number of hollow-eyed, creatures vie for each other's attention and seek to assert themselves. In this work, Mulindwa has created an imaginary space that seems to give concrete form to the artist's intention to "express disgust with what he called 'Aminism'—Aminism being a direct reference to Amin's misrule."[43] More broadly, *Untitled* can be seen as being representative of a felt need for artists during the 1970s and through into the 1980s to express disgust at what they felt were corrupt political regimes.[44] Moreover, and as Kyeyune notes: "Compositional arrangement of the paintings changed from simple pictorial narratives to compact and busy 'visual broadsheets', which took on visionary themes as artists responded to physical and mental brutalities of the time. Formal tenets of pictorial composition like objective and figure drawing, perspective gave way to disguised messages in symbolism taken from myths and legends."[45]

As with artists practicing in America and Europe during the period in question, "the challenges faced by African artists were not monolithic, but instead depended on the specific histories of their countries, as well as on the intellectual, political, and artistic philosophies and ideologies to which they were exposed."[46] Indeed, these challenges extended to artistic developments in Iraq during what was a comparable period.

Together with Shakir Hassan Al Said, Naziha Selim's brother, Jewad Selim was the cofounder in 1951 of Jama'et Baghdad lil Fen al-Hadith (the Baghdad Group for Modern Art). According to Nada Shabout, "Selim emphasized promoting the notion of istilham al-turath—seeking inspiration from tradition—and developed an artistic vision which was historico-cultural as well as modern."[47] Moreover, istilham, a verb which means inspiration or instinct "is a concept that advocates mediation between the past and the present; a negotiation of heritage and of tradition, toward an evolvement of new contemporary aesthetics. Istilham perceives a spiritual relationship between the past and the present regardless of temporal distance."[48]

Having studied at the Baghdad College of Fine Arts (what is now the Institute of Fine Arts) from 1944–1947 where her brother had taught, Naziha Selim was awarded a government scholarship to study at the Ecole des Beaux Arts in Paris. Having graduated in 1951, she remained in Europe before returning to Baghdad in the 1960s where she taught at the Institute of Fine Arts until the 1980s when she retired.

In many respects *Untitled* (1989) (Plate 9) is a continuation of what would be a consistent set of concerns that the artist engaged with over the course of her career. In the painting Selim depicts a series of figures within what we assume to be a domestic setting. Like many other paintings by Selim, the artist demonstrates an interest in the particularities of lived experience for Iraqi women. Achieved through what is both a loose handling of paint and a fluid application line, the partially abstracted figures are perhaps in part indebted to Fernand Leger, an artist whose tutelage she worked under whilst at the Ecole des Beaux Arts.

As the German variant of Neo-Expressionism, the response by artists to political upheaval in Uganda and Selim's own figurative paintings attest, artists in a number of countries were seeking to negotiate with questions of national identity. Certainly, along with a commitment to figuration, discernible within the exhibition catalogue for *The Human Clay* were perhaps some of the first signs of this renewed interest in the medium becoming divided along nationalistic lines.

With respect to Kitaj's attempts at establishing a fully-fledged "School of London," within the same section of the catalogue essay he opined: "There are still those who think that English art can be spoon-fed on the last feeble gruel trickling from the pens of art scribbles in distant places, but New York has its lap full of its own ageing romance and that self-centered art culture, believe it or not, has a lot to learn from over here."[49]

Perhaps, as Michael Compton claimed, writing in the exhibition catalogue that accompanied the Tate's survey show of 1983, simply entitled *New Art*, that it was this very plurality that mobilized artists seeking recourse to, if not nationalistic stereotypes, then certainly recurring and deeply entrenched tropes:

> Qualities of deadpan wit and irony have appeared alongside extreme and direct expressions of sexuality, anxiety, hostility, violence and all that is most disturbing. Styles have been changed and permuted, extemporiszed and imitated. They have been crude and sophisticated. But above all they have been varied to the extent that it has been necessary to fall back on national or regional categories in place of formal definitions.[50]

With regards to what he labelled were the "middle generation German artists," namely Baselitz, Penck, Kiefer, Lupertz and Immendorf, Compton claimed that "we may easily see certain common characteristics that can be considered national."[51] Later on in the text, Compton elaborated upon this claim: "For me, at least, the emptiness of Kiefer's halls and landscapes, the pathos of the hacked wooden figures of Penck and Baselitz, the old and new myths that are invoked in all that work … is universal as well as Germanic."[52]

Within the context of one of the catalogue essays for *Zeitgeist*, a concern to locate the work through the artist's respective geographies proved equally persistent:

> A salutary effect of exhibitions like Zeitgeist is to put in better balance the dialogue between the art of Europe and the United States. Until very recently, American Art was viewed on the American side of the Atlantic within a nationalist vacuum, and the history of art after 1945 seemed to take place only in New York, in much the same way that the history of modern art used to be thought of as taking place exclusively in Paris.[53]

Arguably then, it wasn't so much a case of "painters ... no longer [being] constrained to conceal their native roots" but rather critics being not particularly averse to reverting to issues of nationality as a means by which meaning might be quarried.[54]

Whilst there was a certain inevitability that German artists would have the "Neo-Expressionist" label attached to their work, even if it had been, in certain cases, somewhat artificially grafted, the label did extend to other related instances of painting that were occurring elsewhere both in Europe and in the United States.

Given Italy's history as being steeped within a rich visual tradition, it was perhaps inevitable that artists who were domiciled there would seek to transpose aspects of those traditions within what, in effect, formed their own contribution towards what was happening elsewhere. The term "trans-avantgarde," coined by Achille Bonito Olivia in an article written in 1979 entitled "The Italian Trans-Avantgarde" was, at least according to one commentator, "the Italian equivalent of German Neo-Expressionism."[55]

Whilst certain differences remained between the work of Sandro Chia, Enzo Cucchi and Francesco Clemente, the Italian artists whose work became most readily associated with the term, the over-arching trajectory of their respective practices remained geared towards a lyrical and often classicizing treatment of the figure.

Chia's statement, quoted by Tony Godfrey in his own survey of painting during this decade, can arguably be taken as characterizing not only the artist's own personal set of convictions towards painting, but equally as being more generally emblematic of how painting was now being perceived: "I've been through conceptualism, minimalism, everything. There is a new richness to our perception because we went through all that. Now it's possible to look at paintings again, we see it not only as paint on canvas, but as something else ... A painting is not just an object: it has an aura again. There is light around the work."[56]

Whilst the Italian variant of Neo-Expressionism sought to remodel and at times gently ironize historical forms, their approach, unlike some of their German counterparts, remained invariably resistant to any overt politicization of content. For this reason, the trans-avantgarde, with their "greater tendency to stylistic pluralism," was arguably closer to their American counterparts.[57]

Whilst, according to Fineberg, the "New York art world did not take note of neo expressionist painting of Germany and Italy until the early eighties."

arguably when it did, it was the paintings of Julian Schnabel that appeared to rehearse those sentiments that were prevalent within other instances of Neo-Expressionism.[58]

Adopting Baselitz's vigorous, painterly and often crude facture, Schnabel's paintings equally looked towards the work of Kiefer for the possibilities it offered in terms of how the surface of a particular painting could become a receptacle for unconventional or unorthodox materials. Whilst for Kiefer this included straw, Schnabel chose to cover his supports with broken crockery. This had the effect of providing a fragmented, discontinuous surface upon which imagery ranging from the religious, *St Francis in Ecstasy* (1980), through to the ostensibly autobiographical, as in the case of *Portrait of my Daughter* (1982), was painted.

Though often prone to making somewhat contradictory statements, Schnabel, by his own admission and like his European counterparts, remained indebted to historical precedent: "My painting comes out of the continuum of art that has been ... Different artists from the past have touched me, and I have looked at their paintings ... Vermeer expressed his understanding of light and time in a way that is indelible. If that's Expressionism, then I guess I'm an Expressionist."[59]

Along with the artist's own proclivity to align his practice with a particular reading or interpretation of tradition, others around him were equally inclined to posit what he did and how he did it within the historical parameters of artistic and specifically, modernist production. This entailed the rehearsal of the idea that he was, in effect, a modernist artist operating within a postmodern milieu. To this end, at least one writer at the time claimed that the artist was "taking Pollock's heroic mantle despite all his dilettantism and playboy life-style. In his painting he attempts, like Aeneas, to enter the underworld of the imagination in order to bring back truth."[60]

Whilst Schnabel and more broadly Neo-Expressionism came to dominate the debates that circulated around painting during the 1980s, other approaches towards the medium coalesced during this period. Unlike Neo-Expressionism, these sought to challenge its ostensible lack of criticality, a lack that was on one level symptomatic of its repudiation of the more "cerebral" post-conceptual approaches to art making. Certainly, the question of whether or not painting could be anachronistic without losing its criticality was a question that the Bad Painting sought to address.

Unlike bad painting, Bad Painting, according to Susanne Neuburger, functioned as "project, action and text. It not only questions rules, but also avant-garde dictates, and speculates ahead, either successfully or unsuccessfully, attracting attention or meeting with disapproval."[61] To this end, although what marked the projects of Bad Painting and Neo-Expressionism was a deep-seated commitment to both painting and the place of historical precedent within it, it was arguably the former's more strategic use of historical forms that differentiated it from its more emotionally charged counterpart. Whilst Neo-Expressionism's somewhat anachronistic status remained largely unquestioned, within other interpretive contexts to be anachronistic was not necessarily to be artistically compromised. According to Michael Krebber, this stemmed from painters having assumed a measure of critical distance by way of "opting out of the progressive (abstract) movement at the very moment in which it becomes established and academic." This meant that, for Krebber at least, "anachronism can be revolutionary or even the very means of survival."[62]

The provenance of Bad Painting, if not as a fully fledged movement then, at the very least, as a sentiment or set of attitudes that was brought to what was a predominantly figurative approach to painting, stemmed from an exhibition Marcia Tucker curated in 1978 at New York's New Museum. *"Bad" Painting*, as Eva Badura-Triska notes "included only American artists who had resisted the dictates of the avant-gardes of the 1960s and 1970s by painting figuratively in highly personal idioms, but who generally rejected all canons of painting and refused to develop a signature style."[63]

The significance of Tucker's exhibition rested on the fact that, as Badura-Triska has pointed out, it "foreshadowed the renewed vigor and acceptance of (especially figurative) painting in the 1980s, as well as this period's questioning of the avant-gardes' belief on progress and the acceptance of artistic pluralism."[64]

Whilst for those artists associated with Bad Painting the more conceptually oriented practices were to be avoided, elsewhere it would appear that one didn't necessarily have to throw the baby out with the bathwater. That is, at least according to the organizers of the exhibition *New Image Painting*, one could paint and yet still have one's practice rooted within a set of concerns that first emerged within the respective practices of those artists who were associated with both Minimalism and Conceptual Art.

New Image Painting was staged at the Whitney Museum of American Art between December 1978 and January 1979 and was premised on the idea, according to Richard Marshall writing in the exhibition's catalogue, that "[m]uch of the art of the 1970s has been characterized by artists' inclination toward the use of recognizable images. This has occurred most readily and obviously in those disciplines predisposed to image-making—performance, video, film, photography—and has also become apparent in recent painting and sculpture."[65]

Indeed, this statement is telling to the extent that rather than attempting to distance the paintings of the ten artists that were being shown from what had constituted, in the U.S. at least, a competing set of avant-garde practices, at least part of the rationale that informed this particular exhibition was the claim that Minimalism and painting were not to be understood as being necessarily mutually exclusive. Accordingly, whilst these so-called "imagistic" painters chose as their subject matter the world of appearances, albeit often in an oblique or distorted way, they nevertheless demonstrated, it was claimed, "a closer affinity to Abstract Expressionist, Pop, Minimal, and Conceptual concerns than to traditional figurative and realist work."[66] Elsewhere in the catalogue essay the connection between the "imagists" and Minimalism is made explicit: "The implications suggested by spare forms, perceptual preoccupations, and rational order in minimalistic work have served as a directional indicator for some later painting concerned with imagery."[67] So, for example, and in what is a somewhat tenuous comparison with Minimalism, Marshall suggests that the "weight, simplicity, and ambiguity of images employed in the paintings of Lois Lane recall interpretations similar to those evoked by minimalist objects. In the same way that Donald Judd's reductive, industrial-looking forms announce their objectness, Lois Lane's painted forms announce their imageness."[68] Moreover, Greenberg's theories still appeared, at the very least, to adumbrate a particular historiography of twentieth century American art which "since the mid-'40s has been distinguished by a striving toward the reduction and clarification of all but the most essential qualities of art. Paring down to the most cogent aspects of visual, emotional, formal, and intellectual components has been a consistent objective of recent art."[69]

Along with *New Image Painting*, at the time there were certain other artists who sought to explore how the legacy of modernism and in particular how certain facets that characterized formalism's account of abstract painting could be meaningfully squared with what was ostensibly an image-based practice.

To the extent wherein form was intuited and painting was still construed as being an inherently expressive medium, the paintings of Elizabeth Murray arguably shared the same impetus as that of the Neo-Expressionists. As the artist claimed in 1986: "When things go well, you stop thinking about what you're doing. I was in my last year of art school when I finally put it together and discovered how to get my feelings out. It's not that you learn how to paint—anybody can do that—but you learn how to be *expressive* with paint."[70]

Murray's paintings during this period were characterized by the juxtaposition of several often irregularly shaped panels, sometimes through the abutment of their respective edges, for example in the case of *Painter's Progress* (1981), and sometimes through the artist overlapping their edges, resulting in these latter works protruding somewhat from the wall plane, as with *Fly By*, painted a year later.

Painter's Progress consisted of nineteen panels across which the artist had painted an artist's palette along with three somewhat stylized paintbrushes protruding from the palette's thumbhole. Rather than have a preordained image in mind prior to the work's execution, the choice of a palette appeared to have been arrived at serendipitously: "I went out one night to walk the dog and I walked past Pearl Paint, which had that sign in the window, a neon light shaped like a palette with three beautiful brushes coming out of the palette's hole. And it just hit me: 'that's it. That's my image.'"[71]

Although by that point Murray had very much established her career as an artist, she was seldom invited to show alongside other artists who were being selected to show in group exhibitions. Several explanations for this might be marshalled, including the playful indeterminacy of the paintings that refused to side with either abstraction or representation. In addition, Murray was operating within a predominantly male artistic milieu that meant that she, like other women artists who were painting at that time "were seldom invited to the po-mo painting party."[72] Reflecting on the point at which, as the artist herself noted, "Neo-Expressionism was starting," Murray has claimed that " … I thought I was going to be the leader of the pack—ha ha ha ha—delusional as I was. Instead, suddenly I was over, or that's the way it felt to me. And there these guys were. It was amazing: after all the feminism, the boys were back in town."[73]

Notwithstanding the strictures that Murray was forced to confront and that were aligned with an artist's gender, what Murray's polyptychs demonstrated was the fact that an artist could successfully marry the abstract with the figurative without necessarily having to revert to pastiche, or, indeed, hyperbole. Instead, a more traditional set of techniques and approaches could be adopted without automatically having to place the resulting work in, figuratively speaking, a pair of quotation marks. Whilst Murray's work was by no means a return to Greenbergian formalism, at the very least it offered a welcome antidote to and a separate account of painting that Neo-Expressionism had presented.

What marked the paintings of Murray during the 1980s was their proclivity to treat two seemingly opposing impulses, that is, the representational and the abstract not as mutually exclusive fields of operation, but as two facets that could reciprocally engage in a meaningful dialogue. Rather than being antithetical, a work such as *Painter's Progress* demonstrated how an artist could harness and accord a meaningful role to and for the other. In other words, Murray's work at the time enabled the abstract to dialectically engage with the representational in terms of what was a symbiotic process borne not out of hierarchy, but of equilibrium.

In the same year that *A New Spirit in Painting's* prognosis on art was being foregrounded by a "deep reflection on the traditions of painting," "Figures of Authority, Ciphers of Regression: Notes on the Return of Representation in European Painting," written by the Marxist art historian Benjamin H. D. Buchloh tendentiously sought to oppose such an ambition.[74] What, for Buchloh the hyperbole of such historical retrenchment dissembled was the fact that it serviced a privileged social elite: "Like other objects of cultural history, aesthetic production modes can be wrenched from their contexts and functions, to be used to display the wealth and power of the social group that has appropriated them."[75] Indeed, rather than wanting to instigate the next step in what would be the further advancement of painting, other commentators also interpreted the motivations of the Neo-Expressionists as being arguably more self-regarding.

In terms of Schnabel's proclivity to orient the work's content towards religious iconography, Suzi Gablik professed that "it is difficult to believe in the prophetic consciousness of someone so frankly out to get what he wants—personal success in the New York art world, not metaphysical truths."[76] On one level, whilst Buchloh and Gablik's respective agendas remained markedly different, their deep-seated reservations were equally borne out of the premise that Neo-Expressionism was "market-oriented and regressive."[77]

Adding further weight to such claims was Hal Foster's own interpretation that the purported resurrection of figurative painting in general and Neo-Expressionism in particular was more broadly symptomatic of American cultural politics' "neoconservative postmodernism." To this end, whilst poststructuralism had proffered a politically cognizant account of postmodernism, neoconservativist postmodernism was primarily defined in relation to style.[78] According to Foster, unlike its poststructuralist counterpart, neoconservative postmodernism was reactionary rather than dialectical due to its attempts to reinstate the place of both history and the author–subject.[79] What this produced were paintings, including those made by Schnabel, that were notable for their "use of kitschy historicist references to commodify the usual painting."[80] As such, this purported return to history was in fact, disingenuous: "What, first of all, is this 'history' but a reduction of historical periods to ruling-class styles that are then pastiched?"[81]

Beyond its over-reliance upon the recapitulation of historical forms, the broader implications held by neoconservative postmodernism was that the project of modernism became "bowdlerized," reduced to an abstraction, i.e., "formalism" which, as Foster claimed, was subsequently condemned "as a historical mistake."[82] Indeed, in a sense modernism became a vexing issue not only for neoconservative postmodernism, but for those who represented the poststructuralist account of postmodernism due to the fact that "it was no longer critical enough—it had become the official art of the museums, the favored architecture of the corporations, and so on."[83]

Although modernism evidently no longer held any real critical purchase or favor, the first half of the 1980s was a time when competing claims were being made on behalf of both history and the artist's ability to act both within it and upon it. For whilst Joachimides, writing in the catalogue that accompanied *A New Spirit in Painting* claimed that the artist was "an individual engaged in a search for self-realization and as an actor on the wider historical stage." for others Neo-Expressionism's rehearsal of historical forms was rhetorical rather than instrumental.[84] Or, as Foster would claim, "a postmodern present of hysterical, historical retrospection in which history is fragmented and the subject dispersed in its own representations."[85]

Instead of a costume of rags then, for certain commentators' painting's so-called return to tradition amounted to nothing more than a rehearsal of what one might claim was a case of the emperor's new clothes. For whilst Robert Rosenblum could construe what was at the time painting's "encyclopedic range" as evidence of the generation's prevailing "grasp of every kind of imaginative release ... a windswept field of energies that appears to be caught in mid-air before structures can be regimented, contours regularized, colors clarified, paint strokes refined," others were less willing to interpret the resurgence of the medium within such affirmative terms.[86] Rather than see the return to representation within the context of postmodernism as evidence that artists were still capable of developing their own authentic and individuated style, albeit one that was, to a certain extent, indebted to and authenticated by historical precedent, those that were more skeptical saw the work of the Neo-Expressionists and the paintings of other related artists as merely an almost morbid reiteration, as it were, of an existing back catalogue of stylistic tropes. As McEvilley noted: "Naïve representation—representation that is believed to objectively represent reality—is a kind of dream or hypnosis or wishful thinking. The post-Modern form of representation is not to attempt to represent things in the world but to represent modes of styles of representation: the film, the comic book, the classical painting, the advertising mode."[87]

Whilst there was undeniably a resurgence in painting during the 1980s, this was not something that was unequivocally welcomed. As we will see in the following chapter, such initial misgivings soon became replaced by a wider, more sustained and systematic critique not just of Neo-Expressionism, but of the medium in general.

Notes

1 Thomas McEvilley, *The Exile's Return: Toward a Redefinition of Painting for the Post-Modern Era* (Cambridge: Cambridge University Press, 1994), 7–8.

2 Greenberg, "Modernist Painting" (1960), in Greenberg, *The Collected Essays and Criticism* vol. 4, *Modernism with a Vengeance, 1957–1969*, 86.

3 Ibid, 92.

4 Christos M. Joachimides, "A New Spirit in Painting," in *A New Spirit in Painting* (London: Royal Academy, 1981), 15.

5 McEvilley, *The Exile's Return: Toward a Redefinition of Painting for the Post-Modern Era*, 110.

6 R. B. Kitaj, *The Human Clay: An Exhibition* (London: Arts Council of England, 1976), unpaginated.

7 Ibid.

8 Ibid.

9 Ibid.

10 "Only nine Americans were included, two of them (Kitaj and Cy Twombly) permanently domiciled in Europe, whereas there were no fewer than eleven Germans." Edward Lucie-Smith, *Art in the Eighties* (Oxford: Phaidon, 1990), 10.

11 Joachimides, "A New Spirit in Painting," 15.

12 Ibid.

13 Ibid., 15–16.

14 Ibid., 12

15 Robert Rosenblum, "Thoughts on the Origin of 'Zeitgeist'," in *Zeitgeist: International Art Exhibition*, ed. Christos Joachimides and Norman Rosenthal (London: Weidenfeld and Nicolson, 1983), 13.

16 Ibid.

17 Hilton Kramer, "Signs of Passion," in Joachimides and Rosenthal, *Zeitgeist: International Art Exhibition*, 17.

18 Susan Rothenberg. "When Asked If I'm an Expressionist: An Artist's Symposium" (1982), in *Theories and Documents of Contemporary Art: A Sourcebook of Artist's Writings*, eds. Kristine Stiles and Peter Selz (Berkeley: University of California Press, 1996), 263.

19 Clement Greenberg, "A Public Debate with Clement Greenberg," The University of Ottawa, March 30, 1987, in Thierry de Duve, *Clement Greenberg Between the Lines*, trans. Brian Holmes (Chicago: The University of Chicago Press, 2010), 122.

20 Regarding the provenance of Rothenberg's equine imagery, Rothenberg has claimed that the "way the horse image appeared in my paintings was not an intellectual procedure. Most of my work is not run through a rational part of my brain. It comes from a place in me that I don't choose to examine. I just let it come. I don't have any special affection for horses." Rothenberg, Susan Rothenberg "When Asked If I'm an Expressionist: An Artist's Symposium," 264.

21 Ibid.

22 Ibid., 263.

23 McEvilley, *The Exile's Return: Toward a Redefinition of Painting for the Post-Modern Era*, 124.

24 Georg Baselitz, interview 1983 reproduced in Lucie-Smith, *Art in the Eighties*, 12.

25 Michael Compton, "New Art" in *New Art at the Tate Gallery 1983* (London: Tate Gallery, 1983), 20.

26 Greenberg, "Avant-Garde and Kitsch" (1939), in Greenberg, *The Collected Essays and Criticism Volume 1 Perceptions and Judgments, 1939–1944*, 9.

27 Lisa Saltzman, "Lost in Translation: Clement Greenberg, Anselm Kiefer, and the Subject of History," in *Visual Culture and the Holocaust*, ed. Barbie Zelizer (London: The Athlone Press, 2001), 80.

28 Anselm Kiefer in "A Dialogue with Donald Kuspit" at *Documenta* in 1987, in *Dialectical Conversions Donald Kuspit's Art Criticism*, eds. David Craven and Brian Winkenweder (Liverpool: Liverpool University Press, 2011), 71.

29 Everlyn Nicodemus, "Inside. Outside," in *Seven Stories About Modern Art in Africa*, ed. Jane Havell (London: Whitechapel, 1995), 34.

30 Ibid.

31 Sunanda K. Sanyal, "'Being Modern': Identity Debates and Makerere's Art School in the 1960s," in *A Companion to Modern African Art*, eds.

Gitti Salami and Monica Blackmmun Visonà (Oxford: Wiley, 2013), 256. According to Sanyal, Trowell "rejected the Renaissance pictorial convention for its dependence on the emulation of nature and disregarded modernism for its formal experiments that underscored the artist as the subject, a creative strategy she dismissed as 'soulless superficiality.'" Ibid.

32 "Makerere Art School, Kampala," in Simon Njami, *Africa Remix: Contemporary Art of a Continent* (Johannesburg: Jacana Media (Pty) Ltd, 2007), 239.

33 Katrin Peters-Klaphake, "Collecting Art at Makerere Institute of Heritage Conservation and Restoration, Kampala," *The International Journal of the Inclusive. Museum* 4, Issue 4 (2012): 3.

34 "Makerere Art School," *Africa Remix: Contemporary Art of a Continent*, 239.

35 Wanjiku Nyachae, "Concrete Narratives and Visual Prose," in *Seven Stories About Modern Art in Africa*, 165.

36 Stuart Hall, "Museums of Modern Art and the End of History," in *Modernity and Difference*, eds. Stuart Hall and Sarat Maharaj (London: Institute of International Visual Arts, 2001), 21–22.

37 Ibid.

38 Chika Okeke-Agulu, "The Challenge of the Modern: An Introduction," *African Arts* 39, no. 1 (2006) 15.

39 George Kyeyune, "Artistic Entanglements: Elimo Njau, Theresa Musoke, Peter Mulindwa, and Jak Katarikawe," in Don Handa et al., *Mwili, Akili Na Roho: Ten Figurative Painters From East Africa* (Nairobi: NCAI Publications, 2023), 39.

40 Ibid., 42.

41 Ibid.

42 Ibid.

43 In an interview in 2001, the artist "confirmed that during the late-seventies and early-eighties churches and religious symbols were used to express disgust with what he called 'Aminism'—Aminism being a direct reference to Amin's misrule." Angelo Kakande, "Contemporary Art in Uganda: A Nexus between Art and Politics." PhD thesis 2008, 204.

44 George Kyeyune, *Art in Uganda in the 20th century*. (Unpublished doctoral dissertation.) School of Oriental and African Studies, University of London, London, 2003, p. 155.

45 Ibid.

46 Okeke-Agulu, "The Challenge of the Modern: An Introduction," 14.

47 Nada Shabout, "Jewid Selim: On Abstraction and Symbolism," *Mathaf Encyclopedia of Modern Art and the Arab World*, https://www.encyclopedia.mathaf.org.qa/en/essays/Pages/Jewad-Selim,-On-Abstraction-and-Symbolism.aspx#3u.

48 Ibid.

49 Kitaj, *The Human Clay: An Exhibition*, unpaginated.

50 Compton, "New Art," 17.

51 Ibid., 20.

52 Ibid., 29.

53 Rosenblum, "Thoughts on the Origin of 'Zeitgeist'," 14.

54 Kramer, "Signs of Passion," 18.

55 Lucie-Smith, *Art in the Eighties*, 23.

56 Sandro Chia quoted in Tony Godfrey, *The New Image: Painting in the 1980s* (Oxford: Phaidon, 1983), 69

57 Lucie-Smith, *Art in the Eighties*, 29.

58 Jonathan Fineberg, *Art Since 1940: Strategies of Being* (London: Laurence King, 1995), 418.

59 Schnabel quoted in Diane Crane, *The Transformation of the Avant-Garde: The New York Art World, 1940–1985* (Chicago: University of Chicago Press, 1987), 75.

60 Godfrey, *The New Image: Painting in the 1980s*, 140.

61 Susanne Neuburger, "The First and the Last Painting? An experimental set-up for Bad Painting," in Eva Badura-Triska and Susanne Neuburger, *Bad Painting—good art* (Cologne: DuMont; Vienna: MUMOK Museum Moderner Kunst Stiftung Ludwig Wien, 2008), 12.

62 Michael Krebber, "Wo die Liebe hinfällt," in *Texte zur Kunst*, 36 (December 1999): 223, reproduced in Eva Badura-Triska and Neuburger, *Bad Painting—good art*, 16.

63 Eva Badura-Triska, "Who becomes a Bad Painter, When, Why, and in What Sense?" in Badura-Triska and Neuburger, *Bad Painting—good art*, 78.

64 Ibid.

65 Richard Marshall, "New Image Painting" in Richard Marshall, *New Image Painting* (New York: Whitney Museum of American Art, 1978), 7.

66 Ibid., 8.

67 Ibid., 12.

68 Ibid.

69 Ibid., 8.

70 Elizabeth Murray in Kay Lason, "One From the Heart," *New York Magazine*, February 10, 1986, 43, reproduced in Fineberg, *Art Since 1940: Strategies of Being*, 429.

71 Elizabeth Murray quoted in Robert Storr, *Elizabeth Murray* (New York: Museum of Modern Art, 2005), 175.

72 Ibid., 66.

73 Ibid., 177.

74 Joachimides, *A New Spirit in Painting*, 13.

75 Benjamin H. D. Buchloh, "Figures of Authority, Ciphers of Regression: Notes on the Return of Representation in European Painting," *October* 16 (1981): 55.

76 Suzi Gablik, *Has Modernism Failed?* 2nd edition (London: Thames & Hudson, 2004): 107.

77 Ibid., 99–100.

78 Hal Foster, *Recodings: Art, Spectacle, Cultural Politics*, Seattle (Washington: Bay Press, 1996), 121.

79 Foster, *Recodings: Art, Spectacle, Cultural Politics*, 121.

80 Ibid., 122.

81 Ibid.

82 Ibid., 124.

83 Bois et al., *Art Since 1900: Modernism Antimodernism Postmodernism*, 598.

84 Joachimides, *A New Spirit in Painting*, 14.

85 Foster, *Recodings: Art, Spectacle, Cultural Politics*, 126.

86 Rosenblum, "Thoughts on the Origin of 'Zeitgeist'," 12.

87 McEvilley, *The Exile's Return: Toward a Redefinition of Painting for the Post-Modern Era*, 102.

5

Manic Mourning

Like Baudrillard, I would call them manic mourners. Their return to painting, as though it were an appropriate medium for what they want to address, as though the age of the simulacral could be represented, comes from the feeling that since the end has come, since it's all over, we can rejoice at the killing of the dead.[1]

As the first chapter has already evinced, several artists whose respective practices briefly fell under the auspices of painting, even if it was in some cases a tangential association, adopted an overtly destructive process or set of processes as the primary means of production. In this respect Saint Phalle, for example, somehow sought to turn received wisdom on its head by making an inherently destructive act, namely firing a .22 caliber rifle at a painting, a fundamentally creative gesture. Whilst such actions were placed within the context of those variant, heterogeneous practices that were nevertheless united in their rejection of tradition or artistic dogma, there were subsequent artists who equally strove to radicalize painting through such ostensibly destructive means.

Begun in 1970, with a second series made in 1980, Susan Hiller's Painting Blocks entailed the artist cutting up a number of her earlier paintings and reconfiguring the resulting swatches of canvas into a series of block-like objects. Stencilled onto the front of each were two dates, the earlier of which referred to the date the original painting (from which the Painting Block was subsequently made) was made or exhibited, whilst the latter denoted the year the original painting became reconfigured into a "block." Also stencilled onto the surface were the dimensions of the original painting.

In 1972 and beginning with the Hand Grenades, Hiller embarked on a series of works which collectively were given the name Relics and which arguably extended the blocks' somewhat destructive bent. For the Hand Grenades, the artist burnt her earlier Handpaintings and placed the ashes into a series of grenade-shaped vials.

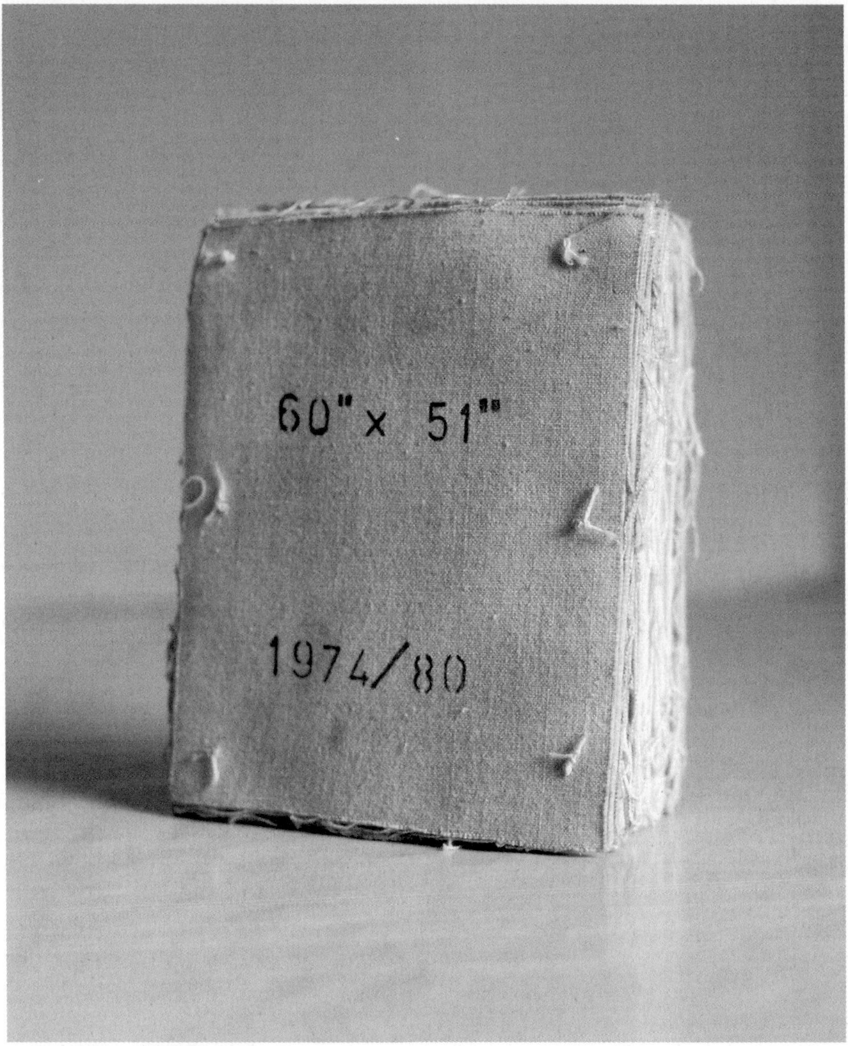

FIGURE 5.1 Susan Hiller, *Painting Block no.6 1974/80: 60" × 51"*, 1980.

On one level, both the *Painting Blocks* and the *Hand Grenades*, like their historical predecessors, entailed a willful and consciously driven destructive process, directed towards a particular set of paintings (it is debatable whether the destruction of Painting per se can be ascribed to either of the two series, or, indeed, whether this was the artists' overarching motivation), either through the act of cutting up or through the arguably more ritualized act of immolation. Either way, Hiller's paintings underwent a transformative process that occurred on both a physical and conceptual level. Although the means remained in many respects conventional, namely oil on canvas, the end result could no longer be buttressed by the various conventions that were ordinarily associated with painting. In this respect, both the *Tirs* and the *Painting Blocks* echoed Conceptual Art and Arte Povera's utilization of painting; not in order to entrench it still further within its own unique area of competence, as Greenberg had prescribed, but rather as a means of opening painting and its incipient materiality out onto the realm of ideas and meanings. For example, and with respect to Hiller's practice, in their final state some of the works took on the appearance, if not the received function, of reliquary.

Indeed, several commentators have read these works through the interpretive prism of the artist's background in anthropology. According to one observer, as a result of their transformation into a seemingly vestigial state, "Hiller returns painting to something nearer its performative functions in pre-Renaissance and indigenous cultures, where it acts as a part of ritual, as a talisman or as a manual, conceived as being impermanent yet as having presence and material effects in the world."[2]

For the purposes of this chapter, the reasoning behind marshalling these works by Hiller resides not in what might be construed as their associative effects, but rather in terms of how they appear to both preface and instantiate, albeit it in a literal way, a certain claim that was made on behalf of painting during the 1980s.

At least since the latter half of the nineteenth century, various figures have proclaimed painting's purported death. One of the first apocryphal instances occurred when the artist Paul Delaroche, who, upon being shown a daguerreotype, an early prototype of the photograph, exclaimed words to the effect of "from this day painting is dead."[3]

Historically, and from that moment, several other instances of painters reaching ostensibly the same conclusions intermittently appeared as the visual arts, and specifically painting developed during modernism and then through into postmodernism.

Within the context of the twentieth century, such proclamations arguably began with the Russian Constructivist Alexander Rodchenko. To accompany the group exhibition 5x5=25 which was held in Moscow in September 1921, the artist had claimed that he had "reduced painting to its logical conclusion and exhibited three canvases: red, blue and yellow. I affirmed: It's all over. Basic colors. Every plane is a plane, and there is to be no more representation."[4] Subsequently, Ad Reinhardt would claim in an interview in 1966 that he was making "the last painting which anyone can make."[5]

Hiller's Measure by Measure, (part I of which is dated 1973–92, part II is dated 1993–12 and part III is dated 2013–32) which is comprised of a series of burettes containing the ashes of paintings that have been burned annually seems especially pertinent here. Irrespective of the frequency of the debate itself, what Measure by Measure appears to acknowledge and moreover, give concrete form to is the iterative nature of the debate. Either way, painting becomes a site of trauma wherein its purported death is periodically rehearsed.

Whilst there were a number of documented instances wherein painting's death was mooted, if not openly declared, for the most part such claims were ostensibly localized and isolated responses to the perceived exhaustion of a medium that remained, for the most part, critically afloat, if not in favor.

Although this chapter will center upon a period of painting's history when this accusation was arguably given most vehemently and with the greatest sense of both urgency and resolve, what precipitated the situation during the 1980s had occurred over at least a fifteen-year period leading up to that point. Certainly, both Minimalism and Conceptual Art had attempted to sound painting's death knell by critically distancing their own operative modes from those of painting. So for example, in 1969 the conceptual artist Joseph Kosuth, an artist who had initially been associated with Art and Language, would assert that "being an artist means questioning the nature of art. If you make paintings, you are already accepting (not questioning) the nature of art."[6]

Be that as it may, it was during the 1980s that the accusations regarding painting's perceived obsolescence were given most vociferously and appeared to emerge from a set of convictions that were held simultaneously by several prominent critics.

Emerging out of a context wherein, as Bois remarked, "one hears endless diagnoses of death," one of the first missives aimed squarely at painting that would, in a sense, set both the tone and the critical agenda for those critiques that would subsequently follow was "The End of Painting" written by Douglas Crimp and published in the American art journal *October* in the spring of 1981.[7]

By way of segueing the reader into the text, the author begins by tactically selecting evidence from the catalogue essay the art critic Barbara Rose had recently written to accompany *American Painting: The Eighties*, an exhibition she had organized in 1979. Certain statements, apropos painting are deployed as being evidence of what is more broadly symptomatic of a malaise that still persisted, for Crimp at least, and worked to privilege the medium by attempting to confer on it a number of outmoded notions. With a faint air of distaste rather than opprobrium, Crimp quotes a passage where Rose claims that the painters whose work was included were "maintaining a conviction in quality and values, a belief in art as a mode of transcendence, a worldly incarnation of the ideal."[8] In effect, Crimp's overarching point of objection and what such a statement was more broadly symptomatic of was that fact that "she, like most people, still *believes* in painting."[9]

On one level, Rose's text seems to affirm Crimp's suspicions, presenting a somewhat traditional account of painting that remained partly organized around a series of anachronisms. For example, under the section headed "The Painter as Image Maker," she makes the following assertion on behalf of painting: "The imagery of painters committed exclusively to a tradition of painting, an inner world of stored images ranging from Altamira to

Pollock, is entirely invented; it is the product exclusively of the individual imagination rather than a mirror of the ephemeral external world of objective reality."[10]

For Crimp, such rhetoric, directly because it was being bound up with a desire to reinscribe a set of humanist and idealized values into the project of painting, was "exclusively reactionary." Moreover, "it reacts specifically against all those art practices of the sixties and seventies which abandoned painting and coherently placed in question the ideological supports of painting, and the ideology which painting, in turn supports."[11] Or, as Henry Sayre has more recently observed: "Deprive art of everything with which Rose wishes to invest it—autonomy, uniqueness, the cult of individuality and 'original' artistic 'vision,' the dream of universality and transcendence—and one has a reasonable definition of what avant-garde art seeks to be."[12]

And so, within *October*'s pages in the spring of 1981 the terms of the debate were set out and were bookended by a period that was loosely sandwiched somewhere after the demise of Abstract Expressionism and prior to the advent of what became labeled "postmodernism." Moreover, leading up to Crimp's claims were, according to the author at least, a number of related events and activities that prefaced, by the time "The Death of Painting" was written in 1981, what had become painting's moribund condition.

Accordingly, the "symptoms were everywhere: in the work of the painters themselves, each of whom seemed to be reiterating Reinhardt's claim that he was 'just making the last paintings which anyone can make,' or to allow their paintings to be contaminated with such alien forces as photographic images: in minimal sculpture, which provided a definitive rupture with painting's unavoidable ties to a centuries-old idealism: in all those other mediums to which artists turned as they, one after the other, abandoned painting."[13] On one level, this contamination worked to loosen the categorical boundaries that up until that point had worked to shore up painting, or at least, had worked to shore up formalism's account therein.

Ostensibly, Crimp's critique of Rose's claims centered on the fact that she still perceived painting as being governed by an inviolable essence. Indeed, when she claims that "the truth of the illusion of painting—and *illusion not flatness, is the essence of painting*" one inevitably sees this both as a rejection of Greenberg's centrally governing axiom of "flatness" and a continuation, albeit by other means, of his criticism.[14] It would appear that, having found the front door of the Greenbergian account of painting locked, the essentializing impulse that still appeared to have a significant claim within painting's conceptualization surreptitiously entered in through the back.

Rather than Crimp's remarks existing in some form a critical vacuum, they appeared to be part of a more broadly held consensus. Although rehearsed at certain moments during the decade and a half leading up to Crimp's proclamations, such claims had arguably reached their greatest cogency by the time the 1980s had begun. Perhaps the question with regards to the text that we will now turn to, published during the same year as Crimp's and foregrounded by the same kind of pronouncements, is whether as a form of criticism it sought to denude painting of its basis within a problematic set of ideologies and assumptions, or, conversely, whether it proffered a strategy by which, in the first instance, it could function as the means by which the medium could still negotiate a viable position for itself within what appeared to be a markedly hostile milieu.

Thomas Lawson's "Last Exit Painting," published in *Artforum* in the autumn of 1981 arguably mitigated painting in ways that Crimp's argument did not. However, that is not to say that Lawson's text was not without its targets. In addition to directing his critique to the Greenbergian version of formalism, Lawson also took as his focus a derivative style of figurative painting. With regards to the former, Lawson claimed that modernist formalism "seems finally discredited, hopelessly co-opted by the social structures it purportedly sought to subvert."[15] With regards to the latter, the "pseudoexpressionists" were to be viewed, according to Lawson, as the "last, decadent flowering of the modernist spirit."[16]

Whilst Crimp's criticism was partly organized around Rose's conviction that painting remained indelibly bound up with the principles of a universalizing and idealizing humanism, Lawson's claims appeared to rest upon the fact that a particular style certain painters were adopting was simply a rhetorical device, divested of any intrinsic communicable meaning. Accordingly, "these artists ... fake recognizable styles and make them over, on a larger scale, with brighter color and more pizzazz."[17] And because it was just that, a form of visual rhetoric, a mimicking, as opposed to a mockery of the modernist canon of painting, this was disingenuous, an "exercise in bad faith [that] succumb[s] to sentimentality."[18]

Whilst Lawson does note the fact that this "wider cultural cannibalism is the topic of another essay," in a sense the text can be read as introducing, albeit tacitly, the terms, or at least some of the terms, upon which postmodernism would be given and subsequently played out.[19]

The root of the author's disillusionment appeared to be the "cultural plundering" of Francesco Clemente, Julian Schnabel, Sandro Chia and Enzo Cucchi, which entailed "the annexation of wide areas of modern art."[20] Such a shift away from modernism's, or at least what Peter Bürger called the historical avant-garde's critique of traditional cultural forms, received ideologies and normative social, psychological and perceptive codes and towards postmodernism's exhaustion of these is evident when he makes the following observation: "Appropriation becomes ceremonial, an accommodation in which collage is understood not as a disruptive agent, a device to question perception—but as a machine to foster unlimited growth."[21]

Whilst the idea of appropriation became virtually synonymous with the more vanguard artistic practices as they became played out during the 1980s, one of the first instances wherein appropriation became marshaled as a term and put to the service of an incipient and yet burgeoning postmodernism was in Craig Owen's text "The Allegorical Impulse: Towards a Theory of Postmodernism," first published in the spring of 1980.

Seeking to posit the allegorical mode of much recent art as that of being interdisciplinary due to the fact that it played fast and loose with received aesthetic conventions and categorical boundaries, appropriation was one of several terms Owens marshaled that were all somehow emblematic not only of the allegorical, but of postmodernism generally. As Owens claimed: "Appropriation, site specificity, impermanence, accumulation, discursivity, hybridization—these diverse strategies characterize much of the art of the present and distinguish it from its modernist predecessors."[22]

Whilst, in the case of Hal Foster a hybridized form of appropriation was evident within the paintings of Phillip Taaffe, an artist who will be considered in greater detail within the next chapter, as a critical term it became more readily applied to the notion of photography. In fact, the affinities appropriation had with the photographic work of art was evident in Owens's selection of artists. Rather than center his discussion on painters who were appropriating other forms of imagery, Owens cites three artists, all of whom during the period in question were involved in making either photographic or photo-based works:

> The first link between allegory and contemporary art may now be made: with the appropriation of images that occurs in the works of Troy Brauntuch, Sherrie Levine, Robert Longo ... artists who generate images through the reproduction of other images. The appropriated image may be a film still, a photograph, a drawing: it is often already a reproduction. However, the manipulations to which these artists subject such images work to empty them of their resonance, their significance, their authoritative claim to meaning.[23]

Such debates were representative of the fact that for those artists who adopted appropriation as a specific strategy, particular accounts of both artist and artwork became engendered as a result. For whilst, as Lawson remarked, appropriation, like collage, relinquishes its efficacy when it is "understood not as a disruptive agent, a device to question perception—but as a machine to foster unlimited growth," its efficacy occurred during those moments when a set of assumptions or values that worked to organize the production and reception of the artwork became fundamentally challenged.[24] To this end, the more overtly aggressive and deliberately provocative use of appropriation could be seen in the photographs of Sherrie Levine, whose wholesale theft of particular photographs from the modernist canon sought to direct a number of fundamental questions towards the images she re-photographed with regards to what was perceived to be their originality, authorship and canonical status.

It is in this respect that Crimp drew a salient distinction between Levine and the cultural borrowings of Robert Mapplethorpe, whose classicizing approach was redolent of Edwards Weston's photographic "style." Whereas, according to Crimp "Mapplethorpe's appropriations ... align him with a tradition of aesthetic mastery, simultaneously referring to that tradition and appearing to renew it ... Levine's work interrupts the discourse of mastery through the refusal to reinvent the image."[25]

Whilst appropriation was primarily associated with those whose respective practices were somehow photographic, there were instances wherein artists who continued to paint, beyond the purview of Neo-Expressionism and its recapitulation of historical forms and traditional motifs, also adopted this strategy.

Along with a small number of painters based in the United States including Mike Bidlo who were working directly with strategies of appropriation, other artists were approaching this particular modus operandi of postmodernism in a way that was arguably more measured and analytical. To this end, rather than a form of cultural borrowing per se, certain artists sought to negotiate the medium through a reiteration of its conventions, its contexts and its histories.

With regards to the latter, Pat Steir's *The Breughel Series* (1982–1984), was comprised of 64 panels, each of which had been painted in a particular style that was characteristic of a particular period from a canonical historiography of painting. To this end, sections were painted in the style of, *inter alia*, Georgia O'Keefe, Jean-Michel Basquiat, Jackson Pollock, Sandro Botticelli, and Henri Matisse. When placed together, and their respective stylistic differences notwithstanding, the amalgamated image that was furnished through the juxtaposition of the sixty-four individual paintings was based on a seventeenth century still life painting by Jan Brueghel the Elder. The connection to this painting was reiterated by the fact that each of the individual panels was the same size as the original painting, namely twenty-one by twenty-six inches.

By organizing the sixty-four panels within a grid, the piece inevitably engaged with modernism's own utilization of and complicity with this compositional device. Of course, the prehistory of modernism's own vested interest in and adoption of the grid had emerged during the Renaissance and accompanied the inception of geometrical perspective. To this end, the recurrent motif of the tiled floor was one means by which the grid could be, as it were, "naturalized" and included within the painting's over-arching composition whilst all the while organizing, rationalizing and, it was hoped, harmonizing pictorial space. Equally, the "gridding up" of the artist's chosen support, which corresponded to an equivalently proportioned grid through which the subject was viewed, as in the case of Albrecht Dürer's famous woodblock print of an artist drawing from a recumbent figure, became an additional means by which the grid worked to underscore the practice of painting during the Renaissance, working to ensure a consistent registration of the world and specifically what was observable within it

Within the context of modernism, the operational character of the grid entailed, as Krauss had noted, an "introjection of the boundaries of the world into the interior of the work; it is a mapping of the space inside the frame onto itself. It is a mode of repetition, the content of which is the conventional nature of art itself."[26] In other words, the grid's utilization was entirely in accordance with modernist painting's valorization of autonomy and pictorial self-sufficiency.

Whilst Steir's own adoption of the grid was inevitably complicit with such a reading, within a climate of postmodernism it worked not to unify and close off the painting from the world, but rather functioned as a means by which it could be read as inherently fragmentary. More broadly, rather than rehearse the understanding of painting's historical development as the progressive unfolding of a causally linked series of movements, each of which were uniquely characterized by a particular approach to the medium, *The Breughel Series* re-presented, non-hierarchically, sixty-four styles that were, in effect, divested of the historical moment from which they had been directly transposed. As one commentator, echoing what had become an increasingly prevalent view noted,

> from the contemporary vantage point, it appears that the history of modern art, with its plurality of styles and isms, demonstrates, not the absolute necessity or rightness of any individual style or original statement, but the equivocal nature of all styles generally and the relative merit of particular styles ... In the 1980s style is but another aesthetic option available to the protean imagination of the artist, not at all the apotheosis of artistic genius.[27]

Although *The Brueghel Series* remained within the operative parameters of appropriation due to its "quotational" status, the work of Alan McCollum sought not to appropriate a particular style that pertained to painting's history, but rather certain normative conventions that pertained to painting.[28]

McCollum's Plaster Surrogates were plaster molds that had been cast in the shape of a framed painting. However, rather than framing an image, a scene, or a figure, the support was painted in a uniform black. Whilst this latter aspect might have been suggestive of an engagement with, if not continuation of, the project of utopian abstraction as it was first propounded by Kasimir Malevich with his similarly styled black monochrome paintings, the opposite was in fact true, for these paintings registered the anonymizing effects of mass production rather than the more individuated and transcendentalist ambitions of early European abstraction. As Foster noted, McCollum's "empty" surrogates made explicit "the reduction of content to form in the exchange of like for like as the general equivalence of objects in a serial mode of production."[29]

On one level, McCollum's own variant strategy of appropriation repudiated modernism's claims of autonomy on behalf of painting by denuding the discourses upon which the medium remained contingent upon "so as to riddle and expose them or to seduce and lead the astray."[30] Whilst Foster was referring here to American art generally, it encompassed the work of Alan McCollum whose practice, albeit in a very particular way, was organized around the painted object. Moreover, and with at the very least a nod to modernist aesthetics and its purported hoodwinking of the viewer, Foster would claim that this "shift in practice entails a shift in position: the artist becomes a manipulator of signs more than a producer of art objects, and the viewer as active reader of messages rather than a passive contemplator of the aesthetic or consumer of the spectacular."[31]

As a strategic counterpoint to what had been, by certain commentators and indeed artists, the repudiation of painting, Lawson positioned within his own thesis the work of David Salle. Unlike painters such as Clemente and Chia who appeared to uncritically rehearse various traditions associated with historical painting, Salle's practice, for Lawson at least, presented a welcome antidote because his work was not willing to be seduced by the multifarious styles and fragments of imagery it collaged together and colluded with. Instead, its chief motivation was the desire to use "established conventions against themselves in the hope of exposing cultural repression."[32] According

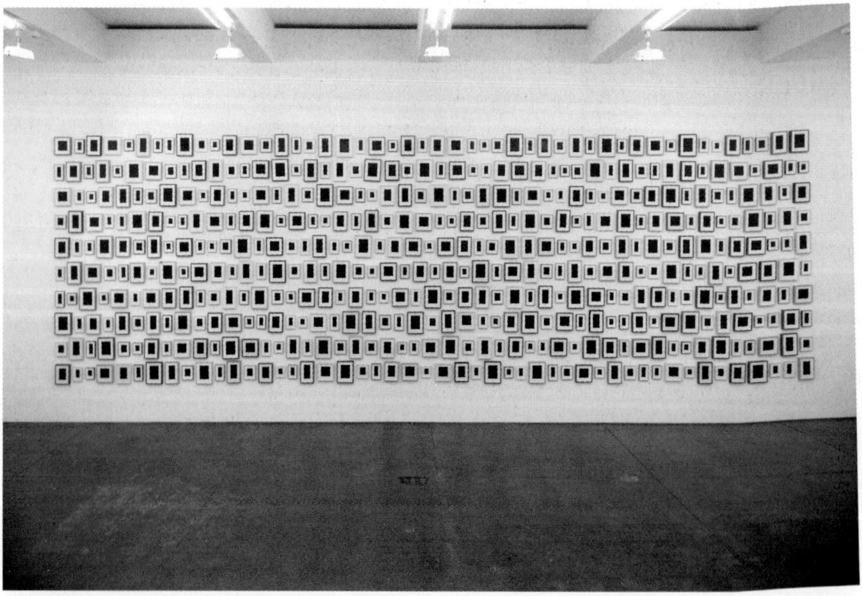

FIGURE 5.2 Allan McCollum, *Collection of 480 Plaster Surrogates*, 1982/1989.

to Sayre, whilst certain instances of painting had the gall to beg, borrow and steal from other moments within its history, these remained marked by a certain aporia: "They have done this, by and large, by insisting on the fundamental *undecidability* of their work and by attempting to 'write between the lines,' as it were, of antecedent painting. One of the best ways to think of painting in the eighties is to see it as consisting in 'doing something to (or with)' other paintings or images."[33]

Notwithstanding those canvases that adopted a more complex method of pictorial structuring, the basis for many of Salle's paintings made during the 1980s invariably entailed the superimposition of a more linear and painterly layer of figurative imagery over another layer of imagery, which, whilst equally figurative, was executed using a more somber and monochromatic palette.

An elaboration on this basic approach is evident within *Muscular Paper* (1985). Functioning in effect as a triptych, the central panel overlays two disembodied heads, rendered in a somewhat garishly putrescent blue and based upon Jusepe de Ribera's *The Club-Footed Boy* (1642) on top of two undressed women whose backs are turned to the viewer and who each appear to be holding one end of a skipping rope whilst also holding hands. Salle's proclivity to quote from other moments pertaining to art history is carried through into the other two panels wherein whilst the left-hand panel is comprised of a painting of a photograph by Brassaï of Pablo Picasso's 1931 sculpture *Bather*, the right-hand panel contains a more illustrative treatment of a bridge that has been directly appropriated from the German Expressionist artist Max Beckmann and placed over a plaid design.

With a juxtaposition of disparate images, motifs and objects that appeared to have been the result of happenstance rather than conscious deliberation, Salle's "postmodern" canvases appeared to adopt Surrealism's own strategy of conflating, both visually and conceptually, seemingly unrelated and for that matter irreconcilable images. However, with Surrealism the resultant imagery invariably became construed as a succession of visual ciphers that were all somehow keyed into and emblematic of Sigmund Freud's model of the unconscious mind. In this sense the imagery, however enigmatic and inexplicable, was able to acquire a measure of purchase within a particular epistemological framework. Moreover, as with other movements associated with modernism that occurred during the first half of the twentieth century in Europe, it adopted technically radicalized means in order to mobilize, it was hoped, emancipatory ends. In the case of Salle's heterogeneous dioramas (as opposed to hybridized—the discrete images within a particular painting by Salle never cohere, are never synthesized but remain held apart, isolated from each other, if not themselves, indefinitely), they never become interlaced within a broader interpretive framework, be it psychic or otherwise. Instead, they appear to rework Claude Levi-Strauss's notion of the floating signifier.[34] That is, rather than work to shore up the paintings by orienting them towards what conventionally would have amounted to the work's meaning, the discordant, seemingly arbitrary nature of the imagery meant that this possibility became indefinitely postponed, held off, deferred. As Robert Rosenblum observed, the paintings of Salle "create an eerie, nowhere environment, part mental, part physical, where incomplete and often almost illegible fragments from the widest range of visual languages wander about like displaced persons."[35]

On one level, Salle's paintings further reiterated what had become, as it were, a critical form of consensus with regards to the ostensible limitations of the artwork and, moreover reality at large within a culture that had become both highly mediated and dependent upon image-based technologies. In real terms, what this meant was a certain existential detachment whereby what one experienced, what was directly and immediately to hand, wasn't the thing itself but a representation of that self same thing. Such an interpretation of postmodernism placed a certain onus upon artists to somehow figure the medium of painting through an increasingly dominant visual culture where received understandings of "high" and "low" no longer carried any credence. As Rosenblum observed in 1986,

> when the original painting in the museum looks like an offshoot of its color reproduction rather than the other way round, when we rush to look at and record a memorable tourist spot with a portable camera rather than see it with our own eyes, then we know that many artists are going to have new things to tell us about whatever it is reality might be today.[36]

For his part, Lawson sanctioned the paintings of David Salle through the claim that they functioned as "disruptive agents" that acted in concert with the artist's own "strategy of infiltration and sabotage."[37] As it was then, the paintings of Salle were able to avoid the more hyperbolic tendencies that characterized certain facets of painting at that time by being able to strike a balance between "an empty formalism of the sort practiced by Clemente and Schnabel and a critical subversion of such formalism."[38] Moreover, as paintings wherein, tautologically, they communicated their inability to communicate, such an admission of a defeat, of purposelessness and of inertia was on one level more broadly symptomatic of postmodernism's relativism and the attempted nullification of received expressive modes.[39] Whilst Crimp's text offered for the most part a pessimistic forecast regarding painting's continued viability and Lawson's text, as we have also seen, attempted to mitigate painting's purported demise by marshalling the paintings of David Salle, Foster's text represented a third, arguably more temperate reading that attended to painting at a time when its legitimacy was sharply being held in question. Indeed "Signs Taken for Wonders," written five years after the publication of both "The End of Painting" and "Last Exit: Painting," on one level presented, relatively speaking, the most robust case *for* painting, or, at least, for a tactical mode of abstraction that by negotiating the strictures and value-laden assumptions of formalism, could redeploy painting within a climate that had deliberately set out to call for its obsolescence.

From the outset, Foster is at pains to distance himself from the possibility of his claims being interpreted as somehow rehearsing a set of debates around abstraction that had first been instigated by modernism. As he makes clear, whilst the artists he initially cites all somehow fall within the purview of this "new abstract painting" (in the text Foster places this designation within inverted commas, the qualification working to ensure that a critical distance is maintained), "it is not new except sometimes in the sense of the novel, it is not properly abstract except in the sense that it sometime simulates or parodies abstract painting; and it is not monolithic—these artists are related by preconditions but diverse in practice."[40] And if the reader was in any way still unsure with regards to the terms upon which Foster was approaching and engaging with abstract painting, the following coda was added: "It is not at all derived, genealogically, from critical abstract painting—that of Stella, Ryman, Marden."[41]

Indeed, Foster used the fact that these so-called critical abstractionists shared a differing artistic blueprint as a means to highlight what exactly separated those antecedental and mutually exclusive figures from his own selection of painters. With regards to the practice of Jack Goldstein, whilst he "makes his abstract paintings structurally as deep as early Stella's (4 to 12 inches thick) and often frames them with painted gold or silver bands ... this stress on 'objecthood' is beside any formalist point, and the metallic elements are formally gratuitous."[42] Indeed, according to Foster, it wasn't only modernist formalism that was pastiched, recycled and divested of any originary meaning. Turning his attention towards the abstract paintings of Sherrie Levine, he would claim that "her abstract paintings simulate modes of abstraction, as if to demonstrate that they are no longer critically reflexive or historically necessary forms with direct access to unconscious truths or a transcendental realm beyond the world—that they are simply *styles* among others."[43] And so, when Foster cited the paintings of Taaffe with regards to their orientation towards Op-art (Foster labels these figures "Neo-Opers"), whereby he claimed that it was "quintessentially twentieth-century: technologically oriented, disruptive, 'about perception,' naïve, superficial, and, by most accounts, a failure," he revealed the crux of the matter—that the so-called death of painting wasn't necessarily a death per se, but was rather a debate that came to be organized around modernist painting's perceived failure with regards to its stated aims.[44] The nub of Foster's argument then was the fact that the new abstract painters "do not appropriate modern abstraction so much as they simulate it."[45]

Like appropriation, "simulation" was another critical term that had emerged out of postmodernism's lexicon and that had slowly acquired a measure of currency within the discourses that had emerged around the status and condition of the artwork after modernism's demise. One of its main advocates was the French philosopher Jean Baudrillard who posited the term in relation to the notion of the "hyperreal," an atrophied version of the real which was read by him as both "that which can be reproduced" but also "that which is already reproduced."[46] Within this process hyperrealism enabled art and reality's mutual fulfillment "through an exchange at the level of simulation of their respective foundational privileges and prejudices" and as such it "is only beyond representation because it functions entirely within the realm of simulation"[47]

If Lawson claimed on behalf of the paintings of David Salle a refutation of a historically received reading of painting that equated to it being somehow indelibly bound up with a set of eternal values, and, moreover, a refutation of formalism's own particular stake within such a reading, the paintings and statements of Peter Halley further legitimized this critical standpoint with respect to the modernist canon and western visual culture generally.

Writing in 1982, a year after Lawson and Crimp's texts had been published, Halley claimed that his paintings functioned as a form of critique that was directed against "idealist modernism."[48] Seeking to make such an intention explicit, within the same text, simply entitled "Notes on the paintings," he stated that in the "'color field' is placed a jail. The misty space of Rothko is walled up."[49]

Halley's basic operative mode for the "cell" or conduit paintings attempted to conflate two seemingly antithetical contexts in order to engender, as is suggested in the artist's statement above, a critique that worked to short-circuit the idealizing tendencies of modernism. Taking as his reference point a series of historical moments wherein artists were working primarily under the auspices of geometric abstraction, Halley's own paintings mimicked the flat areas of color and the grid-like geometrically arranged compositions that became the hallmark of artists working within this particular painterly idiom. However, whilst Halley's paintings had a number of visual or stylistic affinities, they remained deeply hostile towards geometric abstraction's commitment to immanent form. Instead, the visual organization and appearance of these paintings, which spoke of an impulse that marked the project of modernist abstraction, became conflated with a theoretical discourse that centered upon a particular type of socially defined and controlled space. In fact, Halley's paintings presented the concrete means by which certain theories that had been espoused by both Michel Foucault and Jean Baudrillard could be understood.

Halley had oriented his practice towards the ideas of Foucault due to his claims with regards to how historically the social production of space had been understood as a means to organize, control and ultimately determine human agency. As the artist observed in "The Crisis in Geometry," a text that was first published in *Arts Magazine* in the summer of 1984:

> "In *Discipline and Punish*, we find deconstructed the great geometric orderings of industrial society. The omnipresent unfolding of geometric structures in cities, factories, and schools, in housing,

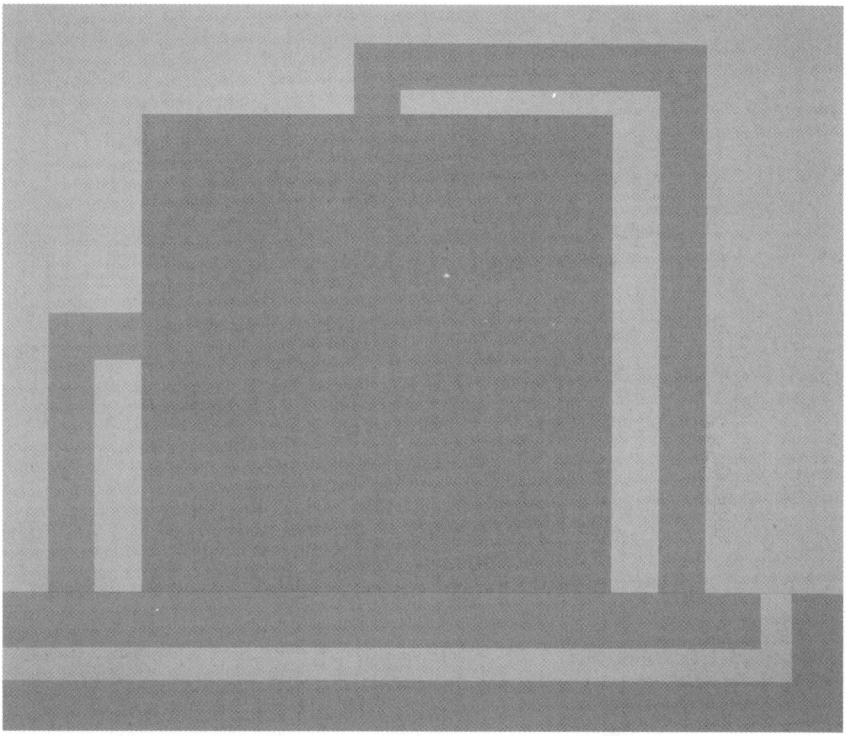

FIGURE 5.3 Peter Halley, *Red Cell*, 1988.

transportation, and hospitals, is revealed as a novel mechanism by which action and movement (and all behavior) could be channeled, measured, and normalized, and a means by which the unprecedented population of the merging industrial era could be controlled and its productivity maximized."[50]

With respect to Baudrillard, Halley's day-glo, stucco-surfaced paintings turned upon the apocalyptic philosopher's ideas of both simulacra and simulation, the bad copy and a reality that had become so attenuated from its illusionistic counterpart that their roles and prescribed functions had become exchanged.

Rather than see geometric abstraction then, as it had previously been understood within an emancipatory set of terms, this category of abstraction for Foster, and specifically the design and designed element of geometric abstraction, codified rather than spoke directly of what was its opposite; restriction, subjugation, and incarceration.

As it stood then, "The End of Painting," "Last Exit: Painting" and "Signs Taken for Wonders" were all organized around, if not painting's purported death, then the question of its legitimacy as a critical form of practice during the 1980s. However, the range of responses to what Bois had claimed had always been a heavily over-determined thesis demonstrated the fact that rather than painting being repudiated *tout court*, a more complex and arguably equivocal set of debates became engendered that brought into question the place and continued relevance of painting and in particular abstraction, given the acknowledged demise of modernist formalism.

In effect, whilst one impulse of painting during the 1980s was towards figuration, another, equally emphatic impulse was directed towards abstraction. Moreover, the recasting of both approaches to the medium of painting sought, in their respective ways, to disinter these respective traditions in order to redefine the place painting could occupy.

Working somewhat against the proliferation of such apocalyptic declarations, Bois, writing in the catalogue that accompanied the exhibition *Endgame: Simulation and Reference in Recent Painting and Sculpture* claimed the following: "Painting might not be dead. Its vitality will only be tested once we are cured of our mania and our melancholy, and we believe again in our ability to act in history: accepting our project of working through the end again, rather than evading it through increasingly elaborate mechanisms of defense."[51] With this in mind, the next chapter will consider instances which, as it were, followed the demise of painting's demise and were once again prepared to "work through" abstraction and revitalize it in the process.

Notes

1 Yve-Alain Bois, *Painting as Model* (Cambridge, MA: MIT Press, 1993), 243. This text first appeared in the catalogue that accompanied the exhibition *Endgame—Reference and Simulation in Recent Painting and Sculpture*, at the Boston Institute of Contemporary Art, autumn 1986.

2 Rosemary Betterton, "Susan Hiller's Painted Work: Bodies, Aesthetics and Feminism," in *Unframed: Practices and Politics of Women's Art*, ed. Rosemary Betterton (London: I. B. Tauris, 2004), 84–85.

3 According to Stephen Bann, this remains an apocryphal story based primarily upon the fact that he was asked to present a report for the French politician François Jean Dominique Arago on the "artistic significance of the daguerreotype." See Stephen Bann, *Paul Delaroche History Painted* (London: Reaktion Books, 1997), 264.

4 Alexander Rodchenko, from the manuscript "Working with Maiakovsky" (1939), quoted in *From Painting to Design: Russian Constructivist Art of the Twenties* (Cologne: Galerie Gmurzynska, 1981), 191, reproduced in Bois, *Painting as Model*, 238.

5 "An Interview with Ad Reinhardt," originally published in *Art International* (Lugano), Winter 1966–1967, reproduced in Rose, *Art as Art: The Selected Writings of Ad Reinhardt*, 13.

6 Arthur R. Rose, "Four Interviews with Barry, Huebler, Kosuth, Weiner," *Arts Magazine* 43 (1969): 22–23; quoted in Joseph Kosuth, Art After Philosophy, in *Conceptual Art* ed. Ursula Meyer (New York: Dutton, 1972), 161.

7 Bois, *Painting as Model*, 229.

8 Douglas Crimp, "The End of Painting," *October* 16 (1981): 73.

9 Ibid., 72.

10 Barbara Rose, *American Painting: The Eighties: A Critical Interpretation* (New York: Vista Press, 1979), unpaginated.

11 Crimp, "The End of Painting," 74.

12 Henry M. Sayre, *The Object of Performance: The American Avant-Garde Since 1970* (Chicago: The University of Chicago Press, 1992), 7.

13 Crimp, "The End of Painting," 75.

14 Rose, *American Painting: The Eighties A Critical Interpretation*, unpaginated.

15 Thomas Lawson, "Last Exit: Painting," reproduced in *Art After Modernism: Rethinking* Representation, ed. Brian Wallis (New York: Museum of Contemporary Art, 1984), 156. Originally appeared in *Artforum* 20, no. 2 (1981): 40–47.

16 Lawson, "Last Exit: Painting," 156.

17 Ibid., 157.

18 Ibid.

19 Ibid.

20 Ibid.

21 Ibid., 159.

22 Craig Owens, "The Allegorical Impulse: Towards a Theory of Postmodernism," in *Beyond Recognition: Representation, Power, Culture* (Berkeley, CA: The University of California Press, 1994), xiii. Originally published in *October* 12 (1980): 67–86.

23 Ibid., 54.

24 Lawson, "Last Exit: Painting," 159.

25 Douglas Crimp, *On the Museum's Ruins*, 4th ed. (Cambridge: MA: MIT Press, 2000), 6.

26 Krauss, *The Originality of the Avant-Garde and Other Modernist Myths*, 19.

27 Howard Fox, "Avant-Garde in the 80s," in *The Post-Avant Garde: Painting in the Eighties*, ed. Andreas C. Papadakis (London: Academy Group, 1987), 29.

28 According to McEvilley and with respect to the painting's modernist as opposed to its postmodernist credentials: "As quotational and learned the *Brueghel Series* is post-modern, involving among other things the rejection of the Modernist cult of pure originality, of the obsessive Modernist quest for new forms, and so on. But the work's passionate incorporation of history as both an icon and a constitutional force shows a fundamentally Modernist reverence for new forms, and so on." McEvilley, *The Exile's Return*, 152.

29 Foster, "Subversive Signs" (1985), in Peter Osborne, *Conceptual Art* (London: Phaidon, 2002), 286.

30 Ibid., 285.

31 Ibid.

32 Lawson, "Last Exit: Painting," 160.

33 Sayre, *The Object of Performance: The American Avant-Garde Since 1970*, 19–20.

34 As Douglas Smith notes, "the floating signifier is the element within a sign-system that itself has no meaning but that serves to guarantee the meaning of the system as a whole by providing a general catch-all term to designate any unknown notion or referent that might otherwise threaten the integrity of the system (in a narrow sense, terms such as *true* or *machin* in French. 'thingummy' or 'whatsit' in English)." Douglas Smith, "Disfigurements: Bacon, Deleuze, Lynch and the Formless," in *Formless: Ways In and Out of Form*, ed. Patrick Crowley and Paul Hegarty (Bern: Peter Lang, 2005), 217.

35 Robert Rosenblum, "Notes on David Salle," in Robert Rosenblum, *David Salle* (Zurich: Edition Gallery Bruno Bischofberger, 1986), unpaginated.

36 Ibid., unpaginated.

37 Lawson, "Last Exit: Painting," 160.

38 Ibid.

39 According to Foster, "Salle's paintings remain significant pointers indicating the last exit for the radical artist. He makes paintings, but they are dead, inert representations of the impossibility of painting in a culture that has institutionalized self-expression." Foster, "Signs Taken for Wonders" in Myers, *Painting*, 33–34.

40 Ibid., 48.

41 Ibid.

42 Ibid.

43 Ibid.

44 Ibid., 49.

45 Ibid.

46 Jean Baudrillard, "The Hyper-realism of Simulation" (1984), in Harrison and Wood, *Art in Theory 1900–2000: An Anthology of Changing Ideas*, 1050.

47 Ibid.

48 Peter Halley, "Notes on the Paintings" (1982), in *Collected Essays 1981–87* (Zurich; New York: Brunobischofberger Gallery & Sonnabend Gallery, 1991), 23.

49 Ibid.

50 Halley, "The Crisis in Geometry," in *Collected Essays 1981–87*, 76; 78.

51 Bois, *Painting as Model*, 196.

6

An-atomising Abstraction

And yet a formalist reading of this new work still seems attractive, if only because formalism itself now seems more capable of disclosing than burying artworks. Perhaps that's because the ideological heat that once soldered the term to a complex of specific names and uses has finally turned lukewarm. The opportunity exists to pry some semantic space between the word and its designations. What, after all, is being referred to—a dated style of art and discredited mode of criticism, or an open-ended, ongoing project?[1]

On one level, the account of painting that was promulgated by Greenberg entailed the understanding that the work of art was cohesive, unified and homogenous. Rather than being conceived in relation to a varying set of characteristics upon which painting was both constructed and understood, a central impulse of the medium entailed a centripetal movement inwards and towards a perceived essence or core that painting was believed to be in possession of. Moreover, within "Modernist Painting," Greenberg was at pains to organize his account of the artwork partly around the idea of "purity":

> It quickly emerged that the unique and proper area of competence of each art coincided with all that was unique in the nature of its medium. The task of self-criticism became to eliminate from the specific effects of each art any and every effect that might conceivably be borrowed from or by the medium of any other art. Thus would each art be rendered "pure," and in its "purity" find the guarantee of its standards of quality as well as of its independence. "Purity" meant self-definition, and the enterprise of self-criticism in the arts became one of self-definition with a vengeance.[2]

However, and as we have already seen, such a reductivist account of painting couldn't be sustained indefinitely, and increasingly the field within which late modernist painting sought to gain a footing within proffered separate modes of production not only of painting, but also of art generally. Consequently, such a heterogeneous range of practices opened art out onto the conditions of possibility that it could operate across, rather than be situated directly *within*, the singularity of any particular medium. In this respect art was no longer understood with regards to the allegiances it had with and to a particular medium, but rather, and as Rosalind Krauss, writing in 1979 would observe, "in relation to the logical operations on a set of cultural terms, for which any medium—photography, books, lines on walls, mirrors, or sculpture itself—might be used."[3]

Within this particular set of debates, which would increasingly become identified with the operative conditions of postmodernism, the term "hybridity" became added to the critical exegeses of the period. As the previous chapter educed, according to Craig Owens, writing in 1980 and at a point somewhere between the exhaustion of modernism and the subsequent wave of practices that fell under the auspices of postmodernism, strategies such as site specificity, impermanence and hybridity characterized "much of the art of the present and distinguish it from its modern predecessors."[4]

To a certain extent, hybridity was symptomatic of a broader set of critical discourses that were organized around the pluralist condition of postmodernism. Certainly during the 1980s aesthetic pluralism, according to at least one commentator, became "the most prevalent approach to the period."[5] Indeed, as Abigail Solomon-Godeau has pointed out, "the 80s was a period in which performance art, installation, video, hybridizations of various media, site specific practice, political artists' collectives, artists books of all kinds and feminist production of all varieties were everywhere in evidence."[6] Moreover this inclusive, if not discursive approach to the production of art continued into the 1990s. As Joanna Drucker notes: "Many new trends came to the fore in the 1990s ... Hybridity became a theme and an attitude, dealing a final death blow to any residual modernist pretense of the purity of form, postmodern critical distance, or clinical theoretical frameworks."[7]

Another notable impulse during this period entailed a renewed interest in abstract painting, its respective traditions and at least some of the precepts that informed modernism's account of it. According to one commentator writing in 1995, " ... today abstraction flourishes. It resolutely maintains a traditional modernist vocabulary by displaying the modernist's interest in purity: the work of art is considered an 'object' that reflects the reductiveness of modernist theory, contemporary abstraction allows a wider referential embrace."[8] Added to a prevailing discourse that was seeking to valorize, once again, abstraction's place within a range of practices that encompassed installation art, performance-based and increasingly new media-based work,

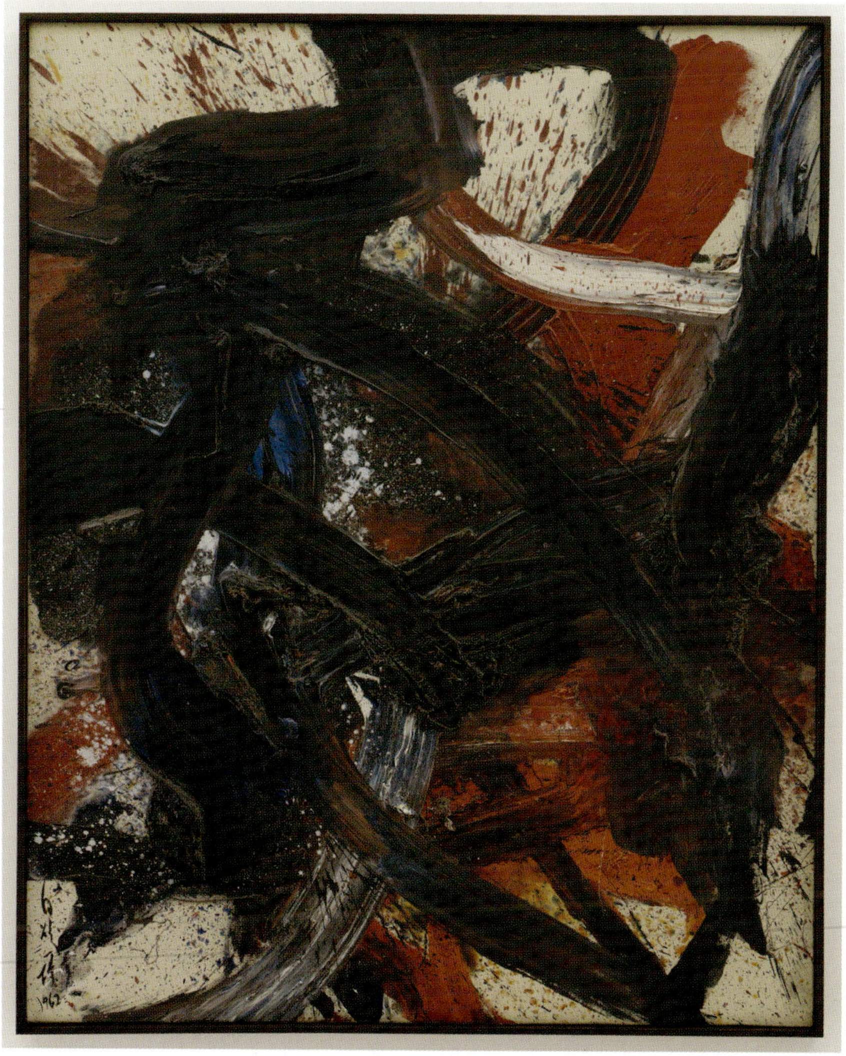

PLATE 1 Kazuo Shiraga, *Chiyusei Byotaichu*, 1962. © The Estate of Kazuo Shiraga.

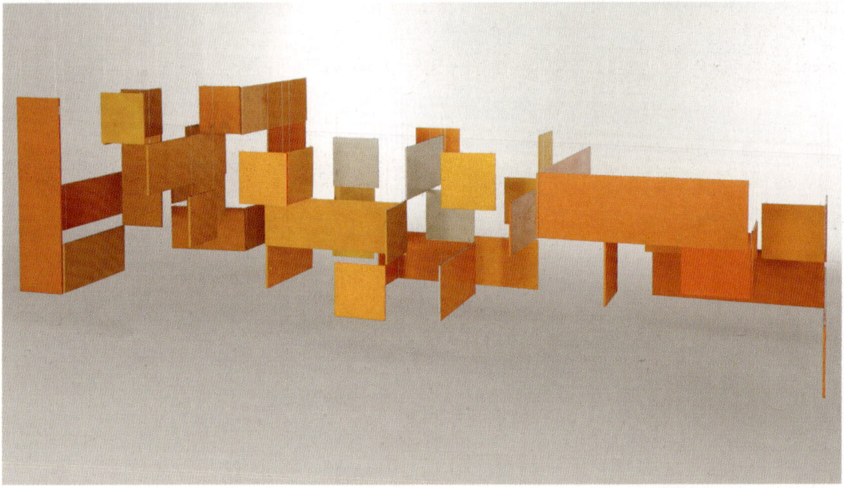

PLATE 2 Hélio Oiticica, *Grand Nucleus, NC3, NC4, NC6*, 1960–63. Oil and resin on wood fiberboard. 670.6 × 975.4 cm (264 × 384 in.). © César and Claudio Oiticica. Courtesy of the Projeto Hélio Oiticica and Lisson Gallery.

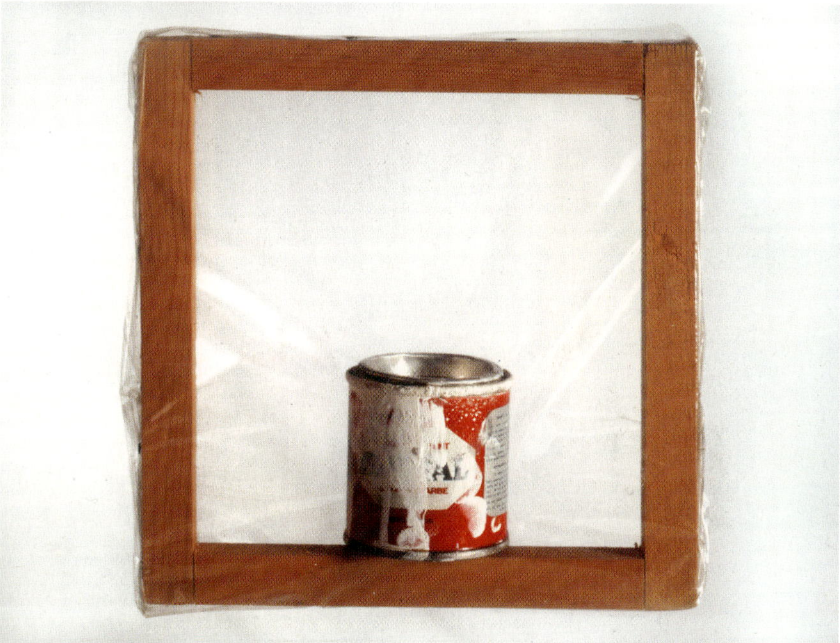

PLATE 3 Giulio Paolini, *Senza titolo* [Untitled], 1961. Tin of paint, stretcher, polyethylene, 21 × 21 cm. Fondazione Giulio e Anna Paolini, Turin © Giulio Paolini. Photo © Paolo Mussat Sartor. Courtesy Fondazione Giulio e Anna Paolini, Turin.

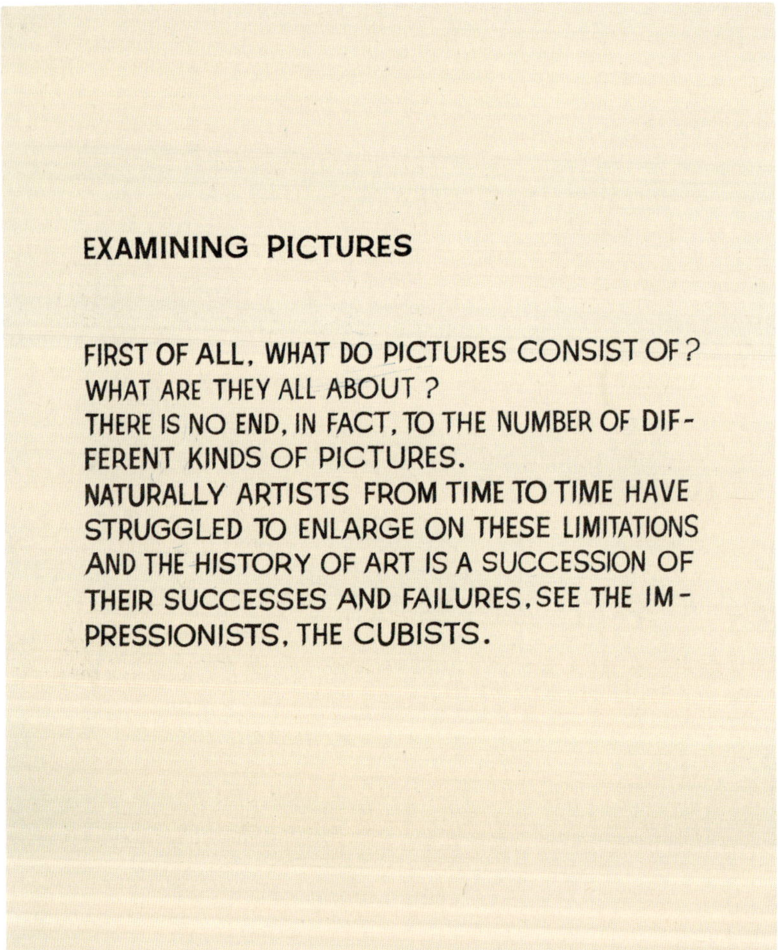

PLATE 4 John Baldessari, *Examining Pictures*, 1966–68. Acrylic on canvas, 172.7 × 143.5 cm (68 × 56 ½ in.) © John Baldessari 1966–68. Courtesy of the Estate of John Baldessari © 2024 Courtesy of the John Baldessari Family Foundation and Sprüth Magers.

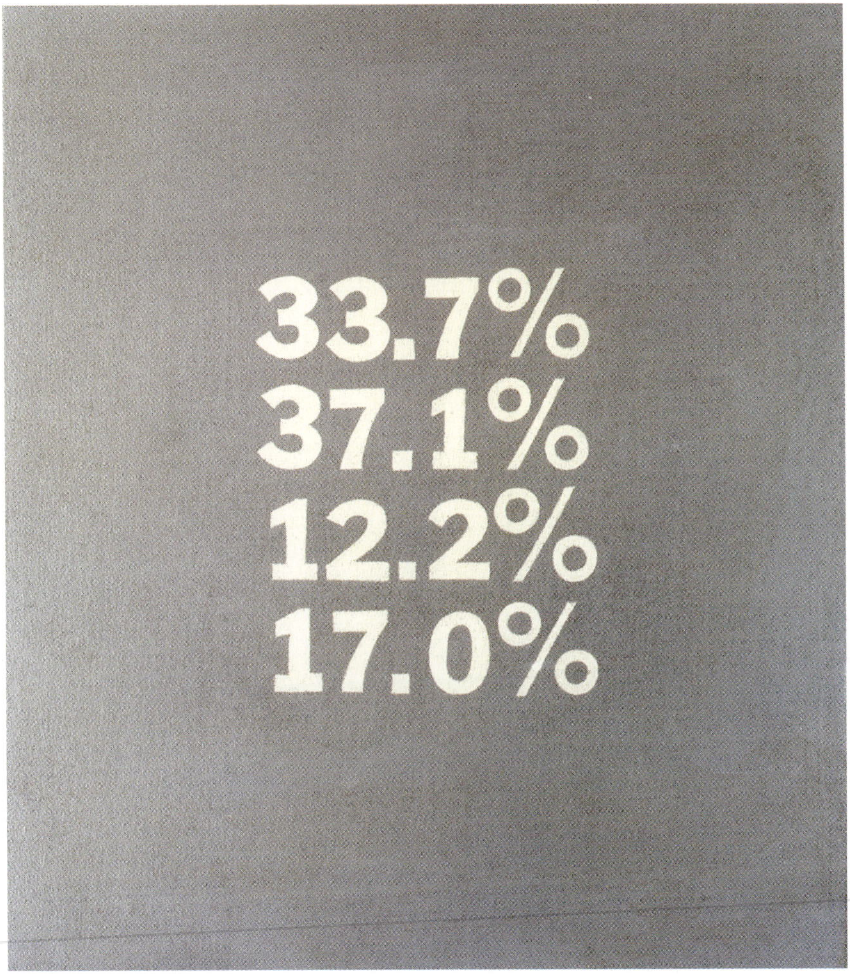

PLATE 5 Art & Language, *100% Abstract*, 1968. Oil on canvas. 45 × 40.5 cm, 68.5 × 61.5 cm (framed); 17 ¾ × 16 in., 27 × 24 ¼ in. (framed). © Art and Language.

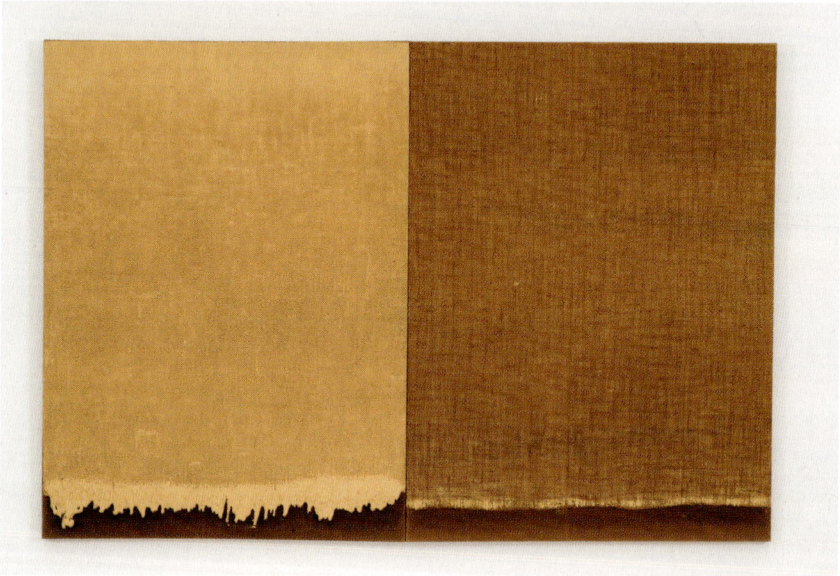

PLATE 6 Ha Chong-hyun, *Conjunction 77-7 (B) Conjunction 77-7 (A)*, 1977. Oil on canvas. 63 × 94 7/8 in. overall (160 × 241 cm). © Ha Chong-hyun, Courtesy of the artist and Blum & Poe, Los Angeles/New York/Toyko. Photo: Joshua White.

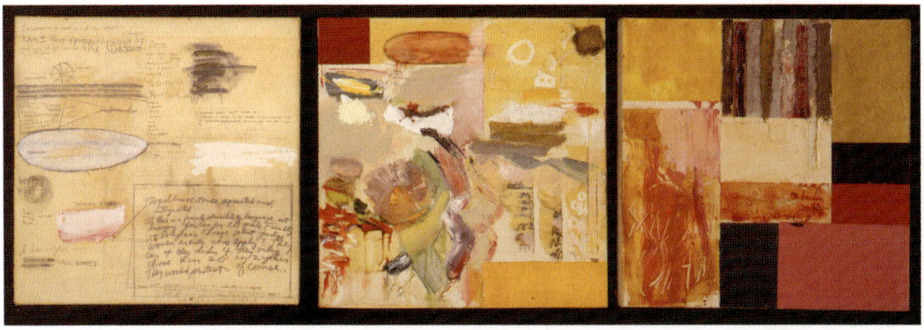

PLATE 7 Joan Snyder, *Small Symphony for Women*, 1974 © the artist. Collection of the Wichita Art Museum, Wichita, Kansas.

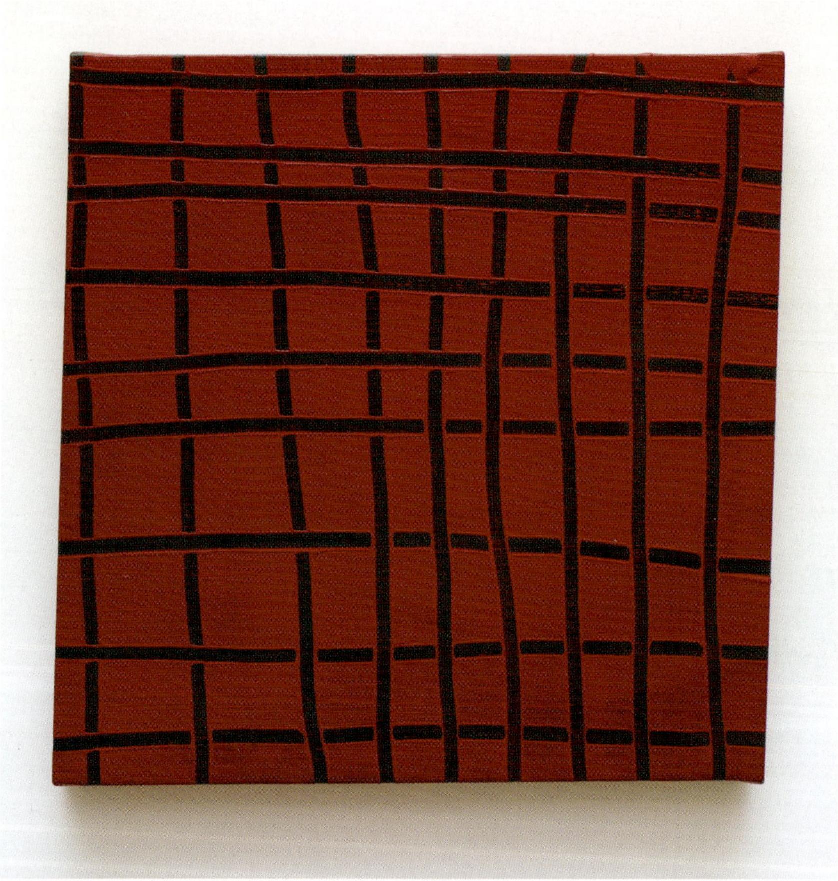

PLATE 8 Mary Heilmann, *Little 9 × 9*, 1973. Acrylic on canvas. 21.875 × 21.875 × 1.75 in. © Mary Heilmann. Photo credit: Stephen White. Image courtesy of the artist, 303 Gallery, New York, and Hauser & Wirth.

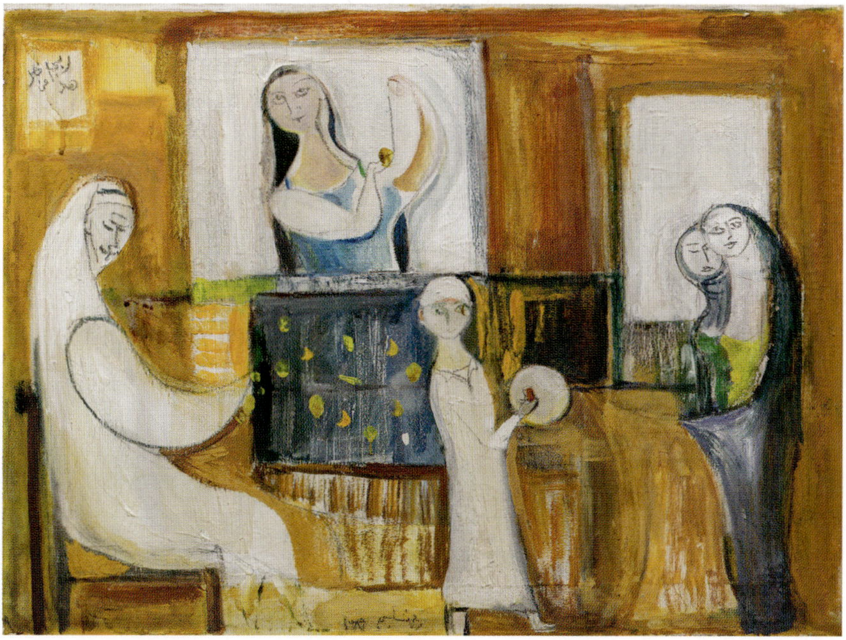

PLATE 9 Naziha Selim, *Untitled*, 1989. © the artist. Image courtesy of Barjeel Art Foundation, Sharjah.

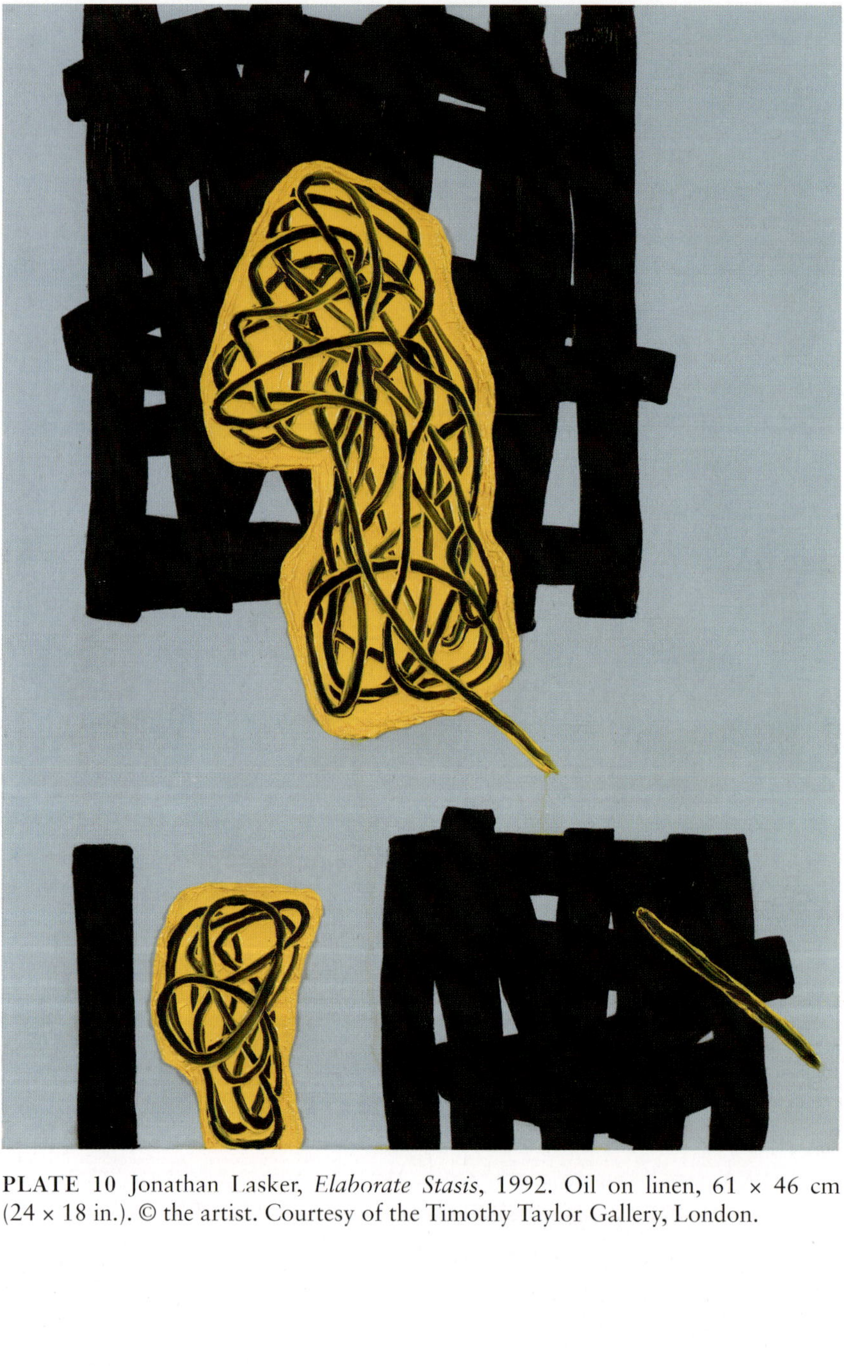

PLATE 10 Jonathan Lasker, *Elaborate Stasis*, 1992. Oil on linen, 61 × 46 cm (24 × 18 in.). © the artist. Courtesy of the Timothy Taylor Gallery, London.

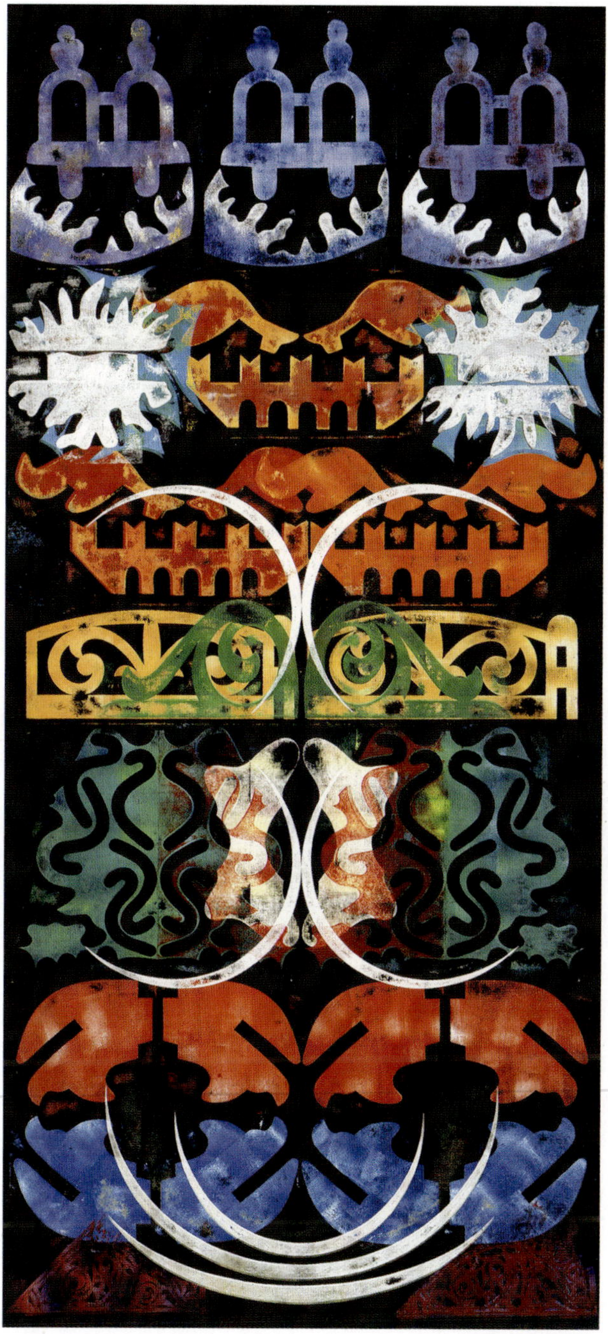

PLATE 11 Philip Taaffe, *Stele*, 1994–95. Mixed media on canvas. 139 × 64 in. © Philip Taaffe. Courtesy of the artist and Luhring Augustine, New York. The Broad Art Foundation.

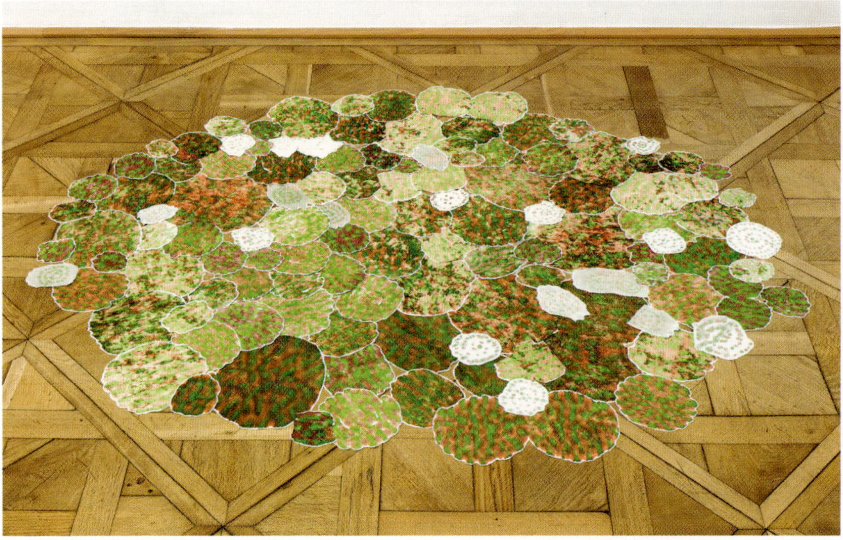

PLATE 12 Polly Apfelbaum, *Snails: Forest Green*, 1999. Synthetic velvet, dye, approx. 122 × 112 cm (48 × 44 in.). Courtesy of the artist and Galerie nächst St. Stephan Rosemarie Schwarzwälder. Photo: Markus Wörgötter. © ARS, NY and DACS, London 2023.

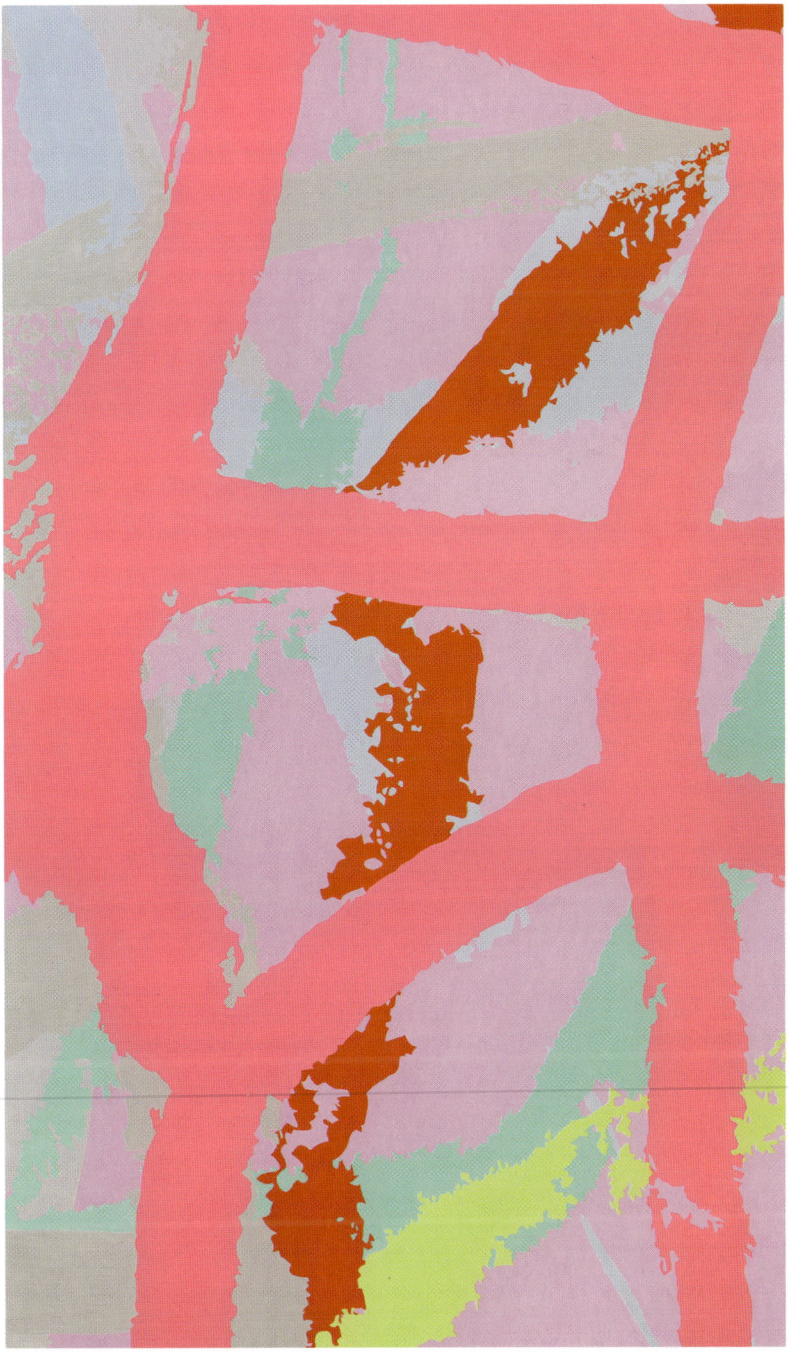

PLATE 13 Ingrid Calame, *Step on a Crack, Break Your Mother's Back*, 2009. Courtesy of the artist.

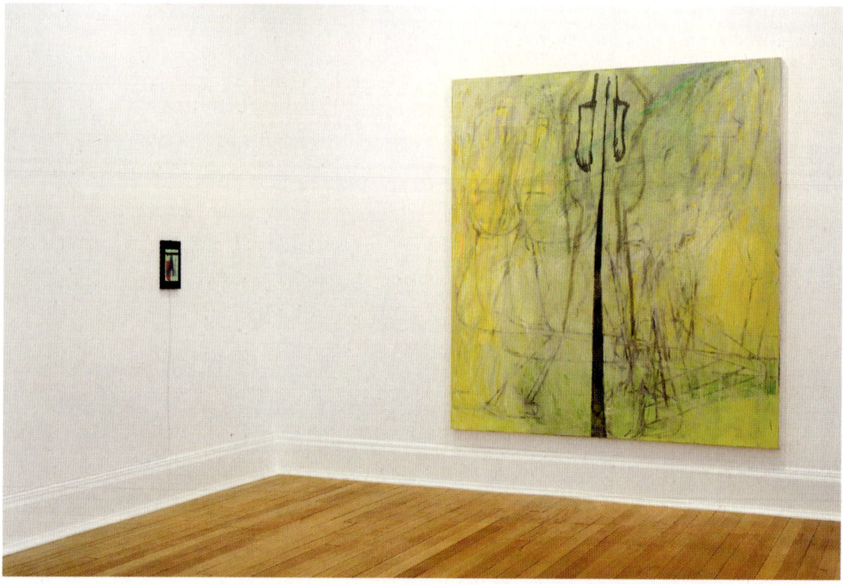

PLATE 14 Installation view, *Amy Sillman: Either or And*, Thomas Dane Gallery, London, England, 6 September–9 October 2013. © Amy Sillman. Courtesy of the artist, Gladstone Gallery, New York and Thomas Dane Gallery. Photo: Thierry Bal.

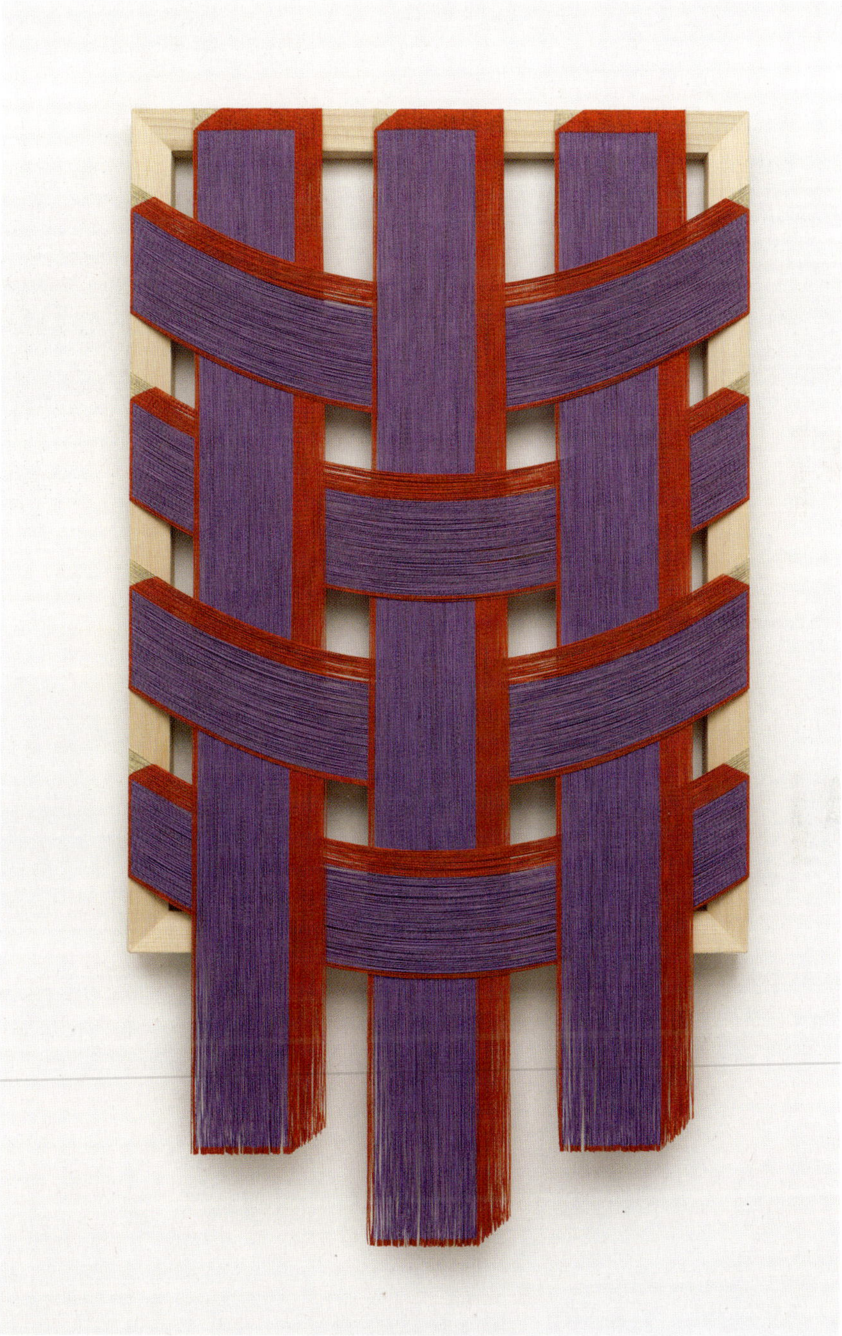

PLATE 15 Dianna Molzan, *Untitled*, 2022. Oil on canvas on poplar. 81.3 × 61 × 3.8 cm (32 × 24 × 1.4 in.). Courtesy of the artist and private collection and kaufmann repetto Milan/New York. Photo: Brica Wilcox.

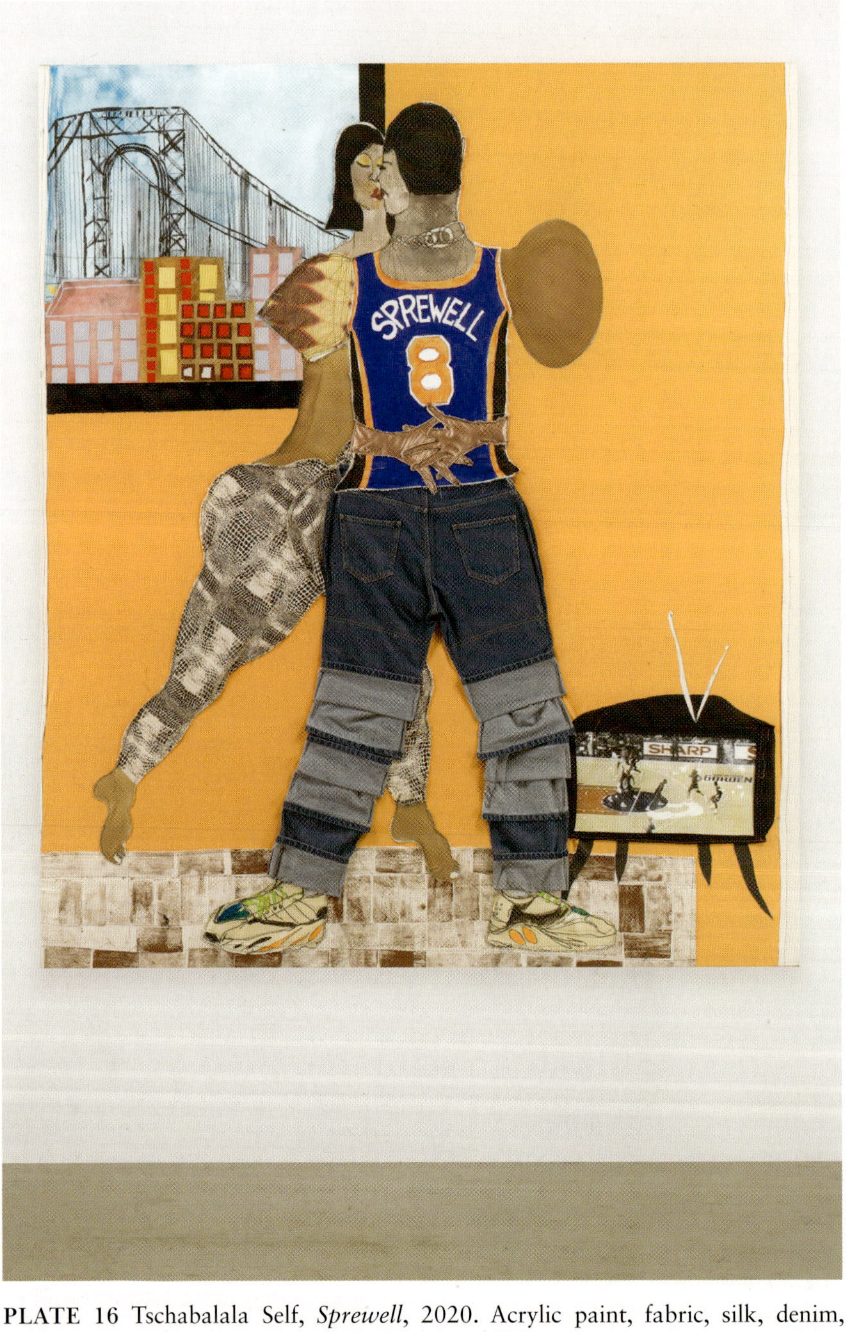

PLATE 16 Tschabalala Self, *Sprewell*, 2020. Acrylic paint, fabric, silk, denim, painted newsprint, paper, thread, photo transfer, painted canvas on canvas. 213.5 × 183 cm (84 × 72 in.). Image courtesy of the artist, Pilar Corrias, London and Galerie Eva Presenhuber, Zurich/Vienna.

a number of exhibitions became staged that attempted to make certain claims on behalf of its currency and continued relevance.

Real Art "A New Modernism" British Reflexive Painters in the 1990s, an exhibition that toured to several venues within the UK included the work of six painters whose work was connected, at least on a technical level, by foregrounding an explicit and for the most part self-evident process. So for example, whilst the monochrome paintings of Jason Martin were the result of the artist having dragged a brush whose width was consonant with the height of the painting across the surface of the canvas, resulting in textured surface akin to that of a vinyl record, the paintings of Torie Begg entailed the systematic application of a number of predetermined layers of paint.

Whilst the work of the six artists selected for the exhibition were engaged with the production of paintings that in some way visually attested to the conditions of their manufacture, the impetus, at least on the part of its curator, Brian Muller, appeared to be premised upon a particular rehearsal and interpretation of Greenberg's proclivity to organize the work of art, and specifically painting, reflexively.

Rather than rehearse Greenberg's own claims with respect to painting's reflexivity, Muller sought to rechannel the reflexive impulse he identified within the work of the artists that were selected away from the actual circuitry of the object and towards "the event of viewing, to the viewer."[9] The corollary as such meant "reflexivity," as used with respect to the six painters, referred to "the viewer as subject, with the painting functioning as a mirror (conceptual mirror and, in some of the high gloss paintings, a physical mirror as well)."[10] Qualifying this claim, Muller, writing in the exhibition catalogue went on to state that although "the use of the word reflexive in the case of Ryman, would be in the sense of 'form is content', painting looking at itself … here it refers to content being shifted to firmly within the viewer's own cognitive process, in which the viewer watches himself/herself, watching himself/herself, looking."[11]

Whilst Muller's claims and, moreover, his somewhat anachronistic positioning of painting in relation to "a new modernism" was arguably the exception rather than the rule, the practical and theoretical renegotiation of abstraction nevertheless remained one salient aspect of what was at the time a much broader and divergent artistic milieu.

However, for the majority of artists who sought to re-engage with abstraction, its histories, discourses and modes of production, their respective practices were premised upon a basic admission that whilst they could still engage with this particular idiom of painting, they could no longer simply rehearse an account of the object that Greenberg had espoused during the 1950s and 1960s. Indeed, it was no doubt because there was a certain historical distance between the period within which Greenberg had first staked out a particular set of claims for the medium and those painters who were seeking to position their respective practices in relation to an abstract pictorial language during the 1990s that afforded and indeed mobilized this critical re-engagement.

So for example, Michael Darling, writing in a review of Monique Prieto's paintings in 1996 observed that: "Sooner or later, the scourge of contemporary art discourse—formalist, Greenbergian painting—had to return for a fresh reappraisal ... it should be no surprise that artists too young to have forged any steadfast ideological aversion to painting theories of the nineteen fifties and sixties might also be able to contribute new interpretations of now archival materials."[12]

Indeed, this renewed interest in certain facets of modernist painting produced its own loose grouping of artists who collectively fell under the heading the "New Abstractionists." According to Enrique Juncosa, in "the nineties [critics applied] the term New Abstractionists to a potent and diverse group of international painters ... who adhere to the formal legacy of modernist painting, but seek to extend it be exploring multiple semantic possibilities."[13]

As it was then, the practices that operated within this artistic milieu became organized around a dialectic that whilst it acknowledged and, to a certain extent engaged with abstraction as it had been formulated within a context of post-war American formalism, it did so not to merely restage its effects and the overarching ambitions it held for painting. On one level, this involved the reiteration of such forms and approaches being undertaken from a strategically depersonalized rather than personalized stance. However, the engagement with history on a set of terms that were critically distanced and semantically disengaged (to the extent that it no longer sought to proffer a comparatively same set of meanings and, moreover, educe a comparable set of readings), was borne out of neither cynicism nor irony. It was perhaps for this reason that the strategy of interlacing certain modernist tropes, or, equally, fixing the work onto a set of concerns that were ostensibly shared with modernism became strategies that, three decades later, remained qualitatively separate from those of their formalist predecessors. Equally, abstraction's engagement with a historically received set of practices that were all, broadly speaking abstract in their orientation differed from those so-called "critical abstractionists" that had adopted ostensibly the same strategy during the 1980s. For although these paintings were complicit with history, they neither sought to maintain the original set of meanings that abstraction proffered, nor did they seek recourse to negation; whilst history was qualified, the activity of painting was ostensibly not.

Somewhat paradoxically then, the 1990s, at least on the basis of what has been loosely sketched out above, became understood by some commentators as the point at which even a residual preoccupation with the theories and ideas Greenberg espoused and which were more broadly organized around the valorization of a particular account of abstraction had all but been bracketed out. Whereas for others, modernist abstraction, Greenbergian or otherwise, became seen as an archive from which it might provide, at the very least, the initial impetus for an artist's ideas to emerge, develop and coalesce. Whilst certain artists dialectically engaged with the legacy of formalism, at the same time they also sought to extend the work's address beyond what had historically been its somewhat prescribed parameters. To this end, and given the fact that, as Drucker remarked, the art that was produced during the 1990s was marked by an aesthetics that was "recombinant," arguably all the artists that will be considered within this chapter, to a lesser or greater extent, adopted a piecemeal rather than wholesale approach.[14] An approach wherein "one thing was placed against another thing."[15] Which, given her overarching approach to artistic production during the period in question, seems a somewhat apt description of Jessica Stockholder's practice. Certainly, her expansive approach to painting worked to extend the medium beyond the limitations of its traditional support and arguably, its received histories.

In certain respects, Stockholder's practice represented the conceptual bridge between those artists who were seeking to disarticulate painting from the confines of the support's surface, amongst whom we would include Gilliam, Carson and Benglis, and those artists, which include Katharina Grosse, who would subsequently refine and rework the claims that were being made on behalf of painting by Stockholder's scattered practice and the "exploded views" it provided the viewer with. Moreover, the artist's installations equally anticipated those respective practices that sought to position the activity, or rather the outcome of painting as somehow fluid and not necessarily geared towards and beholden to the production of discrete objects or artefacts. It is perhaps somewhat ironic then that most of the artists cited by Stockholder as having an affinity with her own practice, ranging from Paul Cézanne, Clyfford Still and through to Frank Stella and Richard Serra, were those, as Barry Schwabsky points out, that emphasized the object's physicality, "whether of the surface of a painting or of the artwork as a three-dimensional artwork—and therefore, perhaps, towards a 'materialist' understanding of artistic modernity."[16]

Initially, Stockholder's early works were somewhat more tentative improvisations, excursions beyond the picture plane that moved into the realm of real space. It was in 1982, in an exhibition at the Open Space Gallery in Victoria in Australia, that Stockholder first sought to approach the gallery as a totality by "consciously address[ing] the space rather than just the wall."[17] From that point on, and as the artist has noted, her work subsequently "developed through the process of making site-specific installations—site-specific sometimes in very specific ways but also just by virtue of being 'art' in a room."[18]

Whilst Stockholder's practice seemed to be organized around a particular understanding of installation art, and whilst her work didn't carry the appearance of paintings, at least in what was the traditionally received sense, a consistent feature of her practice has been its concern with the medium

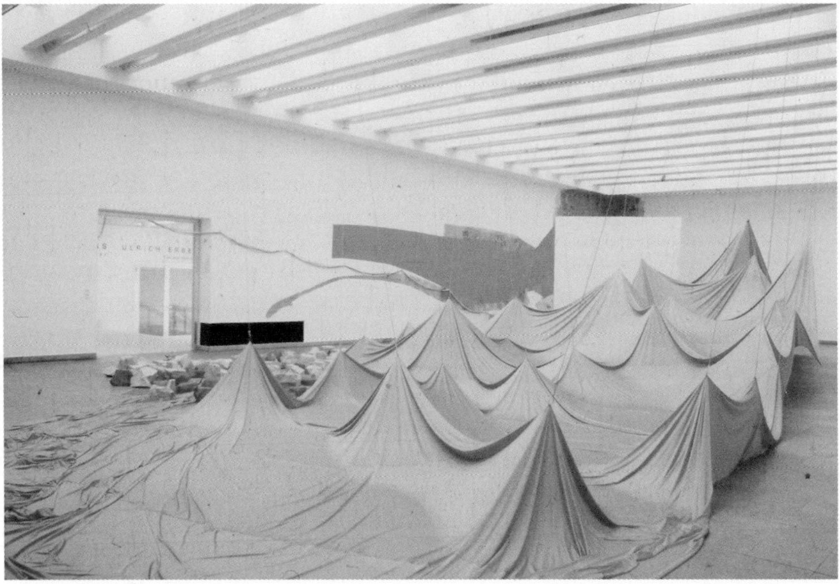

FIGURE 6.1 Jessica Stockholder, *Growing Rock Candy Mountain Grasses in Canned Sand*, 1992.

wherein painting "functions in my work as a pictorial entity laden with history which, among other things, is inextricably bound to the history of the frame."[19] This is not to say that Stockholder's practice merely attempted to recapitulate formalism's account of painting. As the artist has herself claimed, "formal concerns are not interesting unless they carry this other [psychological] information."[20] Nevertheless, on one level Stockholder's practice during the period under consideration remained keyed into questions directed towards the status and condition of painting: "I started as a painter and I never stopped making paintings. And still, part of what interests me is a pictorial way of looking at things."[21]

Rather than insist on her practice being one of making paintings per se, Stockholder's installations provided the viewer with, for the most part, an unregimented yet affective space where they were at liberty to explore and respond to the work in a way that was in accordance with their own embodied situation. In one sense, this was achieved through the artist's very particular use of color which was treated as both a material in its own right and as the means whereby it could frame the viewer's experience of the work. In an interview with Lynne Tillman, and with respect to *Recording Forever Pickled* (1990), Stockholder claimed that as the viewer navigated the piece, "the reflected purple or violet between the wall I made and the wall of the gallery is seen as a volume of color. The violet complements the yellow-orange on the floor. The colors are keyed to carry the eye around; they read across space."[22] Color in this sense is not descriptive; rather Stockholder seeks to exploit the inherent associations a particular color carries, what the artist has described is its "fiction."[23]

Whilst interwoven within the work was a consideration of certain properties that characterized painting, including color, the work often accommodated and was organized around other, more associative layers. To this end, Stockholder's practice didn't necessarily eschew the autobiographical, an aspect of the work that can be discerned as early as 1987 in a piece the artist made for the Contemporary Art Gallery in Vancouver and which, in addition to being constructed within the artist's home town, consisted of objects drawn from the artist's past. It was in arguably this sense that Stockholder's work, whilst by her own admission "doesn't have a frame, in the usual sense," nevertheless could be understood alongside the other paintings that will be considered within this chapter as being foregrounded by what was in effect an aggregative process, a process that directly abutted the physical against the physical whilst at the same time overlaying the conceptual with the psychological.
Stockholder for her part claimed that the

> work grows through the process of making. It is an additive process where each piece is built from nothing to something clear to its foundation ... The construction of each heap within my work involves layering or overlapping many kinds of information. This process creates a conglomeration of elements which arise from absurd relationships between things, from chance occurrences, happenstance and from objects already laden with meaning; and last but not least, from painting.[24]

Such a "conglomeration of elements" seems to be consonant with and have echoes not only of the "recombinant aesthetics" of which Drucker has already spoken of, but also of Jonathan Lasker's description of his practice as "a form of image kit or ... jigsaw puzzles, which offer components of painting as clues pointing the viewer, not to a finished narrative (as when the last piece of the jigsaw puzzle competes a picture of Notre Dame), but rather to a self-awareness of how one construes a painting."[25]

Whereas Lasker's paintings of the 1980s were arguably more lyrical, idiosyncratic and intuitive, although nonetheless considered for that, his practice over the subsequent decade entailed the adoption of a more clearly stated and iterative approach with regards to the various brush strokes, patterns and shapes that collectively went to make up a particular painting.

So for example, *Elaborate Stasis* (Plate 10) is comprised of essentially three coterminous layers. Placed onto a pale blue ground are two areas comprising what appears to be within each a single, swirling black line that has been etched into yellow paint. Partially overlapping and directly adjacent to these areas are two rectilinear, grid-like shapes that have been made using a much thicker black painted line.

Although Lasker didn't necessarily concur with modernism's somewhat more loftier ambitions, he appeared prepared to reengage with specific tropes that had become virtually synonymous with American artistic formalism. With respect to the notion of the archive from which painters operating within an abstract idiom during the 1990s selectively drew from, Konrad Bitterli, writing in 1997, claimed that the artist seemed "to use the artistic vocabulary of modernism and particularly the formal achievements of the art of the twentieth century as a quarry for his artistic activities. He isolates formal elements of the most varied provenance and joins them together to form new, recurrently surprising pictorial conventions."[26] Indeed, with regards to the recurrence of the "gesture" in Lasker's work at that time, Saul Ostrow, writing in 1994 claimed that Lasker understood that "the gestural (even when stilted and studied) was potentially the most privileged signifier of modernism's pictorial paradigm."[27]

In a statement written in 1993, Lasker had reverted to the analogy of the atom, or in his case the molecule as a way of implying that the discursive space art now inhabited was down to society having entered its so-called "decadent" phase, what for the artist consisted of an elemental state or "zero point at which every sub-particle of each social component, each molecule, must be disassembled and analyzed in order to reconstitute an image of reality. At this point we enter 'The Politics of Reality.' Reality is up for grabs. The ball is loose and each molecule is roaming free."[28] It was arguably for this reason that four years later Lasker would claim that rather than deconstruction, he was interested "much more in a situation of reconstruction."[29]

If, according to Peter Schfeldahl, writing in a 1998 catalogue essay entitled "The Rise of Abstraction II" "Abstraction I" began with Wassily Kandinsky and was about "purifications [which] in the 1960s ... attained the only form of purification that was ever truly available to it: more or less complete sterility" then "Abstraction II uses the microbe-free culmination of Abstraction I as a petri dish in which things can grow: selected things, choice contaminants."[30]

With respect to the paintings of Ellen Gallagher, her working method often entailed isolating a particular motif that was imbued with a particular set of associations and repeatedly inscribing it over the surface of the support. However, Gallagher's motives and for that matter her "selected things" were oriented towards political rather than wholly aesthetic ends. For whilst she dialectically engaged with issues around race and representation, her practice was not one of merely re-presenting, but rather, as Thyrza Nichols Goodeve noted, entailed an act of "reinventing, or better distorting, the very terms of representation itself, what [Gertrude] Stein calls the distortion of form."[31] Moreover, according to Goodeve: "In this sense she is decidedly modernist."[32] Developing this observation further, in a conversation with the artist, Goodeve remarked that she associated Gallagher's work with a modernist sensibility to the extent where it appeared to be organized around a so-called "idiolect" or private language. Gallagher responded by claiming that she "was interested in both a painting's immediate appearance and what it can manifest slowly. And maybe that is what links me to a more modernist sensibility ... I'm interested in the way materials manifest meaning. In the paint, the lines, the ink, the drawings."[33]

It is perhaps here that whilst Gallagher's practice can be construed, on one level at least, as bearing some of the effects of a modernist sensibility, her relationship with her subject matter remains equivocal and is premised upon ensuring that there is sufficient critical distance. To this end, "Gallagher's paintings and prints engage the notion of a radically encoded visual vocabulary passed through a subjective structure. By treating these signs as shapes, she strips them of their original associations, reshaping and coaxing them to resignify, otherwise."[34]

However, for the purposes of our argument, it would be worthwhile to take the opportunity to briefly explore Claire Doherty's observation, written in 1998 in the exhibition catalogue that accompanied her exhibition at the IKON Gallery in Birmingham, wherein she claimed: "Though much has been made of the sources of Gallagher's reoccurring motifs (the historical narratives of blackface, vaudeville and minstrelsy), a reading which stops at the historical association and appearance of the references misses the point."[35]

With respect to what has already been claimed, and notwithstanding the admission that there appeared to be some affinity between Gallagher's working methods and modernism's mobilization of ostensibly ambiguous or novel pictorial forms, Doherty's statement seems indicative of the fact that her paintings might conceivably be approached and understood in relation to Schjeldahl's analogy of abstraction as being premised on "choice contaminants."

Within the same catalogue essay, Doherty also noted that the "signs of lips and eyes smother the grid, as if breeding like viruses. The murky rubbings-out and discolorations resemble the formation of cultures on petri dishes or magnified DNA."[36] Of course, rooted within the analogy of a culture growth on a petri dish is the notion of the mutant. Moreover, the mutant is always conceivably understood as a hybridized form, as an amalgam made up of disparate parts or elements that have been fused together to create some semblance, however novel or perturbing, of a whole. If we are to further pursue this line of thinking then we will equally note that hybridity is closely associated with the idea of interdisciplinarity.

Beyond Roland Barthes' admission wherein it eschews "the calm of an easy security," interdisciplinarity, like hybridity, is usually given with regards to how it works to cut across certain categorical boundaries.[37]

According to Joe Moran, although interdisciplinarity as a critical term gained a degree of currency after the Second World War, its provenance was within the context of the social sciences during the mid-1920s.[38] Its subsequent meaning "can suggest forging connections across different disciplines; but it can also mean establishing a kind of undisciplined space in the interstices between disciplines, or even attempting to transcend disciplinary boundaries altogether."[39] So, as with what is implied by the term hybridization, namely an interlacing or enmeshing of mutually exclusive disciplines, interdisciplinarity at least implies an equivalent form of synthesis. In this respect interdisciplinarity could be seen in contrast to one of its related terms, multidisciplinarity, although the latter will also function as a counterpoint to interdisciplinarity's impulse, on one level, to fuse, to blend and to forge. In this sense multidisciplinarity "tends to refer to the simple juxtaposition of two or more disciplines, as one finds on certain joint honors or combined arts degrees ... Here the relationship between the disciplines is merely one of proximity; there is no real integration between them."[40]

With this in mind, and noting the respective differences between, on the one hand interdisciplinarity and, on the other hand, multidisciplinarity, the central impulse of Gallagher's paintings is arguably not one of hybridization, but rather, and perhaps more appropriately, one that is syncretic in both scope and import.

Syncreticism's provenance resides within the political thought of Plutarch and concerned his attempts to make the island of Crete a politically heterogeneous yet cohesive state. Unlike hybridity however, "syncreticism," as Harris reminds us, "implies the recognition that an alliance of peoples *does not* mean a simple identity to or unification of them, but rather a tactical 'co-mingling' of different elements whose separate characteristics are not dissolved within their alliance."[41]

In this respect Gallagher's "'aggregations of materials'—oils, inks, pencil drawings, paintings, and prints" can also be understood and extend to encompass the historical forms that accumulate, grow but arguably never fuse together.[42] Moreover, if indeed Gallagher's "art is driven by the production of history," then the "tactical co-mingling" we see in a painting such as *Untitled* (1998) conveys a certain ambivalence to both its particularities and the possibility of their untrammeled communication as such.[43]

On one level, we can take Gallagher's juxtaposition and iteration of discrete, historically bound elements or "contaminants" as being emblematic of how a number of other painters were approaching their own respective practices during the period under consideration. To this end, Lydia Dona's approach was premised on

> a complex inter-connectedness between different circuitry ... bordering on other circuits and feeding off other ones. So, architecture, literature, film, microbiology are all parallels, for me, of painting, but a painting that has to traverse these different sites. In this way, painting today shows the necessity for conceptualizing its own deterritorialisation, and in this sense, it does have connections with a kind of deconstructive practice.[44]

Conceiving painting as "this molecule that is constantly in the process of its rupture," the palimpsests of Dona appeared to all intents and purposes as intricate amalgams of various codes and materials, some of which were, directly or indirectly, associated with or characteristic of modernist painting.[45]

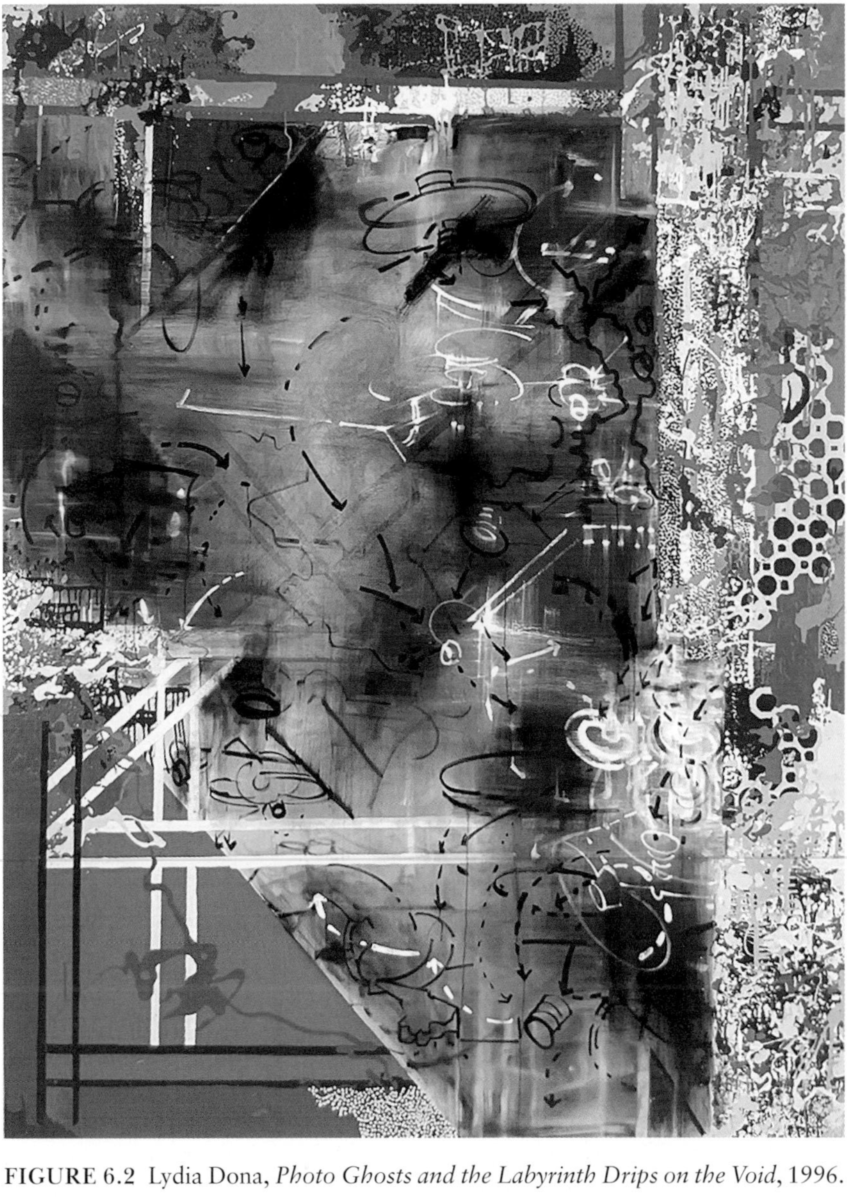

FIGURE 6.2 Lydia Dona, *Photo Ghosts and the Labyrinth Drips on the Void*, 1996.

In works such as *Biochemical Topographies and the Gaps of Dislocation*, 1992, and *Photo Ghosts and the Labyrinth Drips on the Void*, 1996, rather than there being a single focal area, these paintings become organized around spatially indeterminate yet nevertheless markedly vibrant areas or zones of contiguity and confluence. These zones generally played host to a series of abutting, filigree-like painterly marks which at certain points in the painting's composition overlap, in other areas become annexed by more regimented linear structures or denser, more occluded areas that sometimes appear sooty and semi-opaque, at other times ethereal and vaporous.

Whilst the more intuitive range of marks carried by Dona's canvases perhaps once would have been seen as rehearsing the sovereignty of the individuated, painterly gesture, in truth they functioned more as visual ciphers that inhabited a broader, more discursive and mediated interpretive field, a field that had long been divested of the instrumentality, purposefulness and authenticity that characterized the project of modernism. However, for Dona, these paintings operated between or arguably beyond both authenticity and indeed irony. To this end, when asked about the work's relation to "authenticity" and "irony," qualities that, on one level respectively characterized the operative conditions of painting under modernism and postmodernism, Dona replied: "I think that the question of authenticity and the question of irony seem polarized here in a particular way. The polarization is apparent and I'm not interested in that either/or polarity at all."[46]

Nevertheless, the conditions of possibility for the work to affect synthesis remained an open question. For whilst the artist herself would speak of being interested in a point, or indeed place "where the question of synthesis can occur," for others Dona's paintings neither entirely synthesized the multifarious elements that had amassed upon their surfaces nor did they entirely or consistently hold those elements apart.[47] As one commentator observed, writing in 1995: "Her paintings should not improperly be conceived as synthetic or pastiche-based—the now all-too familiar strategies of post-modernism—because with each application of an adopted source, a crucial adaptation occurs."[48]

Such an adaptation arguably occurred on several levels, although in the case of *Photo Ghosts and the Labyrinth Drips on the Void* what it invariably stemmed from was a decision to adopt and work with the historical givenness of, for example, a particular material or visual trope in order to both interrogate its historical prescription so as to allow that its givenness to be thought anew. In this sense one could say, and certainly some of her paintings from the period attest to this observation, the work, rather than being merely emulative, was diagrammatical. Any complicity with modernism in this sense, whilst it stemmed from an impulse that was directed towards a particular facet of its archive, was not reducible to such an impulse. That is, and as David Moos claimed, in Dona's practice some form of regeneration or adaptation invariably occurred. So for example,

Dona's decision to work with acrylic paint "has a lot to do with the history of Minimalist and color-field painting [which] is a historicized type of material that I'm re-utilizing to open up those sign systems."[49]

Like Dona, Philip Taaffe's paintings that were produced during approximately the same period also appear to explore a particular form of "tactical co-mingling" of abstraction's respective traditions and categorical borders. As he claimed himself in a conversation with Robert Creeley in 2000: "I supposed I like working towards certain boundaries of abstraction. This has to do with stretching a pictorial idea until it reaches the end of what it can do. Then I'll break this vocabulary wide open, intervening with it somehow."[50]

One's first impression of Taaffe's paintings of the 1980s, with their proclivity to quote from a received tradition, if not the canon of abstract painting, is to immediately align them with the broader appropriationist stance the period became virtually synonymous with. However, even then, far from functioning as "art-historical facsimiles," Taaffe's practice at the time was motivated by an arguably less cynical set of convictions.[51] According to the artist: "I look upon much historically appropriate work as isolating certain needs that we have with respect to paintings. Not as a parody, but as a tribal ceremonial act. The irony of the gesture did not escape me, but I thought of it rather in terms of liturgical reenactment, a sacred dramaturgy."[52] According to Enrique Juncosa, these canvases "were not nostalgic pastiches, however, but an impassioned attempt at resurrection. For a start, they [were] the result of complex manual practices and not of directives dictated to a group of assistants, which is how many of these works by the most famous figure of Op Art are made."[53]

Indeed, and like Lasker, it would appear that Taaffe's engagement with certain historical forms, be they an Op Art painting by Bridget Riley or a Color Field painting by Mark Rothko, didn't function as a from of critique but arguably served a more heuristic role. With respect to the latter, the artist claimed that "I always derive from his work a tremendous sense of place—the canvas as an inhabitable pictorial situation so that I could almost look inside his paintings [...] This imaginary location, that sense of what his work does on that level, is perhaps what I feel has been his biggest gift to me."[54] By way of elucidating upon this claim, during a talk the artist gave on Mark Rothko at the Whitney Museum in New York 1998 Taaffe showed an image of a painting he had made three years previously, entitled *Stele* (Plate 11). Named after an ancient monolithic stone tablet or pillar, *Stele* was one of a series of paintings the artist had made during this period that were all painted on relatively narrow, vertically oriented rectangular supports. During the talk, Taaffe claimed that the ambition for the series was to "make a series of monolithic gestures that are enterable," and that *Stele* in particular "has this strong frontality of towers and the carapace, it is enterable somehow."[55]

Organized around a vertical axis that bisects the middle of the painting, *Stele* is divided into what is, in effect, a symmetrical composition comprised of a series of ornate and at certain points overlapping forms. Whilst the treatment of the forms has a graphic clarity that is at least in part suggestive of a particular symbolism (traditionally a Stele would carry some form of inscription, often relating to the laws of the society it had been made for), they remain culturally indeterminate.

Evidently then, although the act of cultural borrowing consistently worked to characterize Taaffe's pictorial vocabulary, his use of abstraction in this way, as Juncosa points out, "is instrumental and not an end in itself."[56] So what ends did it serve? Well, firstly, we could arguably square this last observation with the fact that the cultural and historical multi-layering that syncreticism ostensibly affords, indeed, apropos Taaffe's abstraction renders explicable, is such that the medium of painting somehow circumvents a set of received binary oppositions that worked to organize painting according to the categories of abstraction and representation. Certainly, the development of Taaffe's complex pictorial language during the 1990s was such that his canvases refused to be reducible to any singularly identifiable common denominator. Such a position is discernable within the following claim by the artist: "I like syncretist situations, the kind of situation where incursions from many different geographical sources have a layering effect of cultural and historical density."[57] To this end, Taaffe's ambitions for *The Red Desert* (1996–1997) would appear to concur with this observation:

> What I was after in the painting was giving each character a certain depth, making every element seem to play a singular role in the drama. It's a form of theatre with a cast of characters interacting in such a way that they have this proximity, this tension to one another, also this depth—you can look inside each one of these figures and discover a distinct world.[58]

Indeed, *The Red Desert*'s syncretism is further apparent with respect to both Taaffe's claim that the forms within the painting make very particular impressions: "They're not inchoate—they're all very particular" and Creeley's own admission that "they appear to be co-existing."[59]

Taaffe's paintings, whilst on one level clearly engaged with a set of particularities that were drawn from certain key moments pertaining to abstraction's own discursive histories, sought not to rehearse what had become by that point a somewhat well-worn critique, but rather functioned as the means by which a possible future for painting might arguably be imagined. As the artist stated: "I think the power and the possibilities for painting today has to do with binding it to a cultural legacy … Painting is where these symbolic languages or forms somehow crystallize and reveal their ancestry—and that in turn shows a certain sense of future possibility."[60] It is perhaps in this respect that Taaffe's project, with regards to the project of abstraction, remained an essentially humanist one: "However, one thinks about the explicitness or non-explicitness of abstraction, it has certainly moved on to include new themes. I feel an important purpose for art is to demonstrate this range of potential—one that tries to take into consideration archaic realms, but at the same time moves forward to explore unexpected new territory."[61]

If anything, the uncharted territory that the paintings of Pia Fries sought to explore remained readily bound up with the material syntax of painting. For a period of approximately twenty years, Fries has been engaged in an iterative process whereby, according to Iris Wien, "[o]ne painting responds to the next."[62] Whilst canvases that were produced during the early 1990s sought to overlap and meld the various textures and surfaces that invariably resulted in the entirety of the support being covered, the development of Fries's practice over the course of the 1990s entailed a gradual separation or withdrawal of the individual elements away from each other. This withdrawal resulted in the areas of painterly activity being read both in relation to each other and in relation to the areas of the support or ground that remained white. Moreover, as well as this atomization of the constituent areas of paint application, an increased differentiation lent each respective mark with a certain heterogeneity that was in contrast to the earlier, more homogenous "all-over" paintings. That is, glutinous, encrusted areas (which often become read as much as having been borne out of a process of scraping *off* the paint onto the painting's support as much as one of applying *onto* the self-same support), are often seen in proximity to flatter, less vigorous washes or indeed, painterly stains. However, whilst each mark forms part of a particular painting's overall visual circuitry, their organization is such that no mark takes precedence, visual or conceptual, over another. In this sense, and as Wien has noted, the paintings "have no focused hierarchy."[63]

Whilst Fries's syntax of painterly marks, gestures, surfaces and textures appeared to be characteristic not so much of what Dave Hickey had described, with respect to Richter's paintings, as a certain "post-modern doubt," to construe their visual organization in terms of evidencing a particular proclivity for visual fragmentation and non-narrativity remains equally unhelpful.[64] For Fries's canvases, like Lasker's and Taaffe's, were not, in this respect, postmodern pastiches that borrowed and subsequently regurgitated aspects derived from the technical vocabulary of modernist painting's history. However, and as Hickey point outs, as well as her work being resistant to claims that it was "postmodern," it equally negated the conditions of possibility that it might somehow be construed as rehearsing modernism's "reflexive criticality."[65] Although the paintings did not necessarily carry a direct or visually recognizable set of associations, this didn't mean that they were somehow *sui generis* or self-contained, autonomous abstractions engaged in a self-critical process that sought to extract them from the world they inhabited. This is arguably where the paintings of Fries and those of Fiona Rae become marked by a certain kinship. For whilst both worked within what traditionally would be labeled an "abstract" idiom, each of their respective practices encompassed and reverted to a heterogeneous vocabulary of marks and, in Rae's case, pictorial symbols. Indeed, Rae's work was notable for its proclivity to amalgamate an arguably eclectic inventory of visual ciphers. Moreover, the work of both artists could be seen as a renegotiation of painting through an acknowledgment of both modernism's and postmodernism's complicity with a set of debates that centered upon abstraction and which, being applicable to both Fries and Rae, was "clearly self-consciously about the reinvention of painting within the tradition of its demise."[66]

Marti Mayo, writing in the foreword to the exhibition catalogue that accompanied *Abstract Painting, Once Removed*, noted that the curator's thesis centered upon the fact that "the practice of, and critical discussion about, abstract and non-objective painting has been invigorated and broadened by the injection of ideas, forms, processes, tools, and materials from outside the spiritual, expressionistic and/or formalist strands that heretofore dominated twentieth-century abstraction."[67] Such a historical form divested of all or any of its original meanings resulted in artists working within and attempting to reposition what were, in effect, the various husks of modernist practice in the shape of a "tactical co-mingling" rather than a more straightforward process of synthesis. This is not to say that artists even during the 1990s weren't approaching their respective practices with regards to the idea of hybridity. As Polly Apfelbaum, an artist whose practice will be considered in the next chapter, would claim in 1995, her paintings were "hybrid works, poised between painting and sculpture; works not so much attempting to invent new categories but working promiscuously and improperly poaching—in fields clearly defined."[68] Rather, and for the most part, if painting as a material practice remained engaged with a recombinant aesthetic partly through the adaptation of certain tropes belonging to modernist abstraction, then its organization of these materials, both technical and historical, was for the most part aggregative, if not anatomized.

Notes

1 Lane Relyea, "Virtually Formal," *Artforum* 37 (1) (1998): 129.

2 Clement Greenberg, "Modernist Painting" (1960), in Greenberg, *The Collected Essays and Criticism* vol. 4, *Modernism with a Vengeance, 1957–1969*, 86.

3 Krauss, "Sculpture in the Expanded Field," 42.

4 Owens, "The Allegorical Impulse: Towards a Theory of Postmodernism," xiii.

5 Abigail Solomon-Godeau, "The Eighties" in Construction: Difference and Indifference in *The 80s A Topology*, ed. Ulrich Loock (Portugal: Museu de Arte Contemporânea de Serralves, 2007), 91.

6 Ibid., 92.

7 Joanna Drucker, *Sweet Dreams: Contemporary Art and Complicity* (Chicago: University of Chicago Press, 2005), 41.

8 Steven S. High, "The Politics of Space," in Arthur C. Danto et al., *Repicturing Abstraction* (Richmond, VA: Anderson Gallery, Virginia Commonwealth University, 1995), 32.

9 Brian Muller, *Real Art "A New Modernism": British Reflexive Painters in the 1990s* (Southampton: Southampton City Art Gallery, 1995), 7.

10 Ibid., 9.

11 Muller, *Real Art "A New Modernism": British Reflexive Painters in the 1990s*, 12. By way of a coda, Muller does add that: "This does not preclude reflexivity being used in the former sense as a device to inculcate the latter." Muller, ibid.

12 Michael Darling, "Monique Prieto at ACME," *Art Issues* (1996): 41.

13 Enrique Juncosa, "Index and Metaphor Jonathan Lasker, David Reed, Philip Taaffe" in Peter Fischer et al., *Abstraction Gesture Ecriture* (Zurich: Scalo; London: Thames & Hudson 1999), 135.

14 Drucker, *Sweet Dreams: Contemporary Art and Complicity*, 41.

15 "Jonathan Lasker in Conversation with David Ryan" (1997) in David Ryan, *Talking Painting: Dialogues with Twelve Contemporary Abstract Painters* (London: Routledge, 2002), 153.

16 Barry Schwabsky, "The Magic of Sobriety," in Barry Schwabsky et al., *Jessica Stockholder* (London: Phaidon, 1995), 49.

17 "Lynne Tillman in Conversation with Jessica Stockholder," in ibid., 15.

18 "Interview with Klaus Ottmann," in ibid., 116.

19 Jessica Stockholder, "Parallel Parking" (1992), in ibid., 143.

20 "Lynne Tillman in Conversation with Jessica Stockholder," in ibid., 28.

21 "Interview with Klaus Ottmann," 1991, in ibid., 117.

22 "Lynne Tillman in Conversation with Jessica Stockholder," in ibid., 10–11.

23 Ibid., 11.

24 Stockholder, "Parallel Parking," ibid., 143.

25 Jonathan Lasker, "Image Kit" (1986), in Demetrio Paparoni, *Jonathan Lasker Paintings 1977–2001* (Milan: Alberico Cetti Serbelloni Editore, 2002), 154.

26 Konrad Bitterli, "Competitive Codes," in Hans-Michael Herzog, *Jonathan Lasker: Gemälde/Paintings 1977–1997* (Ostfildern: Cantz Verlag 1997), 38.

27 Saul Ostrow, "Jonathan Lasker: A Pre-Fab View," in *Jonathan Lasker: Paintings from 1978 to 1982* (New York: Bravin Post Lee Gallery, 1994), 7.

28 Jonathan Lasker "Paint's Body" (1993) in Paparoni, *Jonathan Lasker Paintings 1977–2001*, 156.

29 "Jonathan Lasker in Conversation with David Ryan" (1997), in Ryan, *Talking Painting: Dialogues with Twelve Contemporary Abstract Painters*, 157.

30 Peter Schjeldahl, "The Rise of Abstraction II," in Dana Friis-Hansen, *Abstract Painting, Once Removed* (Houston: Contemporary Arts Museum, 1998), 35.

31 Thyrza Nichols Goodeve, *Ellen Gallagher* (London: Anthony d'Offay, 2001), 7.

32 Ibid.

33 "This Theatre Where You Are Not There: A Conversation with Ellen Gallagher by Thyrza Nichols Goodeve," in Ellen Gallagher, *Ellen Gallagher* (Birmingham: Ikon, 1998): 19.

34 Ibid., 9.

35 Claire Doherty, "Infection in the Sentence," in *Ellen Gallagher*, 10.

36 Ibid.

37 Roland Barthes *Image-Music-Text*, trans. by Stephen Heath (London: Fontana, 1977), 155.

38 Joe Moran, *Interdisciplinarity* (London: Routledge, 2002), 15.

39 Ibid.

40 Ibid., 16.

41 Ibid.

42 "This Theatre Where You Are Not There: A Conversation with Ellen Gallagher by Thyrza Nichols Goodeve," in Gallagher, *Ellen Gallagher*, 7.

43 "In this sense, Gallagher's art is driven by the production of history: its own (canvas to canvas) as well as the greater social landscape of race and representation." Ibid., 10.

44 "Lydia Dona in Conversation with David Ryan," in Ryan, *Talking Painting: Dialogues with Twelve Contemporary Abstract Painters*, 60.

45 Lydia Dona quoted in David Moos, "Lydia Dona: Architecture of Anxiety," Abstraction issue, *Journal of Philosophy and the Visual Arts*, No. 5, Academy Editions (1995): 43.

46 "Lydia Dona in Conversation with David Ryan," in Ryan, *Talking Painting: Dialogues with Twelve Contemporary Abstract Painters*, 58.

47 Ibid.

48 Moos, "Lydia Dona: Architecture of Anxiety," 44.

49 "Lydia Dona in Conversation with David Ryan," in Ryan, *Talking Painting: Dialogues with Twelve Contemporary Abstract Painters*, 58.

50 "Conversation Robert Creeley and Philip Taaffe," in Philip Taaffe, *Philip Taaffe* (Valencia: IVAM Institut Valencià d'Art Modern 2000), 182.

51 "His replications in the 1980s of existing works by artists well known in the canons of modern art may relate him, for example, not only to Warhol, but to such contemporaries of his as Mike Bildo or Sherrie Levine; yet, unlike their art-historical facsimiles, Taaffe's are involved with an aura of precious refinement and fantasy." Robert Rosenblum, "Another Kind of Abstract Order: Notes on Philip Taaffe" in *Philip Taaffe*, 64.

52 Juncosa, "Painting as Paradise," in *Philip Taaffe*, 24.

53 Ibid., 20.

54 Ibid., 36.

55 https://www.philiptaaffe.net/statements-interviews-2/on-rothko.

56 Juncosa, "Painting as Paradise", in *Philip Taaffe,* 18.

57 Ibid., 32.

58 "Conversation Robert Creeley and Philip Taaffe," in *Philip Taaffe*, 184

59 Ibid.

60 Ibid., 160.

61 Ibid., 166.

62 Iris Wien, "On Color and Space in the Paintings of Pia Fries," in Iris Wien et al., *Pia Fries Paintings 1990–2007* (Dusseldorf: Richter Verlag, 2007), 50.

63 Ibid.

64 Dave Hickey, "The Remains of Today", in Ibid., 129.

65 Ibid.

66 Drucker, *Sweet Dreams: Contemporary Art and Complicity*, 141–2.

67 Marti Mayo, "Foreword" in Friis-Hansen, *Abstract Painting, Once Removed*, 7.

68 Deidre Stein Greben, "Stain Power: with pieces of dyed velvet, Polly Apfelbaum transforms painting into sculpture and beauty into strength," *ARTnews* (2001): 102–5.

7

Situating Painting

So consideration of painting in this extended field centers on the idea that painting no longer exists as a strictly circumscribed mode of expression; rather, it is as a zone of contagion, constantly branching out and widening its scope.[1]

Writing in an article in *Art Monthly* in October 2003, Morgan Falconer put the responsibility for painting's revival squarely at the feet of its propensity to have "expanded beyond the confines of painting's traditional support. Instead of the old metaphorics of dying that were so prevalent only a few years ago—all that dripping, dribbling and entropic collapse—painting has vaulted off the canvas entirely and exploded into life."[2]

Beyond claiming that such a strategy had helped shape the critical reception of Jessica Stockholder's practice during the 1990s, for Falconer "expansion" had "become the underpinning thesis within the new discourse."[3] Whilst Falconer remained skeptical of the rhetoric surrounding a term such as "expansion," making, as he claimed "the sound of weighty theory that the boosters think necessary for its marketplace," the article nevertheless highlighted what had become one salient strategy within painting at the start of the new millennium.

Amidst the roll call of artists Falconer cited as being complicit with painting's leitmotif of expansion was Katharina Grosse, who, like Matthew Ritchie, makes paintings "that entirely envelops the viewer, splattering onto walls, ceiling and floor."[4]

It was in 1998, at the *Projektaum* of Kunsthalle Bern that Grosse first used the technique of spraying selected areas of a particular space. Working with a spray gun, Grosse's paintings mark the spaces and surfaces that she has sprayed thorough a certain spatialization of color, a spatialization that carries with it echoes of Stockholder's own ambitions. Beyond this particular affinity, and notwithstanding the idea that Grosse's practice was at the very least suggestive of how painting might possibly be understood within the new millennium, her work invariably brings with it associations with the legacy of artistic formalism during the 1950s and 1960s in the US.

Perhaps the most self-evident of these can be found in the work of Jules Olitski. As an abstract painter who established his career during the 1960s, Olitski was fortunate enough to have the critical backing of both Greenberg and Fried. Indeed, whereas the former sought to position Olitski's large-scale Color Field paintings within the artistic purview of what he labeled "post-painterly abstraction," Fried showcased Olitski's painting, alongside Frank Stella's and Kenneth Noland's in an exhibition in 1965 entitled *Three American Painters*.[5] Olitski, like Grosse, worked with a spray gun and would cover his canvases with vaporous areas and dense fields of saturated color. Indeed, working tacitly to underscore Greenberg's essentialist annexation of painting, Olitski once remarked that he envisaged a painting that would entail "nothing but some colors sprayed into the air and staying there."[6]

Beyond the fact that both Olitski and Grosse have adopted a comparable set of working methods, as Olitski's statement suggests, both of their respective practices entail an orientation towards disembodied color and, more broadly, the dematerialization of painting on some level. Indeed, beyond the example given by Olitski's paintings of the 1960s, there are arguably other close affinities between Grosse's practice and modernist abstraction.

For example, she has spoken previously of wanting to determine, or rather of wanting the work to determine a certain autonomy or independence from site, from place and from the identity that is invariably conferred onto it just by being located and locatable within a particular space. As the artist has claimed:

> The parameters of autonomy constantly change. My declaration of independence is made visible by the contradiction, by overwriting the existing picture receptacle. My activity, regardless of what I am doing at the time, is extremely non-site-specific, even anti-site-specific, and in that way highlights the intellectual aspects of its pictorial value, i.e., its fragile, ever mutable qualities and its independence from the material outcome.[7]

Interestingly, certain works by the artist appear to utilize the drip as one element within the artist's visual syntax. However, rather than automatically conflate her intentions with Jackson Pollock's own proclivity to harness its effects, Grosse short-circuits, or at least defers such a reading in favor of highlighting the temporal, rather than the spatial dimension of this phenomenon: "It's a kind of indicator of temporality: it might have just been painted, may not even be dry. Perhaps the mingling of colors also gives the idea that control is no longer exerted. It has the look of inability."[8] Arguably however, Grosse's technique remains, to a certain extent, distinct from Jackson Pollock's activities. For whilst the latter's association with a method of working appeared to be conditioned by a highly subjectivized and expressive immediacy and was achieved through the novel range of painterly techniques he had adopted, Grosse's working methods preclude such intimacy with her materials. As the artist has noted, "using spray paint I don't actually touch the space. The only way I'm connected to the space physically is by walking."[9]

However, there remains a certain paradox due to the fact that because Grosse chooses not to apply the paint with a brush, an equivalent from of immediacy becomes automatically implied. As Grosse remarks: "Spray painting is different to painting with a brush, because to some extent the brush gets in the way."[10] Nevertheless, and notwithstanding questions around immediacy, gesture, and mark that Grosse's practice engenders and the relationship with artistic precedent that her work inscribes, the large-scale, expansionist paintings that Grosse produces can be seen as one salient example of how a number of painters within approximately the last ten years have approached the medium in terms of questions around its situational status. That is, how it becomes situated, either within or beyond the gallery's walls and, moreover, what situations it either becomes interwoven with, or, for that matter, elicits.[11] On one level, whilst the former concerns its operational status, that is, what methods or strategies the artist adopts and so in this respect is closer to questions of the artwork's production, the latter is more readily bound up with ideas around context and hence, meaning. In a more plainspoken sense, whilst we might claim that traditionally the medium was geared towards painting and thus depicting situations, the artists whose respective practices we will consider in this chapter attempt to situate painting.

The provenance of the term "situational" arguably stemmed from Victor Burgin's text "Situational Aesthetics."[12] Originally published in *Studio International* in the autumn of 1969, Burgin, who would go on to become a leading exponent of Conceptual Art within England claimed that the two consequences of what he claimed was an aesthetic *system* (original emphasis) were firstly that "the specific nature of any object formed is largely contingent upon the details of the situation for which it is designed," and secondly, "through attention to time, objects formed are intentionally located partly in real, exterior, space and partly in psychological, interior, space."[13] By working directly outwards from Minimalism's phenomenology of the artwork and towards the "psychological," Burgin adopted a stance that was tendentiously antithetical to "the dominant modernist conceptualization of art à la Clement Greenberg, according to which the work of art is constituted as an autonomous object."[14]

The "situational" in one sense worked to critically preface a related term that was prevalent during the latter half of the 1980s and through into the 1990s, namely site specificity. According to Robert Irwin, writing in 1985, the category of site specificity is one whereby the "'sculpture' is conceived with the site in mind; the site sets the parameters and is, in part, the reason for sculpture."[15] More recently, and as Claire Doherty points out, the term entails the theorization of a number of related concepts, including "site, non-site, place, non-place, locality, public space, context and time" resulting in a move from away from the site specific towards what Doherty describes is the "situation-specific."[16]

With regards to the heterogeneity that marked the medium of painting within a critical milieu that one might arguably claim was post-postmodernism, Grosse's strategies of immediacy and distance allowed a certain form to be found that is not restricted to or delimited by the support's framing edge. Moreover, the form's expansion over and across the particular surfaces and planes of the gallery space, and indeed the architectural facades located beyond the rather more static and aseptic confines of the gallery space, allowed Grosse to somehow situate painting and in doing so proffer one means by which its aggregative conditions could become rendered visible and, moreover, arguably held to account.

Whilst Grosse's paintings carry certain affinities with modernist abstraction—its dematerialization of form, its ambitions to render painting optically, its use of color not to convey form but *as* form, by spilling out into the realm of the three-dimensional and, by extension, into a series of spaces that are circumscribed socially, the conditions of possibility for the work to be self-contained, self-sufficient and necessarily autonomous distances the work of Grosse from Greenberg's own ambitions for abstract painting.

Certainly within "Modernist Painting" the work of art became in part understood by a trajectory that was centripetal and that entailed the object's orientation towards what was perceived to be its own essential state or condition. Whilst following its publication this became the cornerstone of Greenberg's ideas, his promulgation of the modernist artwork's inherently autonomous state had begun as early as 1948.

Writing in *The Decline of Cubism*, Greenberg would place the movement within the following interpretive terms: "Cubism, by its rejection of illusionist effects in painting or sculpture and its insistence on the physical nature of the two-dimensional picture plane ... expressed the positivist or empirical state of mind with its refusal to refer to anything outside the concrete experience of the particular discipline, field, or medium in which one worked."[17]

Of course, there is a much longer history to painting's complicity with the realm of three-dimensional space, and in particular how pictorial space was often framed architecturally; one only has to consider how Renaissance artists were often commissioned to work directly onto the interior walls of religious, civic and domestic spaces. Painting's subsequent autonomy was the corollary, as Andrew Blauvelt has noted, of the development of easel painting, which as a self-governing, "portable commodity allowed it to escape its historically subordinate role to architecture and the imposed limits of a specific site. No longer physically attached to a particular architectural surface or structure, painting could develop independently."[18] Indeed, one of the issues that Greenberg was forced to address at a relatively early point in his criticism was how the work of certain Abstract Expressionists, by scaling up what they were doing, were in one sense rehearsing once again painting's affinities with the architectural.

Discussing the work of Barnett Newman in "Feeling is All," an article written in 1952, Greenberg acknowledged and to a certain extent attempted to account for the ostensibly architectural dimension that marked Newman's paintings at that time:

> They may not be easel pictures, or murals in any accepted sense, but what do difficulties of category matter? These paintings have an effect that makes one know immediately that he is in the presence of art. They constitute, moreover, the first kind of painting I have seen that accommodates itself stylistically to the demand of modern interior architecture for flat, clear surfaces and strictly parallel divisions.[19]

Whilst, according to Blauvelt, easel painting and, by extension, modernist painting's reluctance to fully embrace the mural as the necessary means of support "underscores arguments that late-modernist easel painting is the logical product for late-capitalist consumption: big pictures for big collectors that require bigger spaces for exhibition"[20] what has already been evinced were competing modes of abstraction that left behind the confines of easel painting and indeed painting's traditional support in order to engage more dynamically with a set of questions that were organized around the artwork's display. Certainly, and as we have already seen, the paintings of, amongst others, Sam Gilliam and Lynda Benglis sought to expand the physical parameters of abstract painting at the same time as they were attempting, more broadly, to extend modernism's mandate. In this respect, the rightful heir to Benglis's poured paintings was the expansionist practice of Stockholder.

Today, Grosse's practice is to a certain extent more broadly emblematic of a number of artists' practices, all of which, if not present an expanded account of painting, to borrow Falconer's term, are certainly characterized by what we have already claimed is a situated form of painting that operates either somehow within the gallery space, or within a number of sites, spaces and locations that fall beyond it.

With regards to artists using the walls of a particular gallery space as the means of the painting's support, Dominic Morton, writing in *Vitamin P* has claimed that such a strategy

> has developed into a unique and richly varied practice in recent years, moving beyond its abstract, conceptual, and text-based incarnations into a more representational dimension. The pioneering work of such figures as Robert Barry, Michael Craig-Martin, and Sol LeWitt, among others, has provided the impetus to a number of artists working today to explore the introduction of personally and culturally inspired motifs into paintings made expressly for a wall.[21]

Whilst this overview was given within the context of the author's discussion of the wall-based practice of Richard Wright, it seems equally applicable to a number of artists who use the wall plane as their choice of support. Certainly, the wall-based paintings of Arturo Herrera, with their spliced and inverted fragments derived from comic books and Disney animations acquire at least some of their visual cogency from their immediate, expansive and dynamically scaled up physical presence.

Consistently hovering on the cusp of legibility, Herrera's paintings are the result of an image being developed through, as the artist states himself, "sketches, photocopies, bottles of Wite-Out, transparencies, and small drawings directly applied onto scale models."[22]

The sources of Herrera's wall paintings are derived from, amongst other things, coloring books and characters that for the most part have been adapted from Disney films including Snow White and the Seven Dwarfs and Bambi. As Roxana Marcoci notes, Herrera's practice, like that of other American artists, which include Mike Kelley, Paul McCarthy, and Charles Ray, seeks to address a set of issues that are bound up with the attempted conflation of innocence with youth. Most vehemently promulgated and reenacted within the forms of mainstream, popular culture, e.g., the unified field of mainstream, Hollywood cinema, the resulting films such as those made by the Disney studios worked to uphold and maintain a set of culturally encoded social norms, which included the nuclear family.[23]

The provenance of the large-scale painting *All I Ask* (1999) executed in latex paint and commissioned for the *Color Me Blind* exhibition at the Wuttembergischer Kunstverein in Stuttgart, and subsequently shown in the group exhibition *Painting at the Edge of the World* in 2001, was a Snow White coloring book the artist had found at an Odd Jobs store in New York in 1998. With regards to the artist's choice of color for this piece, namely beige and brown, Herrera claimed that as the latter arguably persists as the "world's least popular color," he "wanted this reference to be in dialogue with Snow White's seemingly harmless tale."[24]

If Herrera's paintings tendentiously scramble imagery derived from the fictive realm of cartoons and Disney characters, arguably as a means whereby their proclivity to both idealize and sentimentalize is tendentiously short-circuited, Franz Ackermann's wall-based works are processed from the situation of everyday, lived experience. As the artist claimed in 2008, "I am trying to rework real impressions or events, as well as reevaluate them … real events are represented more effectively using an already conveyed, processed form."[25]

In effect, the "site" of Ackermann's paintings is twofold. Firstly, it consists of the various geographical locations he visits on his travels and which he uses as a means of engendering imagery, however fleeting, impressionistic or oblique. Secondly, the site of Ackermann's paintings often encompass the walls of the gallery space itself. The starting point for Ackermann's practice are what he calls "mental maps," diminutively sized watercolors, which, according to the artist, "seem like my most important companion," and which are executed in wherever city or location the artist happens to find himself in.[26] Indeed, the over-arching theme within Ackermann's paintings is arguably one of attempting to render visually explicable the contingencies of the artist's mobility which is, by his own admission, constantly in a state of flux: "The conditions of travel, and its very notion, exist in a state of radical change: streams of migration meet streams of tourism. In my travels I am trying to clarify these aspects 'on-site'."[27]

What Ackermann's mental maps form the basis of is what he calls "Evasions"—large-scale canvases which are often positioned directly onto more expansive wall paintings. It is arguably with the latter that the artist is able to present a vibrant diorama that simultaneously projects and collapses spatial modes, disjunctions and contiguities. As is implied by the title of his preliminary watercolors and as Douglas Fogle points out, as well as travelling physically, Ackermann "also travels psychically, producing hallucinatory visions of cities that are every bit as accurate as any tourist map."[28] It is perhaps for this reason that the possibility for cartographic similitude is necessarily eschewed in favor of a more subjective and indeed less coherent similitude of a globalized, space-time continuum that is endlessly unfolding and whose economic base is highly dependent upon the cultural activity of tourism. In other words, and if, as Fogle reminds us, tourism "is a particularly contemporary mode of being in the world," then Ackermann's large-scale, multivalent paintings seek to restage the experiential basis of this being through a particular acceleration of color, shape and form.[29] Moreover, the state of flux within which many of Ackermann's paintings appear to reside in is more broadly indicative of a particular lifestyle the artist, and many like him have adopted and which as result characterizes the form and appearance of the paintings he makes. As Jordan Kantor notes, this "quasinomadic life of the post-studio artist" pictures "the artistic self as both traveler and crossroads ... [which characterizes] the itinerancy of many artists today, who travel from biennial to biennial executing site-specific works away from home."[30]

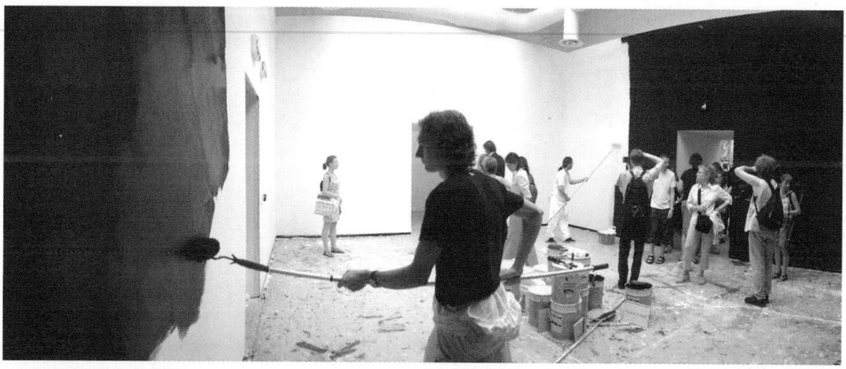

FIGURE 7.1 Nedko Solakov, *A Life (Black & White)*, 1998–.

A somewhat different utilization of the gallery's walls was evident within Nedko Solakov's *A Life (Black & White)* (1998–), which was made for the Venice Biennale in 2001. The piece consisted of two "adult painters," who, working in the recommended clockwise direction, simultaneously painted the walls of the exhibition space, one using undiluted white paint whilst the second followed, using black paint that had the same consistency. Notwithstanding the times during the day when the two painters momentarily, although not concurrently took breaks from their allotted task, this ongoing process, which was as much about painting's undoing as its doing, was undertaken for the duration that the exhibition was open. Whilst the estimated amount of paint was stored within the middle of the exhibition space, the "memorabilia," as Solakov had written in the accompanying "Instructions for Realising A Life (Black & White), 1998–," "the empty paint buckets, the paint brushes and rollers, the plastic and parts of the multi-layered walls—can be kept by the actual owner of the work and used as a kind of visual/physical archive of that very instalment of the piece."[31] In contrast to the other wall-based pieces that we have thus far considered, such a seemingly Sisyphean task worked, if nothing else, to remind its respective audience of a basic truism, namely, that however it is imagined and, in Solakov's case staged, the delimitation of painting occurs iteratively.[32]

If, as Herrera has claimed, the "goal is to activate a space that the architect never intended to be painted by creating an image that feels like it has always been there," it would appear that the corollary of dispensing with the literal framing edge of painting, beyond having certain affinities with installation art, is that the work in situ more specifically foregrounds ideas around the phenomenological, the embodied and arguably the dialogical.[33] Certainly with respect to the latter the large-scale paintings of Michael Lin, based on traditional Taiwanese textile designs segue into Nicholas Bourriaud's own ideas espoused around the "relational." Accordingly, rather than conceive painting as Greenberg arguably had as that which operates within a realm that is autonomous and disarticulated from the rest of society, relational art, according to Bourriaud, consists of a "set of artistic practices which take as their theoretical and practical point of departure the whole of human relations and their social context, rather than an independent and private space."[34]

For the Tapei Biennial in 2000, Lin made a large-scale floor painting for the atrium of the Taipei Fine Arts Museum. By also providing cushions whose floral designs echoed the floral patterns that formed part of the floor's overall design, *Taipei Fine Arts Museum September 9, 2000–January 7, 2001* functioned as a social space which provided momentary respite from the biennial's art-viewing throng. As one commentator has noted, Lin's paintings, "instead of offering the audience an object … gives them a place to daydream, to enjoy moments of freethinking."[35] In this sense Lin's *Taipei Fine Arts Museum September 9, 2000–January 7, 2001* had a certain kinship with other artists, including Rirkrit Tirivanija who has construed the space of the contemporary art gallery not with regards to its received function as a venue wherein objects are displayed, but rather in terms of a more non-object based and reciprocal space that could congenially facilitate an intersubjective set of social relations.

Whilst Michael Lin's floor-based pieces were often based on the visual motifs derived from particular cultural traditions, the traditions from which Polly Apfelbaum's floor-based pieces (Plate 12) emerged remained, in effect, largely modernist in scope and purpose. In many respects *A Pocket Full of Posies*, made in 1990 and consisting of thirteen floor-based, unpainted flower-shaped sections of steel arranged in a circle on the gallery floor adumbrated the artist's subsequent so-called "Fallen Paintings." According to the artist: "'Fallen Paintings' was a term I started using after these pieces first began to be shown in the early 1990s. It was a way of talking about these works as hybrids between painting and sculpture, something that couldn't easily be pinned down to a category."[36] Whilst such a designation worked to organize Apfelbaum's practice during the period in question, what remains notable is the work's variation. For example, whilst *Fine Flowers in the Valley (White Spill)* (1992–1993), with its somewhat crumpled and forlorn appearance appeared to have been the result of painting, to coin a phrase one critic used in a review of Apfelbaum's work in 2000, "spilling its guts," the dappled effect of *Eclipse* (1996) appeared somewhat more considered and closer to the molecular rather than the abject or indeed, the abjected.[37] Certainly the latter was more readily foregrounded by a process whereby small swatches of synthetic velvet were stained with what were usually vibrantly colored fabric dyes, cut out by hand and then strategically placed across an area of the gallery floor.[38]

The situated horizontality of a work such as *Today I Love Everybody* inevitably invites comparison with the works of both Pollock and Benglis.[39] Of course, such a reading of Apfelbaum's work in relation to the all-over canvases of Jackson Pollock requires a measure of qualification; whilst they both share a particular preoccupation with the idea of horizontality, "Apfelbaum's scatters are not expressive gestures or indices of psychic energy—they're closer to self-generating organisms."[40] Nevertheless, arguably Apfelbaum's "Fallen Paintings," along with Pollock's all-over canvases and Benglis's poured pieces all posited the medium of painting not as something that was understood as being universally and innately given, but as a site, was rather necessarily contingent.

Whilst Apfelbaum's paintings on one level appeared to rehearse key moments within the history of artistic modernism, her practice evinced other historical references beyond those artists which included Pollock but logically extended to both the felt pieces of Robert Morris and the Oxidation paintings of Andy Warhol, all of which were somehow organized around particular understandings of horizontality, entropy and dispersal either procedurally, conceptually or with regards to the object's display.

To this end, Apfelbaum's frank acknowledgement and arrangement of her chosen materials echoed Minimalism's proclivity to acknowledge, rather than subvert the intrinsic qualities of a particular material. Moreover, both Apfelbaum's work during the 1990s and Minimalism foregrounded notions of seriality, repetition and a materiality that was usually either industrially based or demotically given. Such a reading of Apfelbaum's practice was evident within the 1994 group exhibition *Sense and Sensibility: Women Artists and Minimalism in the Nineties*, which included Apfelbaum's work along with that of six other women artists.[41] Moreover, the proclivity to read Apfelbaum's work at the time as rehearsing particular aspects that characterized the project of Minimalism, specifically its "truth to materials" credo could arguably be seen in terms of what the artist herself described in 1995 was a "partial taxonomy of abstraction, a taxonomy that included the qualities and characteristics such as 'flows, spots, heaps, fields, patchwork, pointillisms, wrinkles'."[42] Such designations invariably brings to mind the Minimalist sculptor Richard Serra's own list of verbs which for his part included "to roll, to crease, to fold, to store, to bend, to shorten, to twist, to dapple, to crumple."[43]

In addition to having certain affinities with Minimalism, Apfelbaum's floor-based paintings of the 1990s also engaged with the legacies of both Pop Art and Conceptual Art. For example, and with regards to the latter, *Enigma Machine* (1993–1995), which can be configured so that it is set out in a broadly regular grid-like pattern across the floor or, alternately as a series of stacked piles of swatches within what is arguably a more sculptural configuration, is directly comparable to Bochner's *Theory of Painting*. Certainly, both encompass ideas of both reconfiguration and variation within what are a set of material givens.

Given the fact that the artist's expectations of her paintings' respective viewing conditions was premised upon an ambulatory and embodied engagement with the work, an engagement wherein "people have to move through the works so the spectator activates it and participates in the experience," the viewer's complicity with the artwork would mean that the fundamental concerns of her practice, namely "site, scale, and the architectural setting," could be evinced.[44] However, and with respect to the over-arching concerns of this chapter, referring to the fact that all of the work for "Anything Can Happen in a Horse Race," her exhibition in Milton Keynes in 2009 was made in the gallery space itself, Apfelbaum has stated that "I don't really like the word site-specific, I prefer 'situational', but in any event, it's important for me that the work is made in reaction to the place."[45]

This understanding of the "situational" and, moreover, the understanding that the work is somehow made in direct response to certain aspects of a given space is also evident within works Francis Alÿs has made and that stem from and for the most part remains in accordance with the basic premise of painting as a material process that entails particular actions that results in a particular set of visual outcomes. Whilst they often adopt a modest range of working methods, the meanings that inhere within the work as a result are invariably bound up with the contexts from whence they originally came.

In 1991 Alÿs began his *paseos* or walks, temporary actions that generally entailed either something being amassed en route, or, conversely, something being discarded or lost in the process of walking. Like other artists, including David Hammons and Gabriel Orozco who have approached the activity of walking through urban spaces as an embodied form of psychogeographical mapping, Alÿs's practice in this respect seemed characteristic of Miwon Kwon's description of site-oriented methods of artistic production as those that entail the "physical mobilization of the artist to create works in various cities throughout the cosmopolitan art world."[46] So for example, in *Paradox of Praxis* (1997), the artist pushed a block of ice through Mexico City until it had melted. *The Leak,* first performed in 1995 in Sao Paolo in Brazil, entailed Alÿs walking whilst carrying a tin of paint that had been punctured in one end. Whilst the drizzled line indexically registered the artist's route through the city, at the same time it also registered associations that ranged from Pollock's own utilization of line, Paul Klee's oft-quoted aphorism of wanting to "take a line for a walk" to being reminiscent of the twine that Theseus used to guide his way through the minotaur's maze.[47] As the artist has claimed: "My paintings, my images, are only attempting to illustrate the situations I confront, provoke, or perform on a more public, usually urban, and ephemeral level."[48] Increasingly, Alÿs's practice has taken on a more explicitly political dimension which has partly been necessitated by what the artist has described is a particular locality's "political component," which functions as "an obligatory ingredient in addressing the situation."[49]

In 2004 he reenacted *The Leak* by walking the "Green-Line"—a boundary that was drawn up following the Arab–Israeli war in 1948; in real terms and for Alÿs this entailed a fifteen-mile stretch of land in Jerusalem. What intrigued Alÿs

> was the fact that it has at once a very abstract dimension—it's a line drawn on a 1:20,000 map, a treaty that nowadays has got no real space of representation—and at the same time a dramatic, real dimension. The line on the map is the effect of a physical gesture; [Israel's then defense minister] Moshe Dayan drew it with a grease pencil. The lines were three to four millimeters wide and hence represented, on the ground, a band of terrain 60 to 90 yards wide.[50]

Equally, *Retoque/Painting*, made four years later placed what appeared to be the somewhat nondescript act of "touching up" and imbued it with a very particular set of political resonances.

Like *The Green Line* that, on one level, delineated the 1948 armistice line between Israel and Palestine, *Retoque/Painting* was organized around the reiteration, through a physical, painterly act, of what remains a politically demarcated space. By "retouching" over 60 lines that had originally separated an area of land around the Panama Canal, Alÿs rendered visible a set of geographical boundaries by playing the political off of the poetic. And it is arguably Alÿs's decision to revisit the site, rather than simply departing from it that confers onto his practice the nomadic reading that was spoken of earlier in this chapter. According to Gilles Deleuze and Felix Guattari: "Whereas the migrant leaves behind a milieu that has become amorphous or hostile, the nomad is one who does not depart, does not want to depart, who clings to the smooth space left by the receding forest, where the steppe or the desert advances, and who invents nomadism as a response to this challenge."[51]

In one respect Alÿs's actions within the context of *Retoque/Painting* can be related to Federico Herrero's own public interventions within urban space entitled *Carefully Repainted Yellow Areas*, which the artist began in 2001 and that involved repainting sections of curb where the paint had faded or become scuffed. Along with making work within the context of the studio, Herrero's practice has also encompassed other, more socially-oriented pieces including *Mapa Mundi*, a piece made in 2003 for the Havana Biennial that entailed the artist painting a map of the world in orange onto the floor of a public swimming pool.

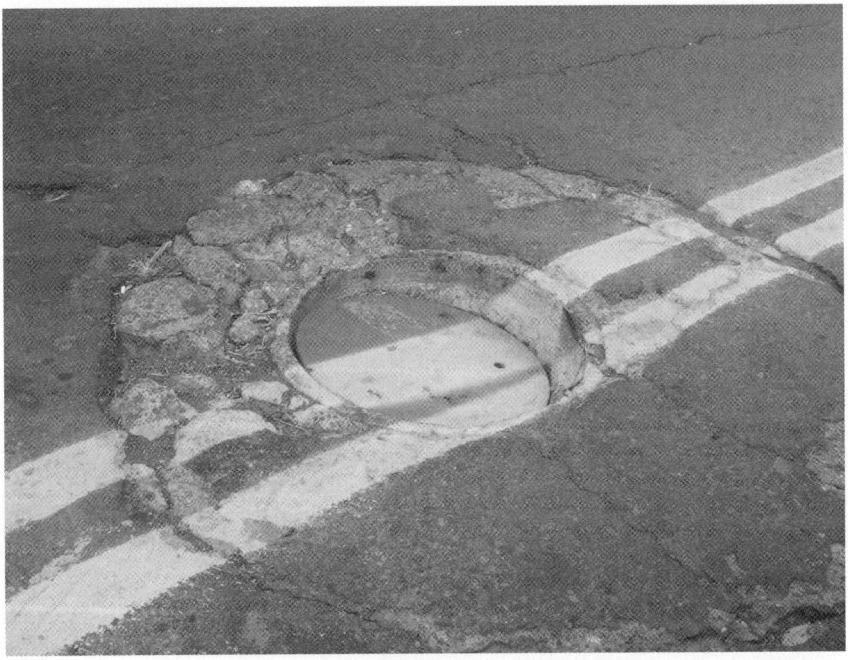

FIGURE 7.2 Federico Herrero, *Found painting*, San Jose, Costa Rica 2004–08.

Comparable to the public interventions through painterly means of both Alÿs and Herrero is *Borrando La Frontera (Erasing the Border)*, 2011 by the artist Ana Teresa Fernández.

Borrando La Frontera began as a solo intervention, with Fernández, sporting a black cocktail dress and black pumps resting a large ladder against a section of the wall that separates Playas de Tijuana from San Diego's Border Field State park and proceeding to paint a section of the wall's metal bars sky blue. According to the artist:

> Erasing the Border was born in 2011. Under the Obama administration, the visits in Friendship Park [a public space between San Diego and Tijuana] were cancelled. After discovering that families' contact was limited to what they could do through the fence with small holes, I felt overwhelmed with anger and sadness. I came up with the idea of using paint as a weapon, as my battle tool, and I decided to erase the border. I wanted to create the illusion of a huge hole in the fence, a visual pause, so that people who came often to the beach could have moments of rest from the beast separating Mexico from the United States.[52]

Since Fernández's initial interaction with the fence, *Borrando La Frontera* has been restaged at various sites dotted along the U.S.–Mexico border where the artist, along with other participants have painted sections of the fence sky blue with the explicit intention of wanting the fence to visually "disappear."

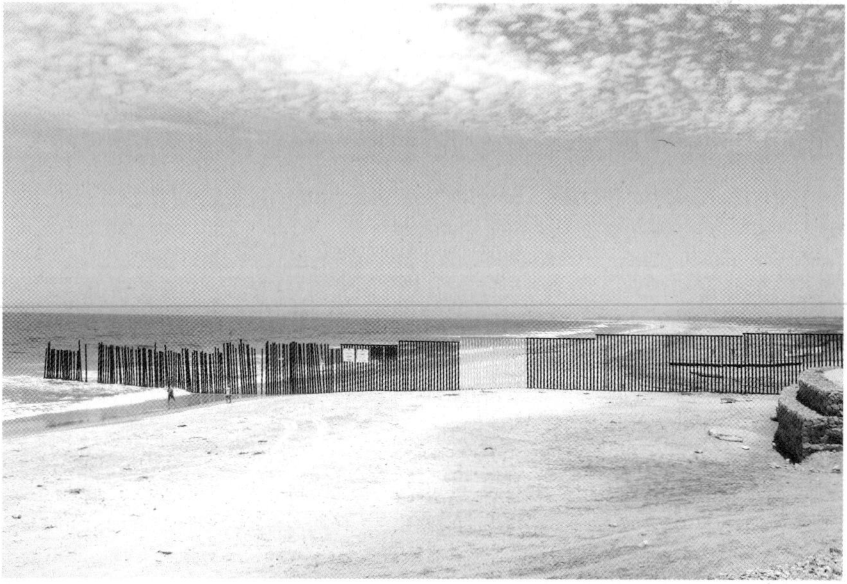

FIGURE 7.3 Ana Teresa Fernandez, *Borrando la Frontera (Erasing the Border) 03*, 2011/2021.

Ostensibly a three-dimensional trompe l'oeil, this basic but nevertheless powerful intervention provides the conditions of possibility, albeit momentarily, for a situation to be imagined where the wall appears to be in the process of being dismantled. As the artist recounts, "I was delighted when, late in the afternoon, a jogger came running from far down the beach and told us that he thought for a moment that part of the wall had come down."[53]

On one level, the interventions of all three artists within public space can be interpreted through what James Meyer has claimed are two competing categories of site, that is the "literal" as against the "functional." To this end, the literal site "is an actual location, a singular place [wherein the] artist's intervention conforms to the physical constraints of this situation, even if (or precisely when) it would subject this to critique. The work's formal outcome is thus determined by a physical place, by an understanding of the place as actual."[54] Whereas the functional site, according to Meyer, is "a mapping of institutional and textual filiations and the bodies that move between them (the artist's above all)."[55] Following Meyer's distinction then, the "literal" dimension of site within Alÿs's walks is organized around and becomes mobilized within a particular location or place whereas the "functional" dimension of site within both *The Green Line* and *Retoque/Painting* can be construed as an interrogation of a particular locality's partisan nature and its complicity with institutional, governmental or ideological contexts. In other words, following Meyer, the "functional" accedes to "a chain of meanings and imbricated histories."[56]

The inherently contingent nature of Alÿs's practice has meant that, as in the case of Lin's installations, the work carries with it a certain dialogical dimension. For example and as Martin Herbert notes in his commentary to *The Green Line*, having showed the video to a number of Palestinians and Israelis, the recordings that were made of their responses to the piece have become part of the work and in addition, have formed the basis of a book of interviews that will be published in Arabic, Hebrew, and English.[57] This dialogical strand to Alÿs's practice, and specifically with regards to his paintings is more readily explicit in the artist's "originals," small-scale paintings based on, as Kitty Scott notes, what the artist has described are "'feasible experiments' where the protagonist, usually a suited man, engages with props or his physical surroundings, for some obscure and apparently irrational, but believable reason."[58] These are then passed on to *rótulistas* or sign painters who paint their own interpretations of Alÿs's paintings. The final stage of this process sees Alÿs making a painting using the *rótulista's* own copy as its basis. Rather than being seen as a straightforward critique or destabilzation of authorship and its corollary, meaning—certainly with regards to the latter meaning in the work of Alÿs is never fixed—these small paintings perform a sort of dialogical relay along Meyer's "chain of meaning."

Whilst Alÿs's and Herrero's urban interventions are deliberate, David Batchelor's Found Monochromes are representative of a more inadvertent and serendipitous situating of painting within the public realm that marries the conceptual practice of situating with the arguably more pragmatic though nonetheless partisan act of sighting.

Since 1997 the artist has taken photographs that vicariously work to inhabit and, indeed extend the history and tradition of the monochrome. Chanced upon rather than deliberately sought out, whilst the monochromes themselves remain, for the most part visually indistinguishable, all characterized by their white blankness, their respective locations diverge considerably; whilst Found Monochrome "19 Islington, London, 01.05.99" is somewhat impromptu, consisting of an A4 piece of paper taped onto the inside of a car's window, the blankness of "331 Star Ferry, Hong Kong, 10.11.08" is more redolent of a projection screen. Speaking of these readymade monochromes, the artist has claimed that: "I prefer to stay and look for the voids in modernity, at the gaps where gaps shouldn't exist, at the blanks which are occasionally carved out of the impacted and replete surfaces of buildings, hoardings, roofs and pavements."[59] In this sense then whilst like Alÿs and Herrero urbanity is conceived as a palimpsest, for Bachelor this particular strand of his practice is directed towards those caesuras wherein the space of modernity in the guise of what was, on one level, the logical end point, if not exhaustion of abstraction, is both sighted and hence sited.

Jonathan Watkins, writing in one of the catalogue essays that accompanied the Tate Triennial in London in 2003, claimed that it is "widely accepted that works of art are not self-contained and that objects and/or gestures traditionally apprehended as art acquire their identity and meaning through what exists around them."[60] Certainly the fifteen diminutively sized works that were painted directly onto adhesive tape and placed both within the gallery space itself and around the vicinity of Tate Britain by Margaret Barron, one of the artists selected to show in the Triennial gave credence to Watkins claim. Indeed, the idea that art, and specifically painting was or could in any way remain autonomous appeared virtually impossible, if not entirely unnecessary. Instead, works by, *inter alia*, Herrera, Alÿs, Fernández and Bachelor foregrounds considerations of their situated context that exist either within, upon or beyond the confines of the gallery space.

Notes

1 Daniel Birnbaum, "Where is Painting Now?," *Tate International Arts and Culture* 1 (2002): 62.

2 Morgan Falconer, "The Undead" *Art Monthly* 270 (2003): 2.

3 Ibid., 3.

4 Ibid., 2.

5 Michael Fried, *Three American Painters* (Cambridge, MA: Fogg Art Museum (1965), 1971).

6 Online at: https://www.tate.org.uk/art/artworks/olitski-instant-loveland-t07244.

7 "Katharina Grosse in conversation with Ulrich Loock Painting on three-dimensional supports" in Ulrich Loock, *Katharina Grosse Atoms Outside Eggs* (Porto: Museu de Arte Contemporânea de Serralves, 2007), 21.

8 Ibid., 34.

9 "How to start and how to stop painting: Jonathan Watkins in conversation with Katharina Grosse," in Katharina Grosse, "*Cool puppen: der weisse saal trift sich im wald ich wüsste jetzt nichts* (Wolfratshausen: Edition Minerva, 2002), 28.

10 Ibid.

11 In this respect, a starting point by which we could begin to apply this interpretive framework with respect to Grosse's practice would be in relation to how the graffitist appropriates and demarcates public space. To this end, Grosse has claimed that: "I come from the history and traditions of painting yet some aspects of my work do coincide with characteristics of graffiti. I am very attracted by its unexpected presence, its uncontrollable generosity, the way it claims space and the fact that it redefines and shifts the function of site." Katharina Grosse in 'Inner Cities, *Art Review* 56 (2006): 63.

12 Victor Burgin, "Situational Aesthetics," in Harrison and Wood, *Art in Theory 1900–2000: An Anthology of Changing Ideas*, 894–7. First published in *Studio International* 178, no. 915 (October 1969): 118–21.

13 Burgin, "Situational Aesthetics," in *Art in Theory 1900–2000: An Anthology of Changing Ideas*, 895.

14 Alexander Streitberger, "The Psychotopological Text: Victor Burgin's Writings in Perspective," in *Situational Aesthetics: Selected Writings by Victor Burgin*, ed. Alexander Streitberger (Leuven: Leuven University Press, 2009), xiii–xiv.

15 Robert Irwin, *Being and Circumstance: Notes Toward a Confidential Art* (1985), in Stiles and Selz, *Theories and Documents of Contemporary Art: A Sourcebook of Artist's Writings*, 572.

16 Claire Doherty, "Introduction/Situation," in *Situation* (Cambridge, MA: MIT Press, 2009), 13. What, on one level is striking about Doherty's compendium of texts, all of which are organized around the idea of the book's title, is the marked absence of discussion of painting or indeed by painters.

17 Clement Greenberg, "The Decline of Cubism" (1948), in Greenberg, *The Collected Essays and Criticism,* vol. 2, *Arrogant Purpose, 1945–1949,* 214.

18 Andrew Blauvelt, "No Visible Means of Support," in Douglas Fogle et al., *Painting at the Edge of the World* (Minneapolis: Walker Art Center 2001): 120.

19 Clement Greenberg, "Feeling is All" (1952), in *The Collected Essays and Criticism: Affirmations and Refusals, 1950–1956*, ed. John O' Brian (Chicago: University of Chicago Press, 1986), 104.

20 Blauvelt, "No Visible Means of Support," 120.

21 Dominic Morton, "Richard Wright," in Barry Schwabsky, *Vitamin P* (London: Phaidon: 2002), 340.

22 Arturo Herrera in Roxana Marcoci, *Comic Abstraction: Image-Making, Image-Breaking* (New York: Museum of Modern Art, 2007), 64.

23 Ibid., 14.

24 Ibid., 66.

25 "Franz Ackermann," in *Altermodern Tate Triennial*, ed. Nicolas Bourriaud (London: Tate Publishing, 2009), 42.

26 Ibid. Ackermann's first international trip was to Asia in 1991, during which time he lived in Hong Kong. It was during this stay that the first series of mental maps were produced.

27 Ibid.

28 Douglas Fogle, "The Occidental Tourist," *Parkett* 68 (2003): 23.

29 Ibid., 20.

30 Jordan Kantor, "Drawing from the Modern: After the Endgames," in Glenn D. Lowry et al., *Drawing from the Modern 1975–2005* (New York: Museum of Modern Art, 2005): 48.

31 Nedko Solakov, "Instructions for Realising A Life (Black & White)', 1998–," http://nedkosolakov.net/content/a_life_black__white/index_eng.html.

32 It is in arguably in this respect that the two participants tasked with painting *A Life (Black & White)* characterize what was for Maurice Merleau-Ponty the particular plight of the artist: Writing in "Eye and Mind," Merleau-Ponty noted that: "His quest is total even where it looks partial. Just when he has reached proficiency in some area, he finds that he has reopened another one where everything he said before must be said again in a different way." Maurice Merleau-Ponty, *L'oeil et l'esprit* (1960) trans. in Douglas L. Donkel, *The Theory of Difference: Readings in Contemporary Continental Thought* (Albany: State University of New York, 2001), 111.

33 Marcoci, *Comic Abstraction: Image-Making, Image-Breaking*, 64.

34 Nicolas Bourriaud, *Relational Aesthetics* (Dijon: Les presses du reel, 2002), 113.

35 Manray Hsu, "Painting as a Place—On Michael Lin," in Daniel Birnbaum et al., *Urgent Painting* (Paris: Paris-Musées, 2002), 88.

36 Polly Apfelbaum in Marcoci, *Comic Abstraction: Image-Making, Image-Breaking*, 42.

37 Terry Myers, "Polly Apfelbaum," *Artext* 70 (2000), 86. *Eclipse* was exhibited in the group show "Painting: The Extended Field" Rooseum Center for Contemporary Art, Malmo, in Sweden in 1996.

38 *Today I Love Everybody* (2003) for example, consisted of approximately 7,000 individual asterisk-shaped pieces.

39 Ibid.

40 T. J. Demos, "Polly Apfelbaum," *Artforum* 42, no. 2 (2003): 176.

41 See Lynn Zelevansky, *Sense and Sensibility: Women Artists and Minimalism in the Nineties* (New York: Museum of Modern Art and Harry N. Abrams, 1994).

42 Polly Apfelbaum, "Varieties of Abstraction: A Partial Taxonomy," in *Abstraction*, ed. Andrew Benjamin, *Journal of Philosophy and the Visual Arts* 5 (1995), 12.

43 Richard Serra, "Verb List, 1967–68,"reproduced in Richard Serra, *Richard Serra, interviews, etc., 1970–1980* Written and compiled in collaboration with Clara Weyergraf (New York: The Hudson River Museum, 1980), 10. First published in "The New Avant-Garde, Issues for the Art of the Seventies." Text by Gregoire Müller, New York, 1972.

44 Apfelbaum in Marcoci, *Comic Abstraction: Image-Making, Image-Breaking*, 42.

45 Morgan Falconer, "New Work: Polly Apfelbaum," *Art World* (2009), 88.

46 Miwon Kwon, *One Place after Another: Site-Specific Art and Locational Identity* (Cambridge, MA: MIT Press, 2004): 46.

47 In this sense, Alÿs is representative of a number of artists, as one commentator observes, who are united by the fact that they "do not face painting as a problem to solve or as an obstacle to their inscription in contemporary processes: on the contrary, they pick these processes up in a spontaneous way, the same way that they might, at one point or another, use photography or turn to installation work." Virginia Pérez-Ratton, "The Urgency of Painting: Federico Herrero," in Birnbaum et al., *Urgent Painting*, 112.

48 "Francis Alys" in Fogle, *Painting at the Edge of the World*, 238.

49 Martin Herbert, "The Distance Between: The Political Peregrinations of Francis Alys," *Modern Painters* 19(2)(2007): 89.

50 Ibid, 87–88.

51 Gilles Deleuze and Félix Guattari, *A Thousand Plateaus* (London: Continuum, 2004), 420.

52 Francesca Dubrock, "Erasing the Border is Possible," *Sol de Medianoche*, https://www.soldemedianochenews.org/erasing-the-border.html.

53 "Borrando la Frontera." https://anateresafernandez.com/borrando-la-barda-tijuana-mexico.

54 James Meyer, "The Functional Site, or, The Transformation of Site Specificity" (1995), reproduced in Suderburg, *Space Site Intervention: Situating Installation Art*, 24.

55 Ibid., 25.

56 Ibid., 24.

57 Herbert, "The Distance Between: The Political Peregrinations of Francis Alys," 87.

58 Kitty Scott, Portrait Francis Alÿs, *Parkett* 69 (2003): 21

59 David Batchelor, "In Bed With the Monochrome," in *From an Aesthetic Point of View: Philosophy, Art and the Senses*, ed. Peter Osborne (London: Serpent's Tail, 2000), 173.

60 Jonathan Watkins, "Unbelievers," in Judith Nesbitt, *Days Like These* (London: Tate Publishing, 2003), 10.

8

Imag[in]ing the Digital

There was once a happy time when painted pictures were seen as windows, portrayals on the screen of the camera obscura, or reflected the world like a mirror. Even when the idea of the picture as a mirror was smashed during the Modernist movement, fragments of external reality were still reflected in the shards. With the advent of the digital age, it seems as if those times are definitely over. So what is the status of a painted picture? What can painting still achieve?[1]

It is perhaps because of the rapid proliferation of digital technology over the last two decades that paintings, even if they aren't the result of a computer-generated program, have become increasingly read in relation to those terms. So, for example, as a means of accounting for Takashi Murakami's paintings' apparent lack of handicraft, Anne Bobzin, writing in the exhibition catalogue that accompanied the exhibition *Painting Pictures: Painting and Media in the Digital Age* that was staged at the Kunstmuseum Wolfsburg in 2003, claimed that "the comic-like figures seem to have been generated by a computer, the main means of communication of today's *screen generation*"[2] [original emphasis].

With this in mind, and in lieu of Gijs van Tuyl's statement that begins this chapter and arguably frames it as a whole, the aim of Imag[in]ing the Digital is to explore both painting's negotiation with and utilization of the digital. To this end, along with considering the work of Ingrid Calame, an artist who like Murakami creates paintings whose synthetic appearances are at least characteristic of the modulated topographies of the digital, the chapter will encompass those artists who use the digital either to image painting within the broader field of contemporary practice or, conversely, imagine it.

Beyond the admission that Ingrid Calame "works within the world of technique now defined by software—the digital processing and printing pictures and paintings—like Photoshop, Paintbox, and Illustrator ...," on one level, the artist's paintings should be understood in terms of how they are able to negotiate issues and particular strictures around both the purported mechanization of the image and historical precedent as it is understood in terms of abstraction during the latter half of the twentieth century.[3]

Borrowing, according to one observer, from "the forms and ideas of post-industrial landscapes and high-tech societies," which, in Calame's case are often the aleatory stains and spillages which mark the surfaces of urban space, this information then becomes transcribed into what amounts to a working drawing.[4] The resulting series of silhouettes then forms the basis for the subsequent painting. Once the "found" forms have been traced out onto either a sheet of Mylar or an aluminum panel, Calame proceeds to paint in the various shapes using gloss paint.

The provenance of *Step on a Crack, Break Your Mother's Back* (2009) (Plate 13) was from when Calame was the Albright-Knox's artist-in-residence in 2008. Working as part of a team, numerous drawings were made of certain locations in and around Buffalo, New York. *Step on a Crack, Break Your Mother's Back*, one of the paintings that was produced as a result of this residency is comprised of a lattice-like design consisting of five layers of overlapping color, ranging from the largest and what is the layer closest to the picture plane executed in pink through to a pale violet that ostensibly functions as the painting's ground. Whilst the title, a reference to the childhood game of not stepping on cracks so as to avoid misfortune alludes to the literal basis of Calame's imagery, it is also suggestive of the way in which, in an embodied sense, we all negotiate urban space.

Beyond the ostensible meanings bound up with this work, Calame's paintings function not as topographies of the digital realm, but rather as topographies of the various incidents that have marked social space. However, although the imagery alludes to the impressionistic, the fleeting and the unintended, Calame's project is characterized by a de-subjectivized, mechanized and systematic delimitation of form.

Several commentators have attempted to conflate what she does with certain precedents that go to make up the history, if not the historiography of modernist artistic practice and in particular how it worked to position a particular account of painting. According to one observer,

> Calame's strategy weaves together key chapters of twentieth-century art. Their amorphous found forms plumb the unconscious and recall the early Surrealists' use of frottage and automatic writing. Most images come from random, probably accidental spills, an incorporation of chance as a compositional strategy that traces an important lineage from Hans Arp and Marcel Duchamp, through Abstract Expressionism, to John Cage and Robert Rauschenberg.[5]

Indeed, the comparison with Abstract Expressionism, which presumably we take to mean Jackson Pollock is given, or at least alluded to partly by way of the fact that like Pollock *ca.* 1947–1950, Calame's enterprise also entails working on a horizontal support. Equally, in addition to the artist's modus operandi, the method by which some of her earlier paintings were presented was such that they would hang down from the wall plane and spill out, into and over the floor.

Furthermore, this affinity also arguably extends to encompass the fact that both are somehow reliant upon the indexical mark for their effect. In Pollock's case, the marks themselves have been read as indexical deposits or traces, vestigial remains of the artist's movements as he oriented himself around the horizontally positioned sections of canvas. Early readings would see Pollock's painterly deposits as evidence of both a certain existential angst and emotional catharsis. Latter, post-structuralist readings would read the self-same indexicality in terms of how it structures and is given over to a "difference" that speaks of a schism within the artwork's temporality. However, in the case of Calame's paintings, whilst visually they are often equally elaborate, they remain resistant to an overtly psychological reading. This is no doubt in part due to the fact that, in effect, Calame traces traces. Such a tautology brings with it a certain critical distance that works against the psychology of the maker somehow becoming imbricated within the paintings. As a result of tracing traces, it is arguably this somewhat depersonalized approach that allows decisions around the formal content of the work and which traditionally would have fallen squarely at the feet of the artist to be, to a certain extent, already given.

However, whilst Calame appears to eschew the personal with regards to her choice of subject matter and working methods, and, moreover, whilst the resulting translation of her topographies appear mechanized, programmatic, technical if not technological, they have been arrived at entirely by way of the artist's hand. As Whitney Davis notes:

> One could do this entirely on a computer—the painting analogizes a possible, if possibly mad, print out—if it were not for the fact, of course, that one *cannot* do it entirely on a computer. Printing in non-computational media hovers nearby: the painting analogizes color lithography or silkscreen as if routed through a disjunctive printer—perhaps a printer that wants to be a painter or a painter who actually is a computer.[6]

Returning to the question posed by van Tuyl and, moreover, notwithstanding the affinities Calame's paintings have with notions of the "digital," there would appear to be at least two possible means by which painting has attempted to open itself up to and, moreover, dialectically engage with the current proliferation of digitally based technologies. Firstly, there are those painters who use digital technology as an instrument by which imagery can be generated. As Amy Cappellazzo notes, writing in "Glee: Painting Now or My Obsession with NASA and Why I think Abstract Painting in the Digital Age Can Help Us Believe in the Future," the catalogue essay that accompanied the exhibition *Glee: Painting Now* exhibition that was staged at The Aldrich Museum of Contemporary Art in Connecticut in 2000: "Abstract painting has opened up its big heart and decided to embrace the digital as a tool, or in family parlance, as a younger sibling (also a tool), able to assist painting in whatever it needed."[7]

For example, and as in the case of Shahzia Sikander, this is arguably true. Sikander has claimed that the digital process is "yet another way for me to explore both formal and subjective issues …"[8] Indeed, one could say that one salient strand or aspect of painting today is the proliferation of artists who use digital technology as a means of generating imagery.[9]

This would be seen in contrast to the second impulse notable within recent painting wherein *ideas* of the digital and a related set of thematics this heralds (which may or may not encompass the artist working directly with digital technology) are bound up with the work's meaning. It is in this sense that we may say that the painting engages in a dialectic with digital media, testing out its claims and exploring both its limitations and its possibilities, even if these are creatively reimagined, in the process. To this end, this second impulse is as much about painting *imagining* as imaging the digital and its attendant processes, contexts and consequences.

As we shall see, for those artists who we might associate with the second understanding, digital code plays an instrumental role. Moreover, unlike the various materialities that attend to painting, as Lane Relyea reminds us, the "operations of a computer … replace the presence of materials with pattern recognition, with code transactions and magnetic polarity switchings that transpire in no time and without regard to distance. They have no visual qualities, no physicality to stage, and no temporality to narrate."[10] The issue then becomes organized around a question of how a painting's physicality might now become ostensibly staged.

Whilst this question perhaps remains most pertinent for those artists who utilize computer code and, as we shall see, eschew the traditional means of a painting's production, arguably the question remains applicable across all of the artists whose respective practices will be considered within this chapter. Indeed, given the fact that interwoven within this study's enquiry has been a question concerning the extent to which Greenberg's claims with regards to painting still continues to inform both its production and reception, it would appear highly apposite to see how the physicality of painting, an idée fixe of Greenbergian aesthetics, continues to be staged approximately half a century later.

One's first impression of Monique Prieto's large-scale canvases that the Los Angeles-based artist made during the latter half of the 1990s is of a certain indebtedness to those painters who emerged directly out of Abstract Expressionism. With their organic, often bulbous forms that seep over and across the surface of the canvas, the connections between these paintings and those of, for example Morris Louis, Helen Frankenthaler and Jules Olitski appear, to a certain extent, self-evident.

Notwithstanding their mutual preoccupation with color, albeit color as Robin Marriner points out whose key is somewhat more pronounced in the work of Prieto, there is much to suggest that the artist's concerns are those of the modernist painter.[11] For not only do they appear to use color non-figuratively, these abstract works are equally foregrounded by their apparent autonomy from the world of recognizable appearances and by their particular fascination with the material effects of painting. Arguably then, they are "modernist" in the way a painting by Frankenthaler is "modernist" because one can perceive an orientation towards those characteristics, formally at least, that were considered to be intrinsic to the medium of painting.[12]

However, the possibility for, as it were, a quid pro quo understanding between the approach, the means adopted by Frankenthaler and an equivalent from of agency that generates Prieto's paintings becomes eschewed when we bring to our discussion the role taken up by gesture and the place within her work that it occupies.

Whilst the canvases of those artists who collectively fell under Greenberg's rubric of "post-painterly abstractionists" still saw the possibility that their actions could be imputed in terms that were direct, unsullied by the various contexts, both social and cultural within which their pourings, their stainings and their sprayings sought to keep at arm's length, "gesture" in the work of Prieto remains indirect, mediated and to a certain extent equivocal. As Marriner claims: "Though in their origins these works embody a degree of gesture (for all their spontaneity and chance), what we actually see in them is a highly mediated version of such a concept."[13] The origins to which Marriner alludes are digital to the extent wherein the provenance for Prieto's paintings during the period under question begin by her drawing onto a computer tablet using the "Painter 3" software.

Prieto began using the computer as a means of expediency shortly after the birth of her first child in 1994. As she recounted in an interview in 2000: "I was grumbling about this [about having less time to make work] and my husband, Michael Webster, said, 'Draw on the computer while you're nursing, at least you've got your thoughts and you can work without them slipping away before you get a chance to duck into the studio.' So I got a stylus and a pad and it was really fun."[14]

As it is then, the operative conditions of Prieto's paintings are such that they render visible in a very particular way the interfacing between the agency of the artist's body, in this case in the form of a stylus or finger the artist uses to "draw" with and a digitized pad. What emerges are a series of visual ciphers that present digitized, and to a certain extent schematic representations of these "drawings." These are then printed off and used as the basis for the painting's subsequent design.

In the case of *High Rolling* (1998) a total of nine, mostly vertical forms are arranged across the surface of the canvas. Whilst each shape is somewhat different and, moreover, their visual contrasts are further emphasized by the

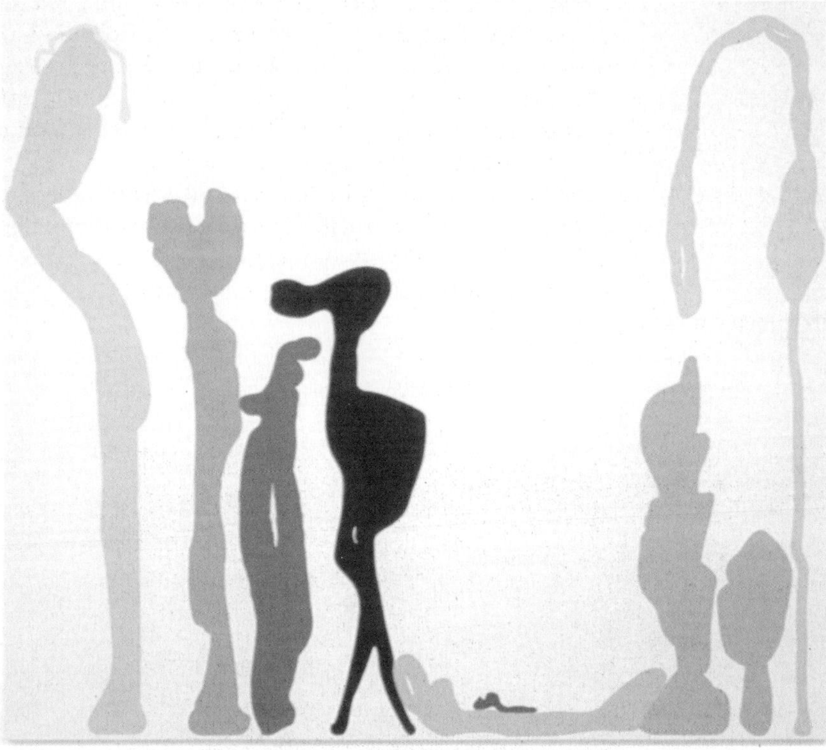

FIGURE 8.1 Monique Prieto, *High Rolling*, 1998.

artist's decision to paint each shape using a different color, collectively they come to be read as Giorgio Morandi's paintings of various pots, jars and other vessels do, that is anthropomorphically as individual members of a family. Moreover, and arguably this reading is given most explicitly with the black vertical shape positioned towards the center of the painting which along with a head, neck and two legs, appears to have a somewhat distended belly. Whilst Prieto initially used a computer for reasons of expediency, her relationship with it developed, and she found that she was able to harness and exploit the particular characteristics it produced:

> In the beginning, using the computer was more like using a pencil or pastel—it was a timesaving device. But over the years I've changed the way that I use the computer. I still use it like a tool, but differently from what we're used to imagining as a tool—it's more like the way a new kind of paint might affect the way you paint, or a new saw the way you cut. It's had an effect on the way I draw.[15]

Earlier in this chapter a claim was made that conveyed the impression that there was a clear distinction between those artists who use digital technology simply as a tool as opposed to those artists who dialectically engage with its processes and the visual effects it educes. However, certainly in the case of Prieto, her utilization of the computer lies somewhere between the two understandings. That is, whilst she never seeks to entirely dissimulate the fact that this imagery is derived from a software program, she equally doesn't intend the paintings to be read solely in terms of what could erroneously be construed as a "digital aesthetic" or indeed, a critique thereof. Instead, the somewhat gauche appearance of her painted forms, whilst they are suggestive of a particular set of technical limitations that the "drawn" mark carries if it is mediated electronically via her choice of software, the resulting forms engage in and with a range of other, albeit oblique meanings and resonances.

FIGURE 8.2 Wade Guyton, *Untitled*, 2007.

Another artist who uses the available digital technology as a means of expediency, but for arguably different reasons is Wade Guyton.

Having made a series of what were somewhat drolly called "drawings" by using an inkjet printer to print either the letter "X" or the letter "U" onto pages taken from catalogues—pages that included imagery derived from the echelons of twentieth-century art, Guyton then went on to apply this depersonalized method of production to develop a series of paintings. Printed on unprimed sections of linen, Guyton's first printed paintings were shown at the Kunstverein in Hamburg in an exhibition entitled *Formalism, Modern Art, Today* in 2004. From having printed directly onto unprimed sections of canvas that when presented in situ were unstretched, as in the case of the artist's contribution for the Kunstverein, Guyton then went on to use pre-primed sections of canvas consisting of a lead white ground as his substrate, a surface that is arguably more receptive to the ink that has been applied directly onto it. This was followed by the decision to fold the support longitudinally down the middle so that the forty-four inch width of the folded section of canvas matched the width of the Epson large-format printer that he was using. Upon which, amongst other things, Guyton printed a black rectangle that he had rendered on his computer using Photoshop. By adopting this method of working, the resulting image produces a vertical line or, to borrow the Abstract Expressionist Barnett Newman's terminology, a "zip," that bisects the two sections and denotes at least a starting point by which the artwork's somewhat unorthodox process of manufacture can be gleaned.

Despite the somewhat deadpan nature of the technique, Guyton manages to elicit from the subsequent mechanized imagery a range of tones, inflections and incidental detail that works against, or at least qualifies their manufactured and depersonalized execution. Subtle variations occur, sometimes by accident, for example when the printer misregisters, and sometimes by design, as in when Guyton deliberately intervenes during the printing process. Indeed, such technical infelicities on one level are arguably evident of the artist's unwillingness to fetishize the digital media he has chosen to work with. As Rothkopf observes, "Guyton's growing investigation of the digital realm and its relationship to our physical one constitutes one of the key fascinations of his recent paintings. Here, it should be said, however, that he has scarcely more mastery of Photoshop than oil painting, and his work shares none of the technophilia evident in so much contemporary art."[16]

In spite of the work's ostensible affinities with certain late or so-called "high" modernist painters such as Frank Stella and their proclivity to be "allocated a place in the history of abstract painting," it is perhaps important to point out that Guyton didn't emerge out of this historical context because modernism, or at least the period wherein the formalist account of modernism was given by Greenberg, remains historically remote.[17] It is perhaps for this reason that certain commentators have attempted to position Guyton's practice instead within the context of the 1980s and the various appropriationist strategies that that period has become identified, if not virtually synonymous with. As Vincent Pecoil has noted, Guyton "is one of the first and most important artists of his generation to have been formed through the postmodern practice of appropriation and for whom abstraction has always existed, above all, as a reproduced image."[18] However, their affinities with late modernist practice remain persistent, and it is perhaps for this reason that Guyton's practice, as one commentator has observed, works to "*make* something of this contested heritage, something that doesn't feel reactionary but right now."[19] And the "now" for Guyton, is of "an everyday screen culture of scanners and scroll bars, layered windows that slip in and out of view, thresholds of information that only reveal themselves when the jpeg loses focus, the printer falters, or the *X* gets a jagged edge."[20]

FIGURE 8.3 Cheyney Thompson, *Chromachrome 7 (5GY/5P) portrait*, 2009.

An interesting counterpoint to Guyton's utilization of the digital can be seen in the Chromachrome paintings of Cheyney Thompson. Certainly, both artists adopt Pop Art's proclivity to adopt banal or deadpan imagery. The visual basis for Thompson's paintings derives from an enlarged digital scan of the warp and weft of the canvas that comprises the painting's support. However, unlike Guyton who decentres authorial presence to the extent wherein a machine, in effect, executes the work for him, Thompson's paintings, like Calame's, steadfastly remain the product of the artist's hand. Whilst the work's ostensibly abstract appearance (ostensible because on one level they are representational to the extent wherein the information that has been painted faithfully, in one sense at least, pictures the appearance of *something*), almost automatically becomes conflated with the tradition of the monochrome, albeit one that is framed according to one commentator with "a surfeit of interference—of noise ..." It is perhaps the iteratively circular nature of these paintings—the digital images, that is, that reproduces the physical grain of the painting's surface, which is painted onto the painting's surface, which then relates back to an intrinsic element of that painting, that conceives the object as some form of self-regulating system that in turn harks back to Greenberg's autonomizing decrees.[21] However, this reading would be perhaps somewhat disingenuous due to the fact that the painting's "noise" seems characteristic of Peter Wieber's idea of "fuzzy logic, that is, the logic of many values, [that replaces] a binary logic. Instead of yes and no decisions you confront several layers, different levels and blurred borderlines, insinuating twilight zones between figure and ground, between layers of paint and painted form, between from and inform, between Gestalt and code."[22]

On one level, the paintings of Prieto, Guyton and Thompson consist of using digital technology as an imaging device. Whilst this is one particular strategy that certain artists have adopted, as was noted in the introduction to this chapter, other artists use the digital as a way of imagining as well as imaging painting.

In this respect, an instructive counterpoint to Prieto, Guyton and Thompson's ambitions for painting are the LCD panels produced by the artist John F. Simon Jr., some of which utilize the digital as the means by which a moment that pertains to painting's history can be reimagined.

Arguably the starting point for these panels was a piece the artist made in 1997. *Every Icon* consisted of a grid that was thirty-two squares long and thirty-two squares wide. Each square or "element" of the grid constantly switched between two antithetical states, that is, they were either "light" or they were "dark." As Michael Rush points out:

> The top line has 4.3 billion variations, which would take sixteen months to display on a continuously operating computer. The second line would take six billion years, and so on. Looking on screen like a kinetic Josef Albers or Agnes Martin, Simon's "art game," in which he invites the viewer

> to watch the grid as it lightens and darkens, can never be completed, but it goes far towards visualizing a notion of infinity.[23]

As an artwork that is essentially "live" and constantly in a state of flux, relaying an infinite range or configuration of permutations that stem from a more straightforward premise, *Every Icon* can be seen as the precursor to Simon Jr.'s subsequent panel pieces.

As with the paintings of Prieto, the provenance for this series was the act of drawing, wherein, as the artist has stated: "I would try to detach myself enough to observe my process, noticing the unspoken rules I was making as I was working. Then, if I could distill some of that I would put it into code."[24]

Produced between 1998 and 2004, these "art appliances," like *Every Icon* that had preceded it were time-based and sought to dynamically engage with a particular idea or, in the case of *Color Panel v1.0* (1999), art historical context. According to the artist, this particular piece was influenced by the Bauhaus movement, and "interprets color 'rules' into software. The software iterates through color possibilities explored in theories proposed by Bauhaus artists including Klee and Kandinsky. The activation of these studies results in a dynamic composition of changing color pallets that never repeat."[25]

ComplexCity, a panel made a year later appears to restage the abstract artist Piet Mondrian's own fascination with the gridded streets and avenues that organize and work to rationalize the city's urban topography. And, like Mondrian's own *Broadway Boogie Woogie*, there is an autobiographical dimension to this piece: "ComplexCity is concerned with the realism of abstraction. A modern day cityscape, including skylines, skyscrapers, and a traffic flow reminiscent of Mondrian's Broadway Boogie Woogie, *ComplexCity* explores the pure abstraction of Mondrian and the abstract realism of Stuart Davis. One of my more autobiographical works, ComplexCity documents my relationship to New York City."[26]

Along with references to the Bauhaus and Mondrian, the artist has spoken of the work's indebtedness to the ideas of the artist Paul Klee: "Klee was embracing dynamism with his use of arrows and lines, but he had no dynamic medium to use … So, I thought, let's take what he's done, try to activate it, and see where it takes us."[27]

Whilst Simon Jr.'s panels are not paintings in what arguably is the received sense of the term's meaning, nevertheless, and in the case of *Color Panel v1.0* at least, the work dialectically engages with painting, and specifically particular ambitions that marked the project of abstract painting at certain points during the twentieth century. Like the canvases of both Prieto and Guyton, Simon Jr.'s panels reference particular instances or moments of modernist or "modern" painting. Moreover, their presentation is somewhat akin to that of painting; they are wall-mounted objects that occupy a comparable viewing space to that which painting has traditionally inhabited. And what is more, and as Cathryn Drake has observed, one interesting paradox with these works is like their analogue counterparts, they are dependent upon first-hand observation to the extent that the "computer screens are contemplated as discrete objects with quirky behaviors, never again repeated ..."[28]

What Drake's observation attests to is the fact that whilst the artist's panels derive from his drawings, the ideas that become manifest as a result get implemented in code.[29] The idea of an underlying code, which forms the ontological basis for most, if not all software programs, operating systems and platforms, is something that certain painters appear to be not only aware of, but also keen to exploit.

For Lev Manovich, there are two fundamental properties or levels that constitute the computer-based image and thus also go to make up what he calls its material status. Firstly, there is a "surface appearance." Secondly, there is an underlying code "which may be the pixel values, a mathematical function, or HTML language."[30] The implications of which, for Manovich at least, is that as the "distribution of all forms of culture becomes computer-based, we are increasingly 'interfacing' to predominantly cultural data—texts, photographs, films, music, virtual environments. In short, we are no longer interfacing to a computer but to a culture encoded in digital form."[31] Indeed, following Manovich's claim that whilst an "image participates in dialog with other cultural objects," hence the claim that they are ostensibly like the late canvases of Mondrian, "in terms of its code, an image exists on the same conceptual plane as other computer objects."[32]

What a work such as *ComplexCity* instantiates is a particular bifurcation between the "surface appearance" and a coded substratum that acts as the driver for what the audience is ultimately privy to. In this sense, Simon Jr.'s panels echo the artist Bill Viola's own observation wherein we are

> leaving the world of optics and visually derived images and arriving at the threshold of a new world that is based on codes and hidden informational substructures. Here the image is literally the top of an iceberg, a temporary surface manifestation of an underlying reality of invisible strata and branching root systems, webs of relationships and histories that we, as social beings, are immersed in but have never been able to represent or model before.[33]

Interestingly, a process, even arguably a thematics whereby the instrumentalization of painting occurs through what it exposes, what it renders visible as much as what it chooses to dissemble echoes both Russian formalism's principle of baring the device and Greenberg's own claims with respect to modernist painting wherein properties such as the flat surface and shape of the support "were acknowledged openly."[34]

Utilizing the material components of a recycled laptop computer with a display housing fabricated from acrylic and a cable extending outwards from the piece, a work such as *Color Panel v1.0* arguably reflects modernism's fixation upon the material identity of the artwork, recasting it within a digital rather than an analogue context.[35] Indeed, as Anna Munster claims: "Modernism is, above all, a mode of calling attention to the conditions and limitations of a medium in order to produce from these something positively different out of the nature of the medium itself. The concentration on technology per se, whether it features as part of the content, the development of a kind of digital style or the emphasis upon computational processes, thus draws the 'cutting-edge' digital artwork back within the modernist tradition."[36]

If the concentration upon technology that occurs within Simon Jr.'s panels can be read in terms of the possibilities offered by digital, algorithmic code, both visually and conceptually, then Tim Head's *Treacherous Light* (2002) presents a comparable set of possibilities that are presented not by computer code per se, but by the basic digital building block, the pixel. To this end, and as Ben Tufnell notes: "Treacherous Light 2002 is a projection in which each pixel of the computer screen has been enlarged to become a distinct visual element."[37]

However, whilst Simon Jr.'s panels are foregrounded by their application of code, whereas Head's isolates the computer screen's pixels, generating a seemingly random, non-hierarchical and constantly evolving series of configurations derived from a palette of over 16,000,000 colors, *Treacherous Light* is organized around an enquiry that seeks to consider, if not establish how the materiality of the digital is given and can be understood. As the artist has noted:

> The work explores certain factors of electronic space, specifically the digital space generated on screen by a computer program. It attempts to isolate some of the intrinsic properties of this electronic space stripping it down to certain prime elements to a carry a raw skeletal message. Attention is focused upon the peculiar and unique physical properties of the digital medium itself and specifically on the computer-generated array of light-emitting pixels that form the elusive fabric of the screen's surface.[38]

According to one observer, writing in the catalogue that accompanied the Tate Triennial in London in 2003, the experiential basis of *Treacherous Light* is, to a certain extent contingent upon the viewer's proximity to the piece. Accordingly:

> Close up, the process is clearly visible and the sensation of movement is strong. At a few meters distance the image becomes a swarming amorphous mass. Areas of color and density coalesce and disperse before it is possible to fix our attention on them. From further back it is a pale grey, still rectangle of light. One is reminded of the pointillist paintings of Georges Seurat, or the densely marked spaces of Mark Tobey or Jackson Pollock.[39]

Though to a certain extent historically remote, on one level this latter observation is comparable to Kasha Linville's description of the paintings of Agnes Martin; certainly both readings confer on the artworks under discussion a separate set of visual effects that are dependent upon the viewer's physical proximity to the work.

Close up, according to Linville's close formal analysis, Martin's "line respects the canvas grain, skimming its surface without filling low places in the fabric so it becomes almost a dotted or broken line at close range. Sometimes she uses pairs of lines that dematerialize as rapidly as the lighter drawn single ones."[40] Further away, "the pairs become single, gray horizontals and then begin to disappear."[41] Moreover, and as this latter observation suggests, both texts are characterized by an observation that entails a degree of visual dissolution. Linville, by way of concluding her discussion with regards to the phenomenological viewing conditions, conditions that nevertheless remain keyed into the material specificity of, in this case Martin's painting of 1967 entitled *Tundra* (1967), provides the viewer with this attentive reading:

> The lines that divide it are dominant at close range, but something very peculiar happens as you move back from this canvas. Because the horizontally brushed, grayish wash on the surface stops near but not against the lines, they seem to have halos around them. These halos actually swallow the lines at middle distance, leaving only their white ghosts. Even the ghosts disappear eventually.[42]

Whilst an artist like Head has attempted to utilize the basic digital building block, namely the pixel, within a set of terms that are dynamic, unfolding and seemingly infinite, situating a visual language in the process that is at least analogous to certain characteristics associated with painting in the process, for example, viewing distance, picture plane and visual field, Dan Hays' *Colorado Paintings* utilizes the pixel finitely, as a means by which a more straightforwardly pictorial vocabulary can be constructed, exposing in the process the pixel's infidelities.

Following the result of an internet search in 1999, Hays discovered his namesake living in Colorado in the United States. Moreover, Hays' American doppelganger had a somewhat homespun website, "Dan's Place," which contained photographs of the surrounding Rocky Mountain area. From a technical standpoint, many of the photographs that had been uploaded were not entirely legible due to having become somewhat pixelated.[43]

Working from computer printouts of the photographs, Hays initially attempted to faithfully reproduce the visual information, that is, a pixelated photograph of a landscape that had been gleaned from his namesake's website. However, for the seventh painting in this series *Colorado Impression 7*, as Hays states, "a slight kink in the grid substrate behind the picture was introduced as a way of subverting it. Then subsequently with

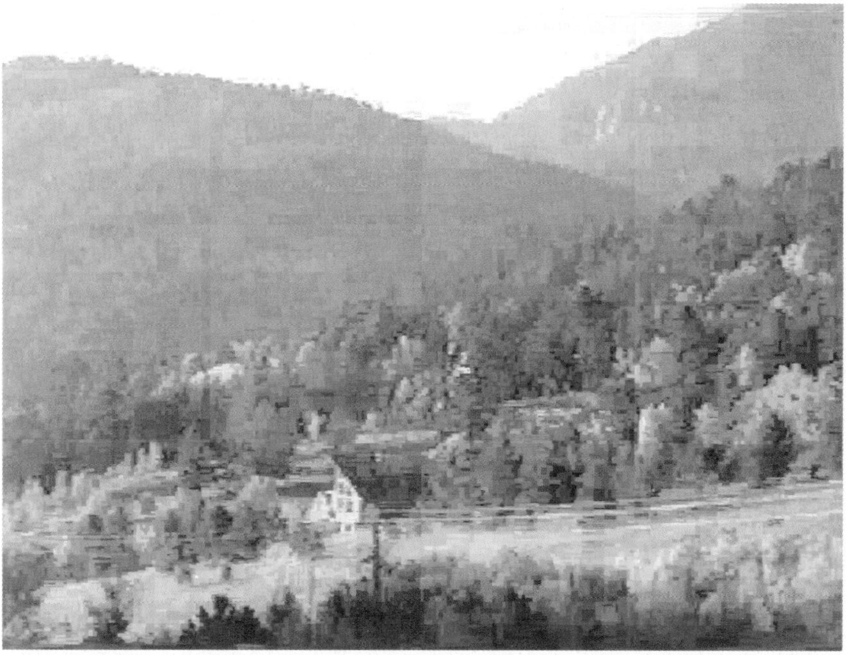

FIGURE 8.4 Dan Hays, *Colorado Impression 5 (After Dan Hays, Colorado)*, 2000.

each painting there was a different formal device, be it in terms of color or painting technique."[44]

Whilst Hays engages with the vicissitudes of what today constitutes a democratized form of image-based technology, the work clearly references, and indeed becomes analogous with the atomization of painting that Impressionism and post-Impressionism mobilized during the latter half of the nineteenth century and that became perhaps became most explicit in the work of the so-called "pointiliists." According to the artist:

> I see an association between digital images and Impressionist painting. They are both anti-iconic; a computer gives every pixel an equal value, which equates closely to the Impressionist approach to depicting a scene where a hierarchy of forms is dispensed with. Also, image compression programs, like Jpeg, serve to reduce the file size of images, speeding up download times, equivalent to the impressionist's restricted palette, used to capture the essence of a scene as quickly as possible.[45]

Of course, as Seitter reminds us, digital also means "*discrete* or *discontinuous*: every number that appears prevents another number from appearing. Similarly, *analog* means: reflecting the continuously variable transition of measured reality in an equally variable way."[46] Whereas we could say Paul Cézanne aimed for the latter but the "pixellated" canvases he produced towards the end of his life were themselves somehow in concert with the first understanding, Hays adopts a form of visuality the digital has become associated, if not directly synonymous with but the paintings approximate the "transition of measured reality." Only the transition of which it speaks is that of the relay of encoded information, in this case involving a series of amateur photographs and a reality measured in pixels. It is in this sense then that Hays' pictorial effects become analogous to the mosaic, a picture technique that, according to Seitter, "has always resisted the desire for the perfect, smooth, seamless connection; and has clearly stood up for and demonstratively displayed the inevitably digital quality of painting."[47]

There is also perhaps a degree of inevitability to the fact that certain artists have chosen to exploit the affinities between the computer screen and a medium that, even today, remains largely wall based. To this end, and as has already been claimed, the categorical positioning of John F. Simon Jr.'s digital panels as painting and, moreover, as abstract paintings, is partly enabled through the means by which they are displayed. Whilst this is arguably the most straightforward way in which the affinity between the computer screen and painting might be construed, other artists have adopted a more conceptual approach, opening up a very different set of possibilities in terms of how painting is given in the process. Hays, for his part has claimed that "Digital images are immaterial and exist in their pure form on a phosphorescent screen. Their rendering in oil paint reveals what is essential to paint: its magical property of representing light. This is hopefully achieved without the distraction of a painting genius getting in the way."[48]

In many respects, the digital screen works to conflate seemingly antithetical ontological categories. Whilst on the one hand it is quite evidently a material object (for now at least), what it proffers is a dense network of data that is inherently immaterial. Equally, whilst devices are reliant upon a real-time, physical interaction by their users, behind the screen's synthetic glow is an endless stream of information which, metonymically, denotes the atemporal and with the advance of quantum computing, the infinite.

What's more, as Lane Relyea points out: "The space of the monitor is neither physical nor illusionistic, neither like a body nor an envelope; it's instead an interstitial space, always between, relaying input and feedback, command and performance, facilitating the call and response of communication."[49]

Since the Renaissance, western painting has been construed as a window through which a likeness of the outward appearance of things could be fashioned. In so doing, the analogy worked to dissemble or disregard the fact that any pictorial likeness afforded was given directly through the physical attributes of the medium. Today, the question that Alex Bacon identifies between what is on the one hand painting-as-object and on the other painting-as-image is played out in practices and debates, which arise out of a creative tension between the physically bounded nature of painting and the virtual status of the digital screen.[50] One such practice which examines the possibilities afforded by this tension is that of Amy Sillman (Plate 14).

Emerging out of the context of post-war American abstraction where, as she recounts, she was "taught by old Ab-Ex guys," Sillman has spent the last four decades exploring the possibilities afforded by an aggregative strategy which both deconstructs and reimagines genre, approach and tradition.[51] In addition to which and using iPhone and iPad apps, she has also made a series of digital animations.

Discussing her single-screen digital video animation *Thirteen Possible Futures: Cartoon for a Painting* (2012) which uses an iPad drawing application, the animation, according to the artist, "takes up where the painting leaves off, the layer of the painting that you see is the beginning of the animation and therefore the animation is a new future. It is of importance to me that people understand the animation as a set of proposals for the future of the painting, as well as a way to reveal its past."[52]

As this statement attests, directly related to *Thirteen Possible Futures: Cartoon for a Painting* is her painting *Duel* (2012) in respect of the fact that her digital animation suggests the various compositional possibilities of the painting. Indeed, this painting has previously been displayed alongside an iPad showing *Thirteen Possible Futures: Cartoon for a Painting.*[53]

In Sillman's practice, the understanding of painting as a time-based medium in respect of the fact that it holds the time of its making becomes imbricated with how time is held, as it were, by the technologies that her practice incorporates:

> It was very productive to have access to a time-based medium because all of a sudden I could keep a layer, add to it, or make a new one. You can approach a painting with a big fat dripping paintbrush thinking, if I put a thin sheet of white over everything, it might not work. You have to be willing to ruin things to see if you can push them forward. Often they can't be pushed forward, because paintings are like that. They're like mules; they're old nags. Whereas with animation you can go backward, you can go forward, and you can press the reverse button. It's a whole different machine.[54]

Whilst such reversibility affords Sillman an opportunity to deconstruct the act of painting so that each image functions, as it were, as a digital pentimento, the juxtaposition of iPad and canvas works to "undercut the idea of the painting as a finished entity."[55] As such, and as Tony Godfrey contends, "the juxtaposition also destabilizes the authority of the screen and, with it, the credibility of the promises that screens seem to offer: to make life more efficient, to allow us to communicate better, and so on … Like the surface of the painting, already thickened with past ideas, the iPad animation keeps on going, refusing conclusions."[56]

By remaining mobile, Sillman's incorporation of animation works to refute the digital's purportedly failsafe outcomes. For the artist Christopher Wool, this lack of fixity is given not through the aesthetic pliability of digital animation, but through the equivocal nature of the visual information contained within the painting's surface. Although arguably more complex, Wool's working methods, like Sillman's, are process-driven.

Emerging out of the legacy of the Pictures Generation, although not sharing their rejection of painting, Wool's work made using a pattern paint roller during the mid-1980s had a shared interest in the vicissitudes of reproduction, a concern that has remained a consistent aspect of his practice.[57]

Towards the latter half of the decade, he began to incorporate stenciled text, either in the form of ambiguous, often terse statements or single words that spanned the entirety of what were often large-scaled canvases. Whilst the stenciled letter presented a relatively early instance of Wool attempting to relate "to the changing state of reproduction," the incorporation of other silkscreened images derived from previous works by the artist into his paintings during the mid-1990s presented a different means by which the mechanical could become inscribed.[58] According to the artist:

> I use silkscreen like a brush. It's just something between my hand and the painting. I do the screening myself and it seems like a very mechanical process. We know from early Warhol that there is an expressive way of working the silk-screen, so I have some control when I'm making the painting—density, focus, all kinds of things. To me, it's one of those kinds of process that you can see, like dripping in the painting, you can see it, you can feel that it is handmade.[59]

It was during this period that Wool began work on the gray paintings, a body of work that emerged out of what was an impasse for the artist. Using a turpentine-soaked rag, he erased a section of his painting. The resulting alteration achieved though Wool's use of turpentine, together with silkscreen "became part of Wool's analog process," a process that ran alongside the digital manipulation of the imagery.[60] In so doing, and as Godfrey notes, "It is hard to know ... what the sequence of these moves has been, or which have repeated ..."[61] Part of this uncertainty is due to the fact that Wool's paintings are often an admixture of techniques, some the direct result of the artist's hand whilst others deriving from a digitally or photo-mechanically manipulated source. This, together with the fact that the information the painting carries and which the viewer receives has an attenuated relationship to its source means that as paintings they remain inherently equivocal statements.

Beyond the more evident connections that the work of Prieto, Simon Jr. and Hays works have with regards to issues around the conditions of possibility for painting to dialectically engage with and for that matter

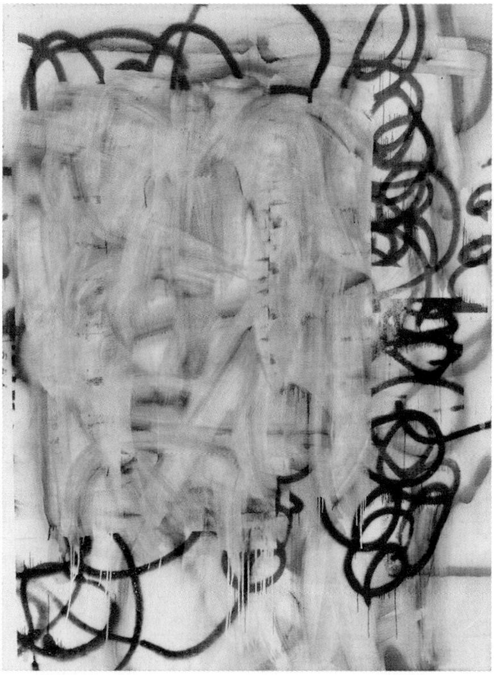

FIGURE 8.5 Christopher Wool, *Untitled*, 2002.

visually imagine realities that are virtual, mediated and digitized, what differentiates the work of all three artists is the distinct types of translation that occurs and that the work, on one level, is premised upon.

For Prieto, artistic agency becomes siphoned through a software program that delimits and, to a certain extent, essentializes her actions into a series of indeterminate, yet nonetheless intriguing visual forms. For Simon Jr., algorithmic code becomes translated into a series of ever-shifting patterns and forms that become played out within the delimited space of an LCD panel. And with Hays, the vicissitudes as much as the ubiquity of the jpeg, in this case derived from a low-res image uploaded onto a website becomes converted into the actual realm of oil paint applied to a canvas support.

The situation outlined above arguably moves beyond Suzanné Page's description in her Foreword to the catalogue that accompanied the exhibition *Urgent Painting* in 2002 wherein the work that was selected remained resistant to "the invasion of those new media that, even so, evidently color their outlooks and sensibilities."[62] If anything, the paintings by Prieto, et al., represent a greater willingness to acquiesce to such an invasion, arguably because this is undertaken with the understanding that the status of the work is not reducible to that of "digital painting." It is in this sense that whilst painting appears willing to adapt to the digital milieu within which it now finds itself, such an adaptation is not undertaken in order to either appease one set of cultural conditions, that is, painting, for another that appears to be all encompassing and rapidly encroaching, in this case, and within this historical moment, the digital. Rather, and beyond the claims that have been made with respect to works that have been marshalled within the context of this chapter, painting's cognizance of itself against that which is other to it has consistently marked the project of painting, certainly from *ca.* 1960 onwards. Indeed, rather than merely being susceptible to other cultural forms, interpretive frameworks and counter strategies, painting, as has now been educed, has always remained resistant to any straightforward form of assimilation within what remained outside of it. For this reason, Caroline A. Jones's statement, written in the same exhibition catalogue remains apposite for the study as a whole:

> Despite its multiple death certificates then, painting refuses to stay buried. However, it must now engage in the same hybridization and "morphing" that confronts the human, adopting technologies and prostheses that were, in the days of high modernism's "purity" and "truth to medium," considered anathema. Rather than "painting" as that stable modernist entity of "colored mud on a flat surface," we must think of hybrid art forms that occupy the cultural space painting once filled. That cultural space may today be occupied by a billboard, by web-based streaming video, or by genetically-altered light sensitive bioorganisms that transfer images to a plane surface. The space of "painting" is only vestigially *that* – it is instead an appetite, a site, a locus of visual power we allocate to cultural forms.[63]

Notes

1 Gijs van Tuyl, "Prologue," in Gijs van Tuyl et al., *Painting Pictures: Painting and Media in the Digital Age* (Kunst Museum: Kerber Verlag, 2003), 8.

2 Anne Bobzin, "Takashi Murakami," in ibid., 211.

3 Whitney Davis, "How to Make Analogies in a Digital Age," *October* 117 (2006), 87.

4 Amy Cappellazzo, *Glee: Painting Now* (Ridgefield, CT: Aldrich Museum of Contemporary Art; Palm Beach, FL: Palm Beach Institute of Contemporary Art, 2000), unpaginated.

5 Friis-Hansen, *Abstract Painting, Once Removed*, 50. This is not to mention, as Friis-Hansen points out, a certain indebtedness the work has to subsequent strategies that sought to reposition artistic practice beyond the purview of discrete, fully bounded mediums. To this end Calame's process which in effect is organized around the activity of walking "echoes Vito Acconci's action of following strangers in public settings ... while her careful registering of the time, date, and location of every stain documented recalls On Kawara's obsessive notebook entries of his daily activities." Ibid.

6 Davis, "How to Make Analogies in a Digital Age," 87.

7 Amy Cappellazzo, "Glee: Painting Now or My Obsession with NASA and Why I think Abstract Painting in the Digital Age Can Help Us Believe in the Future," in Cappellazzo, *Glee: Painting Now*, unpaginated.

8 Homi Bhaba, "Another Country," in Fereshteh Daftari, *Without Boundaries: Seventeen Ways of Looking* (New York: Museum of Modern Art, 2006), 31.

9 For example, Theresa Chong has claimed that the computer "offers a tremendous amount of freedom and control in image making, enabling me to explore freehand gestures in new ways. The computer has liberated me from the traditional way of working as a painter since I never felt aligned with either Western or Eastern methods of making art." "Theresa Chong," in John Yau, *Young+Brash+Abstract* (Richmond, VA: Virginia Commonwealth University, School of the Arts; Seattle, WA: Distributed by the University of Washington Press, 2002), 71.

10 Relyea, 130.

11 Robin Marriner, "LA Law," *Contemporary Visual Arts* 32 (2000): 38.

12 According to Anna Moszynska, Prieto's paintings at this time also reference the so-called "all-over" canvases of Jackson Pollock by way of the horizontality of the computer pad upon which her paintings originated from being akin to the horizontality of the canvases upon which Pollock applied paint. Moreover, for her there is a stylistic comparison to be made between Prieto's paintings and Pollock's *Mural*, painted in 1943. See Anna Moszynska, "Jackson Pollock Revisited," *Contemporary Visual Arts* 22 (1999): 53.

13 Marriner, "LA Law," 38.

14 David Pagel, "Monique Prieto," *Bomb* (2000): 78.

15 Ibid., 76.

16 Scott Rothkopf, "Modern Pictures," in Scott Rothkopf et al., *Wade Guyton: Color, Power and Style* (Cologne: Verlag der Buchhandlung Walther König, 2006), 77.

17 Daniel Baumann, "Wade Guyton—The Lights Are Out in the Land of Necessity," in ibid., 115.

18 Vincent Pecoil, "The American Action Printer," in Wade Guyton: *Le Salle de Bains* Paris: Presses du Reel, 2010), 81. To this end, the artist has claimed that "I didn't learn from reading about Gabo; I learned from Jeff Wall. That work is clearly more important to me than any abstract painting." Rothkopf et al., *Wade Guyton: Color, Power and Style*, 71.

19 Ibid., 82.

20 Ibid.

21 David Joselit, "Blanks and Noise: On Cheyney Thompson," *Texte Zur Kunst* 77 (2010): unpaginated.

22 Peter Wieber, "Pittura/Immedia Painting in the Nineties between Mediated Visuality and Visuality in Context," in *Contemporary Painting in Context*, ed. Anne Ring Petersen (Denmark: Museum Tusculanum Press, 2010), 47.

23 Michael Rush, *New Media in Art* (London: Thames & Hudson, 2005), 214.

24 Dan Tranberg, "Digital Artist Writes Own Code for Endlessly Changing Images," *The Plain Dealer*, February 2006, unpaginated.

25 Online at: http://numeral.com/panels/colorpanelv1.0.html.

26 Ibid. Whilst *Complex City* appears reminiscent of Piet Mondrian's *Broadway Boogie Woogie,* the piece itself, as Simon Jr. points out, was based on code "derived from professional papers on traffic engineering and from existing software of this kind that is used by traffic engineers to study flow." Marcia Caines, "Outside In"—Interview With John F. Simon Jr., *Cluster*, March 10, 2009, unpaginated, https://rhizome.org/community/43654.

27 Tranberg, "Digital Artist Writes Own Code for Endlessly Changing Images," unpaginated.

28 Cathryn Drake, "John F. Simon Jr: Collezione Maramotti," *Artforum* 47, no. 10 (2009), 356.

29 Caines, "Outside In," unpaginated.

30 Lev Manovich, *The Language of New Media* (Cambridge, MA: MIT Press, 2001): 289.

31 Ibid., 69–70.

32 Ibid., 289.

33 Martin Gayford, "The Ultimate Invisible World," *Modern Painters* 16 (2003), 24.

34 Greenberg, "Modernist Painting," in *The Collected Essays and Criticism* vol. 4, *Modernism with a Vengeance, 1957–1969*, 86.

35 Under his "FAQ," Simon Jr. provides the following information: "The electronics are the recycled remains of a laptop computer consisting of a screen (mentioned above), processor, memory, and a disk to store the program. The display housing is fabricated from acrylic. One cable extends from the piece to an electrical outlet." http://numeral.com/panels/FAQ.html.

36 Anna Munster, *Materializing New Media: Embodiment in Information Aesthetics* (Lebanon: UPNE, 2006), 154.

37 Ben Tufnell, "Tim Head," in Nesbitt, *Days Like These*, 96.

38 "Tim Head, unpublished statement, 2002" reproduced in Ibid.

39 Ibid.

40 Kasha Linville, "Agnes Martin: An Appreciation," *Artforum* 9 (1971): 73.

41 Ibid.

42 Ibid.

43 This process whereby the image in effect becomes distorted is due to the fact that, as W. J. T Mitchell points out, a digital image "has precisely limited spatial and tonal resolution and contains a fixed amount of information. Once a digital image is enlarged to the point where its gridded microstructure becomes visible, further enlargement will reveal nothing new: the discrete pixels retain their crisp, square shapes and their original colors, and they simply become more prominent." W. J. T. Mitchell, *The Reconfigured Eye: Visual Truth in the Post-Photographic Era* (Cambridge, MA: MIT Press, 1994), 6.

44 "Colorado at a Distance," Dan Hays interviewed by Ben Tufnell, Spring 2006, http://danhays.org/coloradodistance.html.

45 Ibid.

46 Seitter, "Painting has Always Been a Digital Affair," in Gijs van Tuyl et al., *Painting Pictures: Painting and Media in the Digital Age*, 30.

47 Ibid., 31. Accordingly, "images are encoded digitally by uniformly subdividing the picture plane into a finite Cartesian grid of cells (known as *pixels*) and specifying the intensity or color of each cell by means of an integer number drawn from some limited range ... The resulting two-dimensional array of integers (the *raster grid*) can be stored in computer memory, transmitted electronically, and interpreted by various devices to produce displays and printed images. In such images, unlike photographs, fine details and smooth curves are approximated to the grid, and continuous tonal gradients are broken up into discrete steps." Mitchell, *The Reconfigured Eye: Visual Truth in the Post-Photographic Era*, 5.

48 "Colorado at a Distance," Dan Hays interviewed by Ben Tufnell, Spring 2006.

49 Relyea, "Virtually Formal," 133.

50 Alex Bacon, "Surface, Image, Reception: Painting in a Digital Age," *Rhizome* 24 May 2016, https://rhizome.org/editorial/2016/may/24/surface-image-reception-painting-in-a-digital-age.

51 Imelda Barnard, "'I'm working with and against painting'—an interview with Amy Sillman." *Apollo* (2018), https://www.apollo-magazine.com/amy-sillman-interview-camden-arts-centre.

52 "Amy Sillman. Thirteen Possible Futures: Cartoon for a Painting, 2012," *Tate* https://www.tate.org.uk/art/artworks/sillman-thirteen-possible-futures-cartoon-for-a-painting-t14657.

53 The two works by Sillman were shown in the exhibition *Amy Sillman: Either Or And* which took place at the Thomas Dane Gallery from September 6—October 9, 2013.

54 "Amy Sillman: Abstract Compressionism," *Border Crossings* 34, no. 3, issue 135 (2015): 48.

55 Mark Godfrey, "Statements of Intent," *Artforum* 52, no. 9 (2014): 303.

56 Ibid.

57 As Wool recounts in an interview in 2012 with Nicholas Trembley: "I came from the Studio School in New York, a more traditional, painting-oriented background. A lot of Pictures Generation artists rejected painting. I think I was just young enough—I was a year or two younger—that by the time the idea of rejecting painting had settled in, I didn't need to. I could learn from them, the issues they brought up were important, but it didn't stop me from painting." Nicholas Trembley, "Meet artist Christopher Wool, the master who creates tension between painting and erasing, gesture and removal," *Numéro* 12 (2012), https://numero.com/en/art-design/numero-art-en/meet-artist-christopher-wool-the-master-who-creates-tension-between-painting-and-erasing-gesture-and-removal-2.

58 Bettina Funcke, "Revealed in reproduction: Christopher Wool," *TATE ETC* (2007), https://www.tate.org.uk/tate-etc/issue-9-spring-2007/revealed-reproduction.

59 Trembley, "Meet artist Christopher Wool, the master who creates tension between painting and erasing, gesture and removal."

60 "Christopher Wool," https://www.thebroad.org/sites/default/files/2021-05/TBRO-0043_guide_wool_digital_r2v1_ef.pdf.

61 Mark Godfrey, "Christopher Wool: Stain Resistance," https://thepaintingfactory.net/artists/christopher-wool.

62 Suzanne Pagé, "Foreword," in Birnbaum et al., *Urgent Painting*, 10.

63 Caroline A. Jones, "Still painting," in Ibid., 92.

9

Bodying Back and Forth

In a digital world painting is marked, if anything, by a striking obsolescence. It is an old technology—perhaps the oldest—whose use-value now must seem archaic at best. To paint is to accept something of the medium's impossibility to enact an effect beyond the borders of its own discourse. Yet the compulsion remains.[1]

On December 14, 2014, the exhibition *The Forever Now: Contemporary Painting in an Atemporal World* opened at the Museum of Modern Art in New York. Seeking to explore a "phenomenon in culture that was first identified with the science fiction writer William Gibson," the exhibition understood atemporality as "manifest[ing] itself in painting as an ahistorical free-for-all, where contemporaneity as an indicator of new form is nowhere to be found, and all eras coexist."[2]

Within the context of her catalogue essay penned to accompany the exhibition, Laura Hoptman posed the question as to whether atemporality could afford "us to roam around, instead of plow forward?"[3]

Implicit within this assertion is the repudiation of the expansionism which marked the project of modernism. By being grounded in the pursuit of novelty, modernism's operational logic was construed, on one level, as a series of advances that were both technical and social in orientation. When understood teleologically, implicit in such an understanding was the belief in the necessary evolution of artistic progress that was oriented towards the unique and exceptional character of the art that could be made under such conditions. As Rosalind Krauss remarked, writing in an article in the journal *Artforum* in 1972, modernism was to be conceived as

> a series of rooms *en filade*. Within each room the individual artist explored, to the limits of his experience and his formal intelligence, the separate constituents of his medium. The effect of his pictorial act was to open simultaneously the door to the next space and close our access to the one behind him. The shape and dimensions of the new space were discovered by the next pictorial act; the only thing about that unstable position that was clearly determined beforehand was its point of entrance.[4]

Rather than the modernist promise of linear progress, and with Hoptman's question in mind, the atemporal present, according to Matt Connors, was to be understood as "a kind of super-branched-out questioning."[5]

Within the context of the exhibition, Connors's remarks are given in relation to how the internet "has radically altered visual artists' relationship to the history of art ..."[6] Whether artists choose to roam around or question art history's topography, the "profligate mixing of past styles and genres," according to Hoptman, "can be identified as a kind of hallmark for our moment in painting, with artists achieving it by reanimating historical styles or recreating a contemporary version of them, sampling motifs from across the timeline of twentieth-century art in a single painting or across an oeuvre, or radically paring their language down to the most archetypal forms."[7]

In this respect, such profligate mixing is something that characterizes the practice of Dianna Molzan (Plate 15).

On one level, Bruce Hainley's supposition "that most of Molzan's works are not really paintings at all, but simply sculptures made of wood and canvas and paint ..." acknowledges the works' proclivity to foreground their object-like status.[8] To this end, Molzan's decision to work with a traditional set of materials associated with painting, namely oil paint on either canvas or linen that has been stretched across a wooden frame acknowledges what Hoptman states is painting's "obdurate objecthood."[9] Moreover, this decision acknowledges the works' place in history. According to Molzan:

> Oil paint and linen and the wooden support are all inherited materials that date back to the Renaissance and continue through modernism and all the other styles of painting that are radically different from one another but use the same stuff. I love that I can paint-splatter a canvas and make it look like hard plastic by using more or less the same materials Rousseau used to depict the forest of Fontainebleau in the nineteenth century.[10]

Whilst the visibility of these traditional materials places Molzan's practice within the continuum of history, individual works might bring to the fore any number of art historical references, including, but not necessarily being limited to "Jackson Pollock, Ellsworth Kelly, Lucio Fontana, and Barnett Newman."[11] As such, and as Hoptman contends, "Like [Rashid] Johnson and [Matt] Connors, Dianna Molzan looks at art history from the perspective of a deeply knowledgeable, self-identified enthusiast." In a recent interview, she described the surface of a painting first as a perfume bottle—a container holding a fragrance that is a delicate mix of notes from everywhere—and then as "a platform for a collision of styles."[12]

A synonym of the enthusiast is that of the fan, another identity that arguably one can apply to artists including, but not necessarily limited to Molzan.

Looking towards Henry Jenkins' assertion, made within his text *Textual Poachers: Television Fans and Participatory Culture* that "fans participate in culture by injecting texts with sloppy interpretations, fugitive meanings and mis-readings," Julian Hoeber identifies this proclivity as being equally applicable to contemporary artists who are "fans of art history."[13] With this in mind, Molzan, according to Hoeber "makes a partial use of the fan model by reimaging gestures of traumatic pathos in the works of action painters like Otto Muehl or Shozo Shimamoto as follies and ornaments ... She laughs off the seriousness of canonical interpretation while liberating an old method from its prescribed use in a move that is totally imaginative."[14]

Evidently then, and in accordance with Hoptman's claims made generally on behalf of painting and Molzan's practice in particular, there is a discernible impulse wherein artists today are comparable to a "generation of self-identified cultural pirates and assemblers who, like contemporary Dr. Frankensteins, ransack the timeless tombs of data and cobble together works of art from parts found there."[15] Indeed, Hoptman's thesis that "this is the era of the remix, the mash-up, and the sample" was arguably demonstrated in *Mixing It Up*, a major painting exhibition that was held at the Hayward Gallery in London in 2021.[16]

Featuring the work of thirty-one UK-based artists, according to Ralph Rugoff, writing in the catalogue essay that accompanied the exhibition, what connected them all was a shared "interest in mining their medium's exceptional multiplicity, and exploiting its potential as a format in which things can be mixed up as in no other."[17] So, for example, whilst, according to Rugoff, the practice of Hurvin Anderson "combine[s] aspects of landscape, portraiture and abstraction," a hybridized approach can also be discerned within the paintings of Rachel Jones and Gareth Cadwallader, two artists who contributed work to *Mixing It Up*.[18]

At first Jones' large-scale painting *lick your teeth, they so clutch* (2020) made using oil stick on canvas appears reminiscent, albeit on a markedly

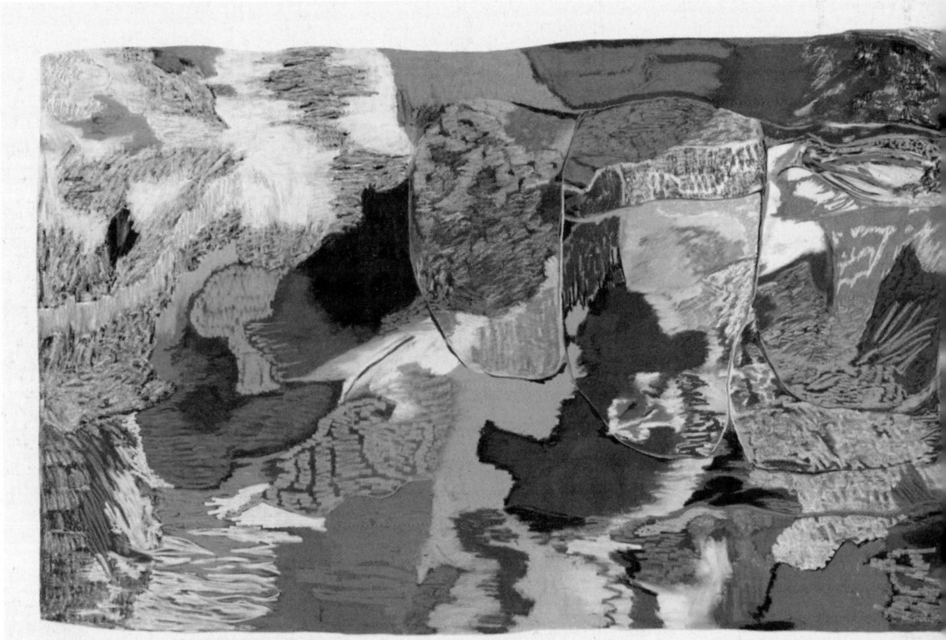

FIGURE 9.1 Rachel Jones, *lick your teeth, they so clutch*, 2021.

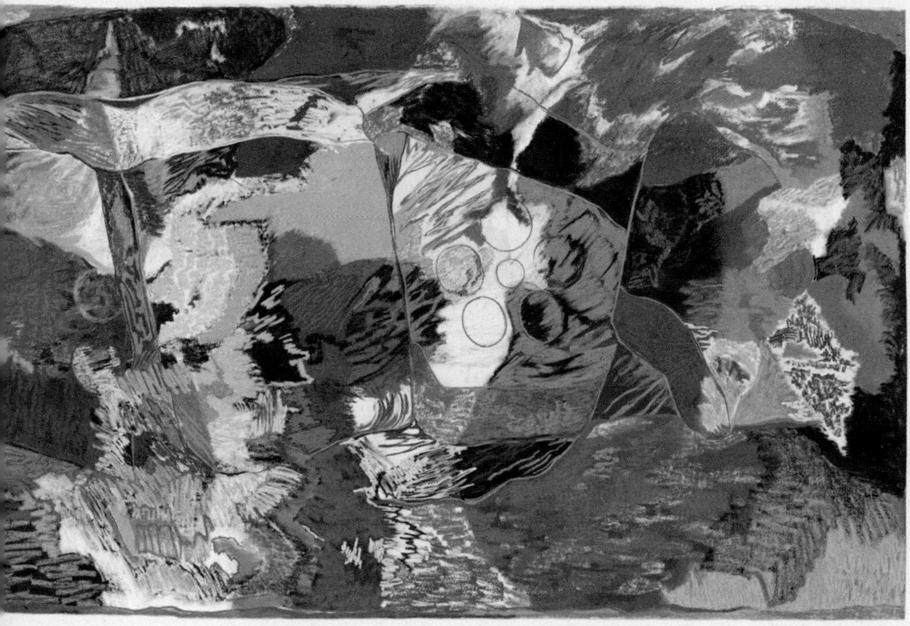

different scale, to some of Wassily Kandinsky's painterly abstractions; certainly, in both cases there is the suggestion, rather than the depiction, of a landscape. However, upon closer inspection, and as the title of the work denotes, one can discern within the overarching and highly colorful composition a row of teeth.

In the case of Gareth Cadwallader's painting *Shave* (2019–23), the gable end wall of two buildings is adorned with geometric designs that appear to be reminiscent of the Chevron paintings of Frank Stella. These structures work to frame the two figures that inhabit what one assumes is someone's front garden (a landscape of sorts, as implied by the gate). This forms the backdrop against which the younger of the two men stands as he shaves the seated, older man who is seen in profile. Although individually they appear, as it were, unremarkable, as with Jones's painting, when seen in combination they imbue the work with a level of ambiguity.

Taken collectively, the aggregative approaches of Anderson, Jones and Cadwallader, like those of the other artists included in the exhibition all seem to support Rugoff's claim that their paintings

> blur the boundaries between different genres. They do so not merely to make a rhetorical point about the limits of existing categories, but to open up the possible range of frameworks through which their audiences can read these paintings ... By blending and remixing genres, artists essentially provide competing sets of instructions, inviting us to examine a particular work from a number of possible perspectives.[19]

Whilst the examples derived from *Mixing It Up* drew on and ranged over multiple contexts, genres, histories and approaches, we can also discern what Amy Tobin has described as a "referential complexity" in the work of those artists whose paintings are aligned with or seem representative of the resurgence of interest in figurative painting.[20]

Tobin's description was applied to an approach she was able to discern within the context of the exhibition *Radical Figures: Painting in the New Millennium*.

Foregrounding modernism's pursuit of novelty, whilst seeking to reaffirm the role of the body within representational painting, the exhibition *Radical Figures: Painting in the New Millennium*, staged at the Whitechapel Gallery in 2020 allied a so-called "new generation of artists" to the pursuit of figuration and its expressive potential. Whilst rehearsing a particular set of tropes that historically had worked to frame painting, including but not necessarily limited to the primacy of the medium and its proclivity to endure in the face of its detractors, *Radical Figures* was arguably more broadly symptomatic of what has been a renewed interest in using painting as a vehicle to depict the human form.

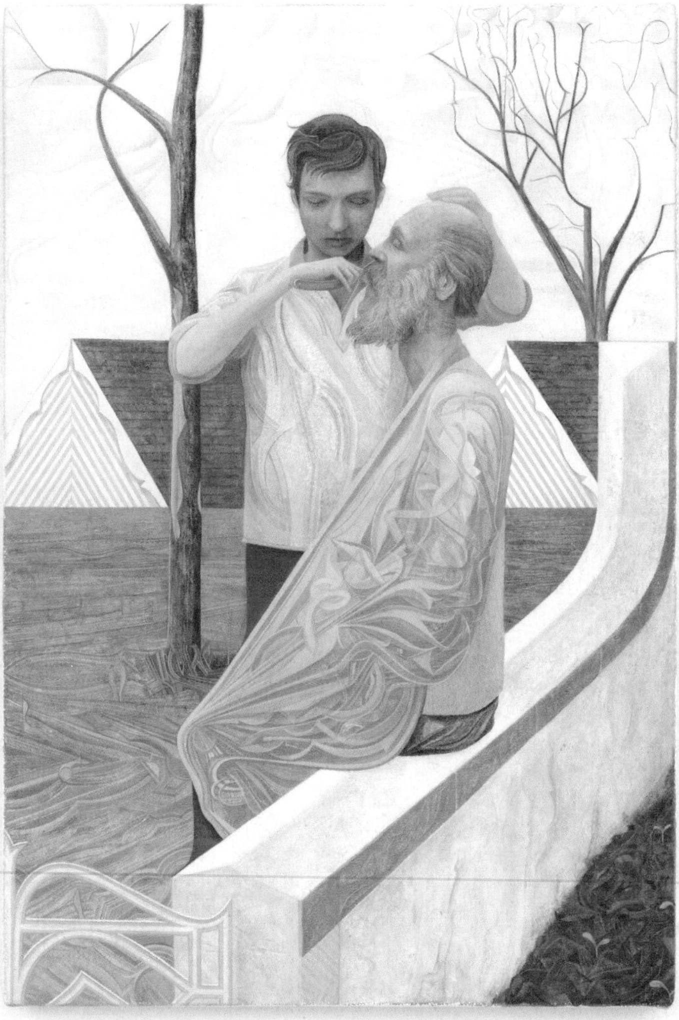

FIGURE 9.2 Gareth Cadwallader, *Shave*, 2019–23.

Despite the proclivity for the market to reduce a complex set of practices into a series of catch-all terms, the artist Didier William has acknowledged the inherent complexity and lack of cohesion within this renewed interest:

> Artists are using the body in various ways, citing history, mythology, citing personal narrative, working within the realm of memorial, working within traditions of surrealism, etc. I think it's unfair to sort of lump all of those different uses of the body under one broad category of figuration. I think the market wants to do that, for sure, for the sake of economy and legibility.[21]

Although William's own visually complex paintings are often centered around a body or a series of bodies, they remain only partially legible, both with regard to them being recognizable as such and with respect to the ostensible meanings they might engender. As such, and according to the artist: "The acts of figurative distortion, collage/patterning, and ornamentation, synchronize to form a permeable membrane between the psychological body and its failed container (anatomy.)"[22]

William's proclivity to represent the human figure by working across a range of media and through his adoption of a number of different techniques is an approach that is shared with the artist Tschabalala Self.

Before producing work utilizing collage and assemblage-based processes, and whilst at graduate school in Yale, Self was predominantly involved with the medium of print in the guise of handmade colorgraphic plates, the matrices of which were comprised of various different materials.[23] Through wanting to "find a way back to painting," Self realized that the route was already present, namely that she could adapt the processes that had initially been working with in print in order to produce a series of appliqué elements that could be incorporated into her paintings.[24]

Although collage was, on one level indicative of modernism's pursuit of technical radicalism, the social dimension, if not radicalism of the technique was due to the fact that it necessarily entailed extracting aspects derived from the everyday and inserting these aspects into the context of the artist's studio and by extension, into the context of art. This shift in the material's import that characterizes our understanding of collage is equally applicable to the practice of Self. When asked as to whether the act of repositioning everyday materials engenders a connection between pictorial and social or political spaces, Self acknowledges the fact that "there's a social and political dimension to every art practice regardless of whether the artist admits to it or is even aware of it … I want to make my figures as complex and multi-dimensional as possible."[25]

It is by working with textiles and fabrics that the artist, as she says herself, is able to build her subjects.[26] Indeed, and whilst we have acknowledged, the materials that Self avails herself of in order to make her paintings are often quotidian, they nevertheless are imbued with a number of cultural, historical and social meanings.

For example, *Sprewell*, a work the artist made in 2020 (Plate 16) is comprised, in part, of denim. Using a pair of her own jeans, the concertina-like effect has been achieved through repeatedly folding the fabric so the lighter hue of the inside of each trouser leg is visible as well as the more familiar darker indigo that we associate with denim. The jeans are used to depict the back of a man who wears a Sprewell Jersey—a reference to the former professional basketball player Latrell Sprewell who gained notoriety due to an incident where on December 1, 1997, he attempted to choke the Golden State Warriors coach P. J. Carlesimo. Viewed in tandem with the pair of Yeezy sneakers the man also wears, the jersey, as she says herself, "is meant to invoke a memory of and a conversation about Latrell Sprewell the individual. I conflated Sprewell's narrative with the narrative of Kanye West through the gesture of having the male protagonist in the work wear Yeezy sneakers. I want to explore the idea of the 'rogue negro'; the Black person that is acting opposite to how they're expected to act, going against their programming."[27]

Echoing Self's own method of gathering materials from a number of different but familiar sources, Lynette Yiadom-Boakye works from both scrapbooks and from the images that she has collected. As such, and as Yiadom-Boakye acknowledges, "I work from life a little bit, I seek out the imagery I need. I take photos. All of that is then composed on the canvas."[28] Speaking of the scrapbooks that the artist has amassed over a number of years, Andrea Schlieker, director of exhibitions and displays at Tate Britain, has likened to what is contained within them, namely "photographs of friends and family but also postcards of famous paintings she admires, or something ripped out of a magazine," as "visual ledgers."[29] Indeed, this description could equally be applied to the figures that Yiadom-Boakye paints to the extent wherein they are themselves collages or to use the artist's description, "composites" of different reference points collapsed, or perhaps rather distilled into a single body.[30] Moreover, as the figures that the artist paints are usually imagined rather than being necessarily real, they are, to borrow Schlieker's description, "invented characters."[31]

Several commentators, including Schlieker, have noted the ostensible timelessness of Yiadom-Boakye's paintings.[32] Acknowledging the importance of this characterization of her practice, Yiadom-Boakye has said that it is

> partly about removing things that would become in some way nostalgic. There aren't really any markers of time, like furniture or a particular style of shoe that denote a particular period or place. I think that's why I like the outdoors, because it removes a sense of time and I want the painting to feel timeless, because it increases that sense of omnipotence. Part of it is, I do think of the work as political, and we think we know what political art is supposed to look like, but I think there are many ways to make it.[33]

What the political in Yiadom-Boakye's work looks like, at least according to JaBrea Patterson-West, is indelibly bound up with questions of both representation and agency: "Neither struggle, nor statement. Instead, blackness is a state of being punctuated by thoughtfulness, reflection, intimacy, community, and repose. In a world where countless images of Black bodies exist as brutal evidence of pain and suffering and are circulated without regard, Yiadom-Boakye's conscious decision to create images of Black bodies in moments of atemporal pleasure and tranquility is cathartic."[34]

As such, timelessness is not an attempt to withdraw from the world but rather is the point from which a meaningful relationship to the world can be imagined: "There is a necessity for new and different representation of the Black body grounded in futurity which Lynette Yiadom-Boakye fulfils through her timeless scenes of Black life. Her work visualizes an alternate space where Black bodies can exist undisturbed and undefined by contemporary or historical sociopolitical landscapes."[35]

Whilst the paintings of Self and Yiadom-Boakye have reinvigorated figurative painting and in so doing, have sought to explore questions around identity, agency and selfhood, the means of production, to a lesser or greater extent remains consistent with collage. In addition to utilizing collage as a means to generate form, whether it is through sewing in the case of Self or working from scrapbooks in the case of Yiadom-Boakye, the corollary of both strategies is that an ostensible set of meanings are pictured in a particular way. Indeed, the proclivity for artists to orient their respective practices towards the formal possibilities afforded by collage extends beyond those artists who are working with or from the figure; Self's claim that sewing "is a kind of collaging" is keyed into a practice that is cognate with a certain worldview that, as we have seen, underscored the exhibition *Mixing It Up*.[36] To this end and remaining with the notion that the activity of sewing is more broadly indicative of Self's collagist impulse, Rugoff has claimed that a similar process of stitching together that derives from a "principle of collage" informs a number of artists whose work was selected for the *Mixing It Up* exhibition.[37] Moreover, as well as the activity of stitching being synonymous with collage, the activity can also function as the means by which an artist seeks to reconstruct a sense of self. William's attempts to

> make images of things that I haven't seen before are arrived at through this process of retrieval and reconstruction: Things that I've heard about, things that I've read, things that I might sort of loosely remember, things that have been inherited certainly from my parents. And I think, as someone who immigrated to this country and is sort of trying to access those lost memories, some of which are personal and individual, and some of which are cultural and collective, I'm sort of constantly trying to stitch it together into a particular kind of presence

in the moment. A presence that gets rebuilt onto and literally inscribed into the painting's surface.[38]

In addition to figurative painting today being given, in part, through a relationship to collage, one might reasonably extend this claim to encompass a relationship with montage as well.

The affinity painting today has with modernist montage stems from what was its exploration and reworking of representation's narrative possibilities. As Patrizia C. McBride notes:

> While it is customary to relate montage to strategies of interruption and disarticulation that challenge basic narrative criteria of consistency and continuity, an examination of the discourse and practice of montage in the 1920s and 1930s shows that its imitative strategies were often a means for rethinking narrative beyond the conceptual and experiential constraints imposed by the novel and other literary genres bound to the print media.[39]

Indeed, montage's strategies of interruption and disarticulation are echoed in the following statement by Rugoff:

> A number of artists in *Mixing It Up* make paintings that commingle tropes from different historical eras in order to engineer temporal dissonances that disturb our ability to 'place' the picture in a recognizable time frame ... Because their historical coordinates seem perplexingly indeterminate, paintings like these [Graham Little's *Blue Bulb Lady*] can destabilize our sense of their 'contemporary' character. In its place, they advance a notion of a heterogenous or unstable contemporaneity, a multi-layered present that unfolds in conversation with a confluence of various trajectories and influences from the past.[40]

The challenge to conventional narrative structures that montage arguably brought about and that has as its analogue in the "temporal dissonances" that painting today is organized around both echo Walter Benjamin's concept of "constellation" (*Konstellation*) which he used to account for the practice of montage.[41] According to Pelagia Goulimari, what Benjamin, writing in *The Arcades Project* and in "Theses on the Philosophy of History" "considered particularly urgent was the task of constellating the present with repressed fragments of the past."[42] Whilst Benjamin reserved an "aesthetic constellation" for the practice pf montage, the temporal dimension of the idea has as its counterpart today in works that borrow elements derived from the past.[43] For example, William has claimed that the sites of his paintings "where the body is formed through cuts, stains, and the residue of historical narratives—become sites of convergence and collision, marking both the fragility and the persistence of Black humanity."[44] To this end, and asked whether with regard to his subject matter, there was a "constellation of things" that he was dealing with, the artist replied "that constellation is always at work."[45] That said, whilst painting today bears certain affinities with both collage and montage, in certain respects it remains separate from both. For example, whilst the paintings of Self and William do, as it were, combine a number of heterogeneous elements, this strategy does not entail, as in the case of montage, a dialectical juxtaposition nor do the artists seek to combine such elements, as collage had, in response to what was "a crisis of representation."[46] Instead, where more broadly painting today seems to echo the montagist's approach is in the recognition that what they produced was an "affirmation of the work of art in the age of technological reproducibility."[47]

Echoing montage's proclivity to evoke "the world of the machine," artists' interest in the reprographic today, as opposed to the autographic (although the latter is never entirely eschewed), is given through our interaction with a set of technologies that are arguably becoming ever more ubiquitous.[48]

According to Simon Morley: "Not surprisingly, paintings in the era of the LERD-backlit computer and smartphone often engage with the kind of spaces and effects that the electronic screen generates. As a result, many paintings today seem to be hybrid constructions, bringing together maps, diagrams, windows, movie and computer screens, abstract constellations of information, and the chaotic randomness of garbage dumps."[49]

As such, whilst we have already observed elsewhere in this chapter the proclivity for painters to "reassemble in individual canvases already-existing art histories," the potential for this to occur has perhaps increased due to the ease by which we can access such histories.[50] As such, and as Wells Chandler points out, the "internet and social media have allowed for 'mashup' to be a genre of the twenty-first century."[51]

In one respect, such hybridity challenges a received set of histories including, but not limited to the "medium specificity" of formalist abstraction that constituted painting through a clearly demarcated series of categorical and aesthetic boundaries.

If painting today still has such boundaries, then they have been rendered sufficiently porous to allow different genres to be "remixed."[52] According to Alex Bacon, "If there was ever a firm line between abstraction and representation, it is at an all-time low today."[53] Moreover, the dissolution of discrete genres also affords painting to become "a site of interchange and slippage," according to Rugoff, between "subjective and objective perspectives."[54]

Whilst some fifty years ago the "willful eclecticism" that Rosalind Krauss diagnosed was symptomatic of a repudiation of the "collective effort" that one could discern in modernist movements such as Abstract Expressionism and Minimalism, the "multiple options now open to individual choice" are in part due to an embeddedness within a network of technological structures.[55]

Indeed, such multiplicity applies not only to what combination of genres or perspectives goes to make up any particular painting, but also acknowledges the fact that the physical object has, so to speak, a virtual alter ego. According to John Kelsey:

> now that the work and time of painting have become so immersed in the 24-7 temporality of digital networks, it can only operate in an immanent and immediately participatory way, without the luxury of any clearly demarcated temporal or spatial gap between the proper time and place of its own work and nonplace of info networks that seem to abolish these. So it involves itself in boundary confusion, haunting and stalking itself, happily confusing itself with its selfie.[56]

According to Manuela Ammer, writing in the catalogue that accompanied the exhibition *Painting 2.0: Expression in the Information Age*, "[i]n spirited opposition to canonical investments in medium specificity, twenty-first-century painting has incorporated a broad range of 'alien' objects, such as readymades, advertisement, film, video, and performance, into its procedures."[57]

Although as we have seen, at least some of these so-called "alien objects" infiltrated painting during the latter half of the twentieth century and moreover, this description now encompasses any number of elements derived from the electronic screen, what Ammer's claim points towards is a basic admission, namely that painting has never been either a static or singular category of art.

Of course, this claim rehearses what we have previously established, namely that painting today is a site of categorical interchange and slippage. A separate understanding, and one that John Berger sought to advance, writing in the journal *New Society* in 1979 is that this stasis stems from the "uniqueness of the experience of looking at a painting repeatedly—over a period of days or years [wherein] in the midst of flux, the image remains changeless."[58]

More recently, the curator Hans Ulrich Obrist has sought to address this purported immutability of painting and moreover, what Berger claims is the "strange contrast between static and dynamic."[59] In an interview with Andrew M. Goldstein for *Artspace* in 2016, Obrist observed the fact that although artists are painting in a "digital age" wherein "everything moves now—everything is in continual transformation … paintings just don't change."[60] However, in an attempt to qualify this claim, it is Obrist's contention "that just because paintings don't move doesn't mean they are still. They're very dynamic things—they come, they go, they approach, they recede, they disappear—and that's because they are pure feeling, like a fog or a cloud."[61] In so doing, and in conclusion, such bodying back and forth brings with it and is organized around, to paraphrase Berger, "the sensuous, the particular and the ephemeral."[62]

Notes

1 Quentin Sprague, "Six False Starts For An Essay On Painting. More Painting," *Painting. More Painting*, Melbourne: Australian Centre for Contemporary Art, 2016, p. 14.

2 "*The Forever Now: Contemporary Painting in an Atemporal World*," Museum of Modern Art, New York, https://www.moma.org/calendar/exhibitions/1455.

3 Laura Hoptman, *The Forever Now: Contemporary Painting in an Atemporal World* (New York: MoMA, 2014), 18.

4 Rosalind Krauss, "A View of Modernism," in Harrison and Wood, *Art in Theory, 1900–2000: An Anthology of Changing Ideas*, 978.

5 Hoptman, *The Forever Now: Contemporary Painting in an Atemporal World*, 14.

6 Ibid.

7 "*The Forever Now: Contemporary Painting in an Atemporal World*," Museum of Modern Art, https://www.moma.org/calendar/exhibitions/1455.

8 Jonathon Griffin, "Dianna Molzan," *Kaleidoscope* (2011): 80.

9 Hoptman, *The Forever Now: Contemporary Painting in an Atemporal World*, 22.

10 *Bologna Meissen* exhibition brochure, Whitney Museum of American Art, New York, 2011 https://whitneymedia.org/assets/generic_file/192/molzan_brochure.pdf.

11 Katie Kitamura, "Dianna Molzan: Deconstructed canvases and layers of reference," *Frieze* 140 (2011), https://www.frieze.com/article/focus-dianna-molzan. According to Roberta Smith, writing in *The New York Times*, this list extends to encompass the Surface/Support group of the 1960s. According to Smith, Molzan's "piquant explorations of canvas, stretcher and paint" actually "improve upon" the French group's deconstructionist approach. Roberta Smith, "The Paintbrush in the Digital Era," *The New York Times*, December 11, 2014, https://www.nytimes.com/2014/12/12/arts/design/the-forever-now-a-survey-of-contemporary-painting-at-moma.html.

12 Hoptman, *The Forever Now: Contemporary Painting in an Atemporal World*, 42.

13 Henry Jenkins, *Textual Poachers: Television Fans and Participatory* Culture (New York: Routledge, 1992), 52–54 cited in Julian Hoeber, "The Fan Club," *Frieze* 174 (October 2015): 205.

14 Ibid., 208.

15 Hoptman, *The Forever Now: Contemporary Painting in an Atemporal World*, 47.

16 Ibid.

17 Ralph Rugoff, "Mixing It Up," in *Mixing It Up: Painting Today* (London: Hayward Gallery Publishing, 2021), 6.

18 Ibid., 9.

19 Ibid.

20 Amy Tobin, "Radical Figures: Painting in the New Millennium," *Art Monthly* 435 (2020), 34.

21 Jason Stopa, "'I Don't Go to Crisis Just Yet': Four Painters Discuss the Rise of Figurative Painting, *MOMUS*, April 30, 2021 https://momus.ca/i-dont-go-to-crisis-just-yet-four-painters-on-the-rise-of-figurative-painting.

22 "Didier William," *Art At A Time Like This*, https://artatatimelikethis.com/building-a-better-monument/didier-william.

23 "Tschabala Self with Natasha Becker," *The Brooklyn Rail*, March 2021, https://brooklynrail.org/2021/03/art/TSCHABALALA-SELF-with-Natasha-Becker.

24 Ibid.

25 "Tschabalala Self in Conversation with Lydia Yee" in *Radical Figures: Painting in the New Millennium*, ed. Lydia Yee, Cameron Foote and Candy Stobbs (London: Whitechapel Gallery, 2020), 142.

26 "Tschabala Self with Natasha Becker."

27 Ibid.

28 "An Introduction to Lynette Yiadom-Boakye," *Tate*, https://www.tate.org.uk/art/artists/lynette-yiadom-boakye-16784/introduction-lynette-yiadom-boakye#:~:text=Yiadom%2DBoakye%20works%20with%20oil,as%20sources%20for%20her%20work.

29 Andrea Schlieker in Kelly Grovier, "Lynette Yiadom-Boakye's portraits that question history," BBC Culture, January 17, 2023, https://www.bbc.com/culture/article/20230116-lynette-yiadom-boakyes-portraits-that-question-history.

30 Antwaun Sargent, "Lynette Yiadom-Boakye's Fictive Figures," *Interview*, May 15, 2017, https://www.interviewmagazine.com/art/lynette-yiadom-boakye-new-museum.

31 Schlieker in Kelly Grovier, "Lynette Yiadom-Boakye's portraits that question history."

32 Ibid.

33 Sargent, "Lynette Yiadom-Boakye's Fictive Figures."

34 JaBrea Patterson-West, "Rest as Revolution: The Speculative Nature of Lynette Yiadom-Boakye's Figurations," *Flash Art* (Summer 2020) https://flash--art.com/article/lynette-yiadom-boakyes For her part, Yiadom Boakye has expressed a greater interest in "Black thought" rather than "Black bodies." See Sargent, "Lynette Yiadom-Boakye's Fictive Figures."

35 Ibid.

36 "For me, sewing's a kind of collaging. Before I found this way of working, people used to ask, "How do you see yourself in relation to your figures?" Maybe I have a Pygmalion-like relationship to the work—to the idea that you can actually build something that's outside of you but is also an expression of an ideal figure or persona you have in your mind. Plus, people interact with sewn objects every day. And it does have this association with my mom, who's

one of the most important people to me. Working this way feels like honoring her." M. H. Miller, "Tschabala Self," *New York Times Magazine*, New York April 24, 2022, 97.

37 "These artists treat the canvas not as a base for iconic, self-evident imagery, but as a site of assemblage, a landing pad where references converge from diverse territories and time periods. A principle of collage informs this approach, with imagery typically fashioned in a composite manner: a single figure on a canvas, say, may be seamlessly stitched together with details derived from a variety of sources." Rugoff, "Mixing It Up," 6.

38 Jason Stopa, "'I Don't Go to Crisis Just Yet': Four Painters Discuss the Rise of Figurative Painting."

39 Patrizia C. McBride, *The Chatter of the Visible: Montage and Narrative in Weimar Germany* (Ann Arbor: University of Michigan Press, 2016), 8.

40 Rugoff, "Mixing It Up," 8.

41 Pelagia Goulimari, *Literary Criticism and Theory from Plato to Postcolonialism* (London: Routledge, 2015), 171.

42 Ibid.

43 Ibid., 172. "Benjamin seems to outline at least three sorts of constellation: a revolutionary political constellation of the *now* with past moments of special affinity … an aesthetic constellation (e.g., avant-garde montage and collage); and a historiographic constellation …" Goulimari, *Literary Criticism and Theory from Plato to Postcolonialism*, 172

44 "Didier William," *Art At A Time Like This*.

45 Stopa, "'I Don't Go to Crisis Just Yet': Four Painters Discuss the Rise of Figurative Painting."

46 Martino Stierli, *Montage and the Metropolis: Architecture, Modernity, and the Representation of Space* (New Haven, CT: Yale University Press, 2018), 18.

47 Ibid.

48 "To the radical artists associated with Dada and Constructivism, montage appeared preferable to the clumsy translations of the French *collage* because it directly evoked the world of machine, industrial production, and mass consumption, thus emphasizing the constructed quality of artifacts and their reliance on found materials and ready-made parts …" McBride, *The Chatter of the Visible: Montage and Narrative in Weimar Germany*, 14–15.

49 Simon Morley, "The Brain is Wider Than the Sky," in *Chaos and Awe: Painting for the 21st Century*, ed. Mark W. Scala (Cambridge, MA: MIT Press, 2018), 28.

50 "Simultaneously, a wide range of artists began to recuperate and reformat—often through mechanical means—modernist forms, ranging from geometric icons to Op art patterns. Such a strategy of *using* the history of art as a fully available archive, rich in materials that might be manipulated and recontextualized, has emerged as a mode of generating 'user-based content,' through which painters do not simply invent their paintings from scratch but reassemble in individual canvases already-existing art histories." Manuela Ammer, Achim Hochd örfer, David Joselit, "Introduction," in *Painting 2.0 Expression in the Information Age: Gesture and Spectacle Eccentric*

Figuration, Social Networks, ed. Manuela Ammer, Achim Hochdörfer, David Joselit (Munich: Prestel Books, 2016), 10.

51 Stopa, "'I Don't Go to Crisis Just Yet': Four Painters Discuss the Rise of Figurative Painting."

52 Rugoff, "Mixing It Up," 9.

53 Alex Bacon, "Surface, Image, Reception: Painting in a Digital Age."

54 Rugoff, "Mixing It Up," 10.

55 Rosalind Krauss, "Notes on the Index: Seventies Art in America," *October* 3 (1977): 68.

56 John Kelsey, "The Sext Life of Painting," in *Painting 2.0 Expression in the Information Age Gesture and Spectacle Eccentric, Figuration, Social* Networks, eds Manuela Ammer, Achim Hochdörfer, David Joselit (Munich: Prestel Books, 2016), 269–70.

57 Ammer, Hochdörfer, Joselt, "Introduction," 10. *Painting 2.0: Expression in the Information Age* that was staged at the Museum Brandhorst in Munich November 14, 2015–April 30, 2016 and the Museum moderner Kunst Stiftung in Vienna from June 4, 2016–November 6, 2016.

58 John Berger, "Painting and Time," *New Society* 49, no. 886 (1979): 684.

59 Ibid.

60 Andrew M. Goldstein, "Curator Hans Ulrich Obrist on What Makes Painting an 'Urgent' Medium Today," *Artspace*, Sept. 26, 2016, https://www.artspace.com/magazine/interviews_features/expert_eye/supercurator-hans-ulrich-obrist-on-what-makes-painting-an-urgent-medium-today-54218.

61 Ibid.

62 Berger, "Painting and Time," 685.

Conclusion

The historical point of departure for *After Modernist Painting: The History of a Contemporary Practice* was Clement Greenberg's text of 1961, "Modernist Painting." Whilst there continues to be a measure of interest in his legacy, it would be difficult to argue the case that Greenberg remains an influential figure, both with regard to painting generally and in particular the version of abstraction his criticism is most readily associated with.

The question with regard to whether his ideas maintain a level of respect is perhaps less clear cut. For whilst today many have freely spoken of the shortcomings of his criticism, following his death in 1994 there remain those individuals who feel that his ideas still hold some appeal and moreover, are still prepared to come to his defense. For example, Arthur C. Danto, writing in *Artforum* in 1998 makes the following claims on Greenberg's behalf:

> From the perspective of quality, none of the critics who came after him, with their borrowed philosophies and poststructuralist prose, were in his class as thinkers. They exemplified without in any particular way clarifying the moment to which they belonged. Moreover, for all the lapses in judgment, for all the moral insensitivity and pugnacity, Greenberg wrote the abiding philosophy of art for the period in which he flourished, and he did so in language that embodied the virtues of the aesthetic it enjoined.[1]

In 2010, Thierry de Duve prefaced his text *Clement Greenberg Between the Lines* in part with the admission that "the doctrinaire Greenberg, who very early on formed a conviction as to the role of the avant-garde … is the one I admire the most."[2] More recently, John Yau writing in his online text "How Soutine Showed de Kooning a Way Out," for *Hyperallergic* acknowledges the fact that Greenberg was "one of the most influential critics of the period …"[3]

Whilst, anecdotally at least, it would appear that there are those individuals who are still prepared to acknowledge the legacy of his criticism, for today's generation of artists, his theorization of painting must appear to many as historically remote, if not all but moribund. However, although "Modernist Painting" and Greenberg's theories arguably no longer hold sway, the period within which the text was published is widely acknowledged as being characterized by the dissolution of what had been up until that point the organization of art into a series of aesthetic categories, for example, painting, sculpture, etc. As Donald Judd's previously remarked comments that "Half of the best new work in the last few years has been neither painting nor sculpture" indicate, the production of art during the period in question flouted and worked to upend the various conventions that historically had organized the status and condition of art.[4]

No longer aligned to a particular medium or discipline, the art of the 1960s was marked by a heterogeneity in approach, media and form and became played out against a backdrop that, according to Alex Potts, was comprised of a series of "tensions between the modernist insistence on medium specificity and the avant-garde negation of traditional medium-based categories ..."[5]

In one respect, the question artists were faced with during this period was as to whether they should continue to adhere to Greenberg's position wherein the work of art was to be understood centripetally, that is, as moving increasingly towards that which has been deemed to be essential to its identity. Or, conversely, should it move centrifugally outwards towards what Greenberg, in his own formulation of the artwork under modernism, had proscribed.

According to certain commentators, Greenberg's attempts to face down the latter was given through what became an increasingly entrenched and doctrinaire approach. In part, this entailed proscribing those movements which were deemed to be antithetical to his version of modernism.[6] Whilst the "School of Paris," namely Cubism and the likes of Paul Klee, Wassily Kandinsky, and Piet Mondrian were named as Abstract Expressionism's antecedents, Greenberg, and for that matter Michael Fried were hostile to the so-called "other tradition" which encompassed but was not limited to Dada.[7]

Whilst such antagonisms no doubt would have been keenly felt during the historical moment within which they were played out, today a malaise, if not exhaustion of these competing factions and for that matter artistic strategies associated with modernism is evident in the following statement by Hal Foster:

> Once seen as an absolute break with representational art (or its necessary overcoming), abstraction now appears, in art museums as well as in college surveys, as a historical interlude, and in artist studios as just one more option among countless others, including all manner of figuration.

> The readymade has suffered a different fate; too much with us, it is emptied out by overuse, a once-critical probe of the commodity structure of modern life transformed (often through super-expensive reproduction) into a cynical bauble of the luxury market.[8]

"Modernist Painting" prefaces the study not on the grounds that it is representative of any form of artistic zenith, but because it provides the basis by which subsequent approaches to painting can, on one level, be compared against, if not understood. This is not to say that the subsequent contexts of practice and for that matter debate can *only* be considered through the prism of Greenberg's criticism but rather, and at the very least, the measure of proximity or distance to that body of writing functions as the means by which what's at stake with a particular approach to or category of painting can begin to be gauged. Whilst this affords the opportunity to lay bare the advantages, if any, formalism can offer, the production and interpretation of painting (together with what were its perceived shortcomings), more fundamentally "Modernist Painting" functions as a critical point of departure against which subsequent developments in painting have been mapped out.

Contained within the historical moment when the ramifications of Greenberg's theories were felt most keenly (and arguably had most influence), was the question of how the artist might focus upon painting's necessary and sufficient conditions. In one sense, this forms the basis of what many have construed was the basis of the reductivism within Greenberg's approach. Nevertheless, it is also indicative of a broader aim that has been consistently applied across each of the study's nine chapters, namely what are the terms by which we might apply to painting in order to gain a measure of understanding.

Although Greenberg's narrow determination of painting eventually fell out of critical favor, the attempt to understand what sets painting, as an aesthetic category, apart from the various other forms art takes has remained a principal concern of this study.

Having said that, whilst it has remained necessary to pay close attention to painting's material conditions, what some might argue, as Greenberg once had, was its "form," what has been equally integral to the enquiry has also been the acknowledgement that these self-same conditions are borne out of and find themselves situated within a broader set of contexts which the study has sought to address.

By concurrently seeking to examine both, the either/or binary is replaced by what is instead an acknowledgment that painting inhabits a space that is both material and contextual.

This twofoldedness has been geared towards what has been the study's overarching aim, namely to consider the importance of painting both after "Modernist Painting" and also after modernist painting. For whilst, as Schwabsky acknowledges, painting "was terribly important" to modernism, a response to the question of its continued importance within an arguably more antagonistic set of contexts has been necessary in order to chart painting's course over approximately the last six decades.[9] In so doing, it has been with the hope that what has emerged as a result is a version of events as it were, rather than a comprehensive survey as such.

Notes

1 Arthur C. Danto, "Clement Greenberg." *Artforum* 36, no. 7 (March 1998): 14

2 Thierry de Duve, *Clement Greenberg Between the Lines*. Translated by Brian Holmes (Chicago: The University of Chicago Press, 2010), 8.

3 John Yau, "How Soutine Showed de Kooning a Way Out," *Hyperallergic*, July 24, 2021. https://hyperallergic.com/664044/how-soutine-showed-de-kooning-a-way-out.

4 Donald Judd, "Specific Objects" (1965), in Charles Harrison and Paul Wood (ed.), *Art in Theory 1900–2000 An Anthology of Changing Ideas*, 2nd ed. (Oxford: Blackwell, 2005), 824.

5 Alex Potts, "'Tactility': The Interrogation of Medium in Art of the 1960s." *Art History* Vol. 27, No. 2 (April 2004): 286

6 In an article published in the journal *Art History* in January 2021, John Curley describes Greenberg's formalist interpretation of the Morris Louis's paintings as being beholden to the former's "critical straightjacket." John J. Curley, "'Banner of an Atomic Regiment': Morris Louis, Greenberg's Modernism, and Science, ca. 1962." *Art History* Vol. 44, Issue 1 (February 2021): 134.

7 Between January 27 and March 7 1966, the art critic Gene Swenson curated the exhibition "The Other Tradition" at the Philadelphia Institute of Contemporary Art. Within the context of the exhibition Swenson had "two positive goals in mind: (1) seeing certain twentieth-century works of art which have been overlooked or neglected by art historians, and (2) suggesting alternative 'intellectual' rather than formal ways of dealing with those works." G. R. Swenson, *The Other Tradition* (Philadelphia: Institute of Contemporary Art, University of Pennsylvania, 1966), VII. Writing in the catalogue essay, Swenson would make the following assertion: "It is less easily appreciated with the familiar critical tool known as formal analysis. Its major importance lies outside or beyond 'significant form', and its application is useful chiefly to non-abstract art: that is, in general it deals more with the movements known as Dada, Surrealism and Pop Art than with those known as Cubism, Early Abstraction (Mondrian and Kandinsky) and Abstract-Expressionism." Ibid.

8 Hal Foster, "Modernism in a Non-Melancholic Key." *October* 186 (Fall 2023): 197.

9 Barry Schwabsky, *The Observer Effect On Contemporary Painting* (Berlin: Sternberg Press, 2019), 7.

BIBLIOGRAPHY

Alan Charlton, *Annely Juda Fine Art*, https://www.annelyjudafineart.co.uk/artists/39-alan-charlton/overview.

Albero, Alexander and Sabeth Buchman (ed.) *Art After Conceptual Art*. Cambridge, MA; London: MIT, 2006.

Alberti, Leon Battista. *On Painting*. Translated by Rocco Sinisgalli. Cambridge: Cambridge University Press, 2011.

Ammer, Manuela, Achim Hochdörfer,and David Joselit. (ed.) *Painting 2.0 Expression in the Information Age: Gesture and Spectacle, Eccentric Figuration, Social Networks*. London; New York; Munich: Prestel Books, 2016.

"Amy Sillman: Abstract Compressionism," *Border Crossings* 34, no. 3, issue 135 (2015): 46–50.

"Amy Sillman. Thirteen Possible Futures: Cartoon for a Painting, 2012," *Tate*. Accessed October 20, 2023. https://www.tate.org.uk/art/artworks/sillman-thirteen-possible-futures-cartoon-for-a-painting-t14657

"An Introduction to Lynette Yiadom-Boakye." *Tate* Accessed October 20, 2023. https://www.tate.org.uk/art/artists/lynette-yiadom-boakye-16784/introduction-lynette-yiadom-boakye#:~:text=Yiadom%2DBoakye%20works%20with%20oil,as%20sources%20for%20her%20work.

Armstrong, Elizabeth et al., *Mary Heilmann: To Be Someone*. Newport Beach, California: Orange County Museum of Art, 2009.

Armstrong, Philip et al., *As Painting: Division and Displacement*. Cambridge, MA: MIT Press, 2001.

Bachelor, David. "On Paintings and Pictures: An Interview with Robert Ryman." *Frieze* 10 (1993): 42–6.

Bacon, Alex. "Surface, Image, Reception: Painting in a Digital Age." *Rhizome* 24 May 2016, https://rhizome.org/editorial/2016/may/24/surface-image-reception-painting-in-a-digital-age.

Badura-Triska, Eva and Susanne Neuburger, *Bad Painting—good art*, Cologne: Dumont; Vienna: MUMOK Museum Moderner Kunst Stiftung Ludwig Wien, 2008.

Bakargiev, Carolyn Christov. *Arte Povera*, London: Phaidon, 1999.

Baker, Kenneth. "Rosemarie Castoro. Tiber de Nagy Gallery." *Artforum* 10, no. 9 (May 1972): 86–7.

Barnard, Imelda. "'I'm working with and against painting' – an interview with Amy Sillman."*Apollo* (2018), https://www.apollo-magazine.com/amy-sillman-interview-camden-arts-centre.

Barson, Tanya. "Rosemarie Castoro 1964–79: An Obstacle Course for a Dancer?" Accessed October 20, 2023. https://img.macba.cat/public/uploads/20180606/Tania_Barson_Rosemarie_Castoro_eng.0.pdf.

Barthes, Roland. *Image-Music-Text*. Translated by Stephen Heath. London: Fontana, 1977.
Battcock, Gregory (ed.) *Minimal Art: A Critical Anthology*. London: Studio Vista, 1968.
Benjamin, Andrew (ed.) *Abstraction. Journal of Philosophy and the Visual Arts*, no. 5, 1995.
Berger, John. "Painting and Time." *New Society* 49, no. 886 (1979): 684–5.
Betterton, Rosemary (ed.) *Unframed: Practices and Politics of Women's Art*. London: I. B. Tauris, 2004.
Birnbaum, Daniel. "Where is Painting Now?" *Tate International Arts and Culture* 1 (Sept/Oct 2002): 60–63.
Birnbaum, Daniel et al., *Urgent Painting*. Paris: Paris-Musées, 2002.
Binstock, Jonathan P. *Sam Gilliam: A Retrospective*. Berkeley: University of California Press, 2006.
Bois, Yves-Alain et al., *Art Since 1900: Modernism Antimodernism Postmodernism*. London: Thames and Hudson, 2004.
Bois, Yves-Alain. *Painting as Model*. Cambridge, MA: MIT Press, 1993.
Bologna Meissen exhibition brochure, Whitney Museum of American Art, New York, 2011. Accessed October 20, 2023. https://whitneymedia.org/assets/generic_file/192/molzan_brochure.pdf.
"Borrando la Frontera." Accessed October 20, 2023. https://anateresafernandez.com/borrando-la-barda-tijuana-mexico.
Bourdon, David. "Fling, Dribble and Drip." *Life* 68, February 27, 1970.
Bourriaud, Nicolas (ed.) *Altermodern Tate Triennial*. London: Tate Publishing, 2009.
Brennan, Marcia. *Modernism's Masculine Subjects: Matisse, the New York School, and Post-Painterly Abstraction*. Cambridge, MA: MIT, 2004.
Burton, Johanna et al., *Open Systems: Rethinking Art c. 1970*. London: Tate, 2005.
Butler, Cornelia and Schwartz, Alexandra (ed.). *Modern Women: Women Artists at the Museum of Modern Art*. New York: Museum of Modern Art, 2010.
Caines, Marcia. "'Outside In'"—Interview With John F. Simon Jr, *Cluster*, March 10, 2009, https://rhizome.org/community/43654.
Cappellazzo, Amy. *Glee: Painting Now*. Aldrich Museum of Contemporary Art & Palm Beach, FL: Palm Beach Institute of Contemporary Art, 2000.
Carrick, Jill. "Phallic Victories? Niki de Saint Phalle's Tirs." *Art History* 26, no. 5 (November 2003): 700–29.
"Christopher Wool." Accessed October 20, 2023. https://www.thebroad.org/sites/default/files/2021-05/TBRO-0043_guide_wool_digital_r2v1_ef.pdf
Coelho, Maria Luísa. "Woman-Body-Paint: Helena Almeida and the Visual Inscription of Sexual Difference." *Luso-Brazilian Review* 54, no. 1 (2017): 55–77.
Colpitt, Frances (ed.) *Abstract Art in the Twentieth Century*. Cambridge: Cambridge University Press, 2002.
Colpitt, Frances. *Minimal Art: The Critical Perspective*. Seattle: University of Washington Press, 1993.
Colpitt, Frances. "The Shape of Painting in the 1960s." *Art Journal* 50, no. 1 (Spring 1991): 52–6.
Compton, Michael. *New Art at the Tate Gallery 1983*. London: Tate Gallery, 1983.

Cotter, Holland. *Robert Kushner: Garden of Earthly Delights*. New York: Hudson Hills Press, 1997.

Cottingham, Laura. *Seeing through the Seventies: Essays on Feminism and Art*. London: Routledge, 2003.

Crane, Diane. *The Transformation of the Avant-Garde: The New York Art World, 1940–1985*. Chicago; London: University of Chicago Press, 1987.

Crimp, Douglas. "The End of Painting." *October* 16 (Spring 1981): 69–86.

Crimp, Douglas. *On the Museum's Ruins*, 4th ed. Cambridge: MA: MIT Press, 2000.

Curley, John J. "'Banner of an Atomic Regiment': Morris Louis, Greenberg's Modernism, and Science, c. 1962." *Art History* Vol. 44, Issue 1 (February 2021): 130–62.

Darling, Michael (ed.) *Target Practice: Painting Under Attack 1949–78*. Seattle: Seattle Art Museum, 2009.

Davis, Whitney. "How to Make Analogies in a Digital Age." *October* 117 (Summer 2006): 71–98.

Daniel Buren: Intervention II Works in Situ. Oxford: Modern Art Oxford, 2007.

Daftari, Fereshteh. *Without Boundaries: Seventeen Ways of Looking*. New York: Museum of Modern Art, 2006.

Danto, Arthur C. "Clement Greenberg." Artforum 36, no. 7 (March 1998): 13–14.

de Duve, Thierry. *Clement Greenberg Between the Lines*. Translated by Brian Holmes. Chicago; London: The University of Chicago Press, 2010.

de Duve, Thierry. *Kant After Duchamp*. Cambridge, MA: MIT Press, 1998.

Delaquis, H. Ato. "Dilemma of the Contemporary African Artist," *Transition* 50 (October 1975–March 1976): 16–30.

Demos, T. J. "Polly Apfelbaum." *Artforum* 42, no. 2 (October, 2003): 176.

"Didier William." *Art At A Time Like This*. Accessed October 20, 2023. https://artatatimelikethis.com/building-a-better-monument/didier-william.

Doherty, Claire (ed.) *Situation*. London; Cambridge, MA: Whitechapel Art Gallery; MIT Press, 2009.

Drake, Cathryn. "John F. Simon Jr: Collezione Maramotti." *Artforum* 47, no. 10 (Summer 2009): 356.

Drucker, Johanna. *Sweet Dreams: Contemporary Art and Complicity*. Chicago: University of Chicago Press, 2005.

Dubrock, Francesca. "Erasing the Border is Possible" *Sol de Medianoche*. Accessed October 20, 2023. https://www.soldemedianochenews.org/erasing-the-border.html.

Elger, Dietmar. *Gerhard Richter: A Life in Painting*. Translated by Elizabeth M. Solaro, Chicago: University of Chicago Press, 2009.

Elger, Dietmar and Obrist Hans Ulrich. *Gerhard Richter: Text, Writings, Interviews and Letters, 1961–2007*. London: Thames and Hudson, 2009.

Falconer, Morgan. "New Work: Polly Apfelbaum." *Art World* (April/May 2009): 88.

Falconer, Morgan. "The Undead." *Art Monthly* 270 (October 2003): 1–4.

Field, Richard S. *Mel Bochner: Thought Made Visible 1966–1973*. New Haven, CT: Yale University Art Gallery, 1995.

Fineberg, Jonathan. *Art Since 1940: Strategies of Being*. London: Laurence King, 1995.

Fogle, Douglas. "The Occidental Tourist." *Parkett* 68 (2003): 20–31.

Fogle, Douglas et al., *Painting at the Edge of the World*. Minneapolis: Walker Art Center 2001.

Foster, Hal. "Modernism in a Non-Melancholic Key." *October* 186 (Fall 2023): 197–204

Foster, Hal. *Recodings: Art, Spectacle, Cultural Politics*. Seattle, Washington: Bay Press, 1996.

Fried, Michael. *Art and Objecthood*. Chicago: University of Chicago Press, 1998.

Fried, Michael. *Three American Painters*. Cambridge, MA: Fogg Art Museum (1965), 1971.

Fuller, Diane Burgess and Daniela Salvioni (ed.) *Art, Women, California, Parallels and Intersections, 1950–2000*. Berkeley and Los Angeles, California: University of California Press, 2003.

Funcke, Bettina. "Revealed in Reproduction: Christopher Wool." *TATE ETC* (2007). https://www.tate.org.uk/tate-etc/issue-9-spring-2007/revealed-reproduction.

Gaiger, Jason & Paul Wood (ed.) *Art of the Twentieth Century: A Reader*. New Haven, CT: Yale University Press, 2003.

Gaiger, Jason. "Constraints and Conventions: Kant and Greenberg on Aesthetic Judgment." *British Journal of Aesthetics* 39, no. 4 (October 1999): 376–91.

Gallagher, Ellen. *Ellen Gallagher*. Birmingham: Ikon, 1998.

Gayford, Martin. "The Ultimate Invisible World: Interview with Bill Viola." *Modern Painters* 16, issue 3 (Autumn 2003): 22–5.

Gerhard Richter Paintings. Chicago: Museum of Contemporary Art Toronto: Art Gallery of Toronto, 1988.

Godfrey, Mark. "Christopher Wool: Stain Resistance." Accessed October 20, 2023. https://thepaintingfactory.net/artists/christopher-wool.

Godfrey, Mark. "Statements of Intent." *Artforum* 52, no. 9 (2014): 296–303; 344.

Godfrey, Tony. *The New Image: Painting in the 1980s*. Oxford: Phaidon, 1983.

Goldstein, Andrew M. "Curator Hans Ulrich Obrist on What Makes Painting an 'Urgent' Medium Today." *Artspace*, September 26, 2016, https://www.artspace.com/magazine/interviews_features/expert_eye/supercurator-hans-ulrich-obrist-on-what-makes-painting-an-urgent-medium-today-54218.

Goldstein, Ann and Anne Rorimer, *Reconsidering the Object of Art: 1965–1975*. Cambridge, MA: MIT Press, 1996.

Goodeve, Thyrza Nichols. *Ellen Gallagher*. London: Anthony d'Offay, 2001.

Goulimari, Pelagia. *Literary Criticism and Theory from Plato to Postcolonialism*. London: Routledge, 2015.

Greben, Deidre Stein. "Stain Power: with pieces of dyed velvet, Polly Apfelbaum transforms painting into sculpture and beauty into strength." *ARTnews* (June 2001): 98–105.

Greenberg, Clement. *The Collected Essays and Criticism*, edited by John O' Brian. vol. 1, *Perceptions and Judgments, 1939–1944*. Chicago: University of Chicago Press, 1986.

Greenberg, Clement. *The Collected Essays and Criticism*, edited by John O' Brian vol. 2, *Arrogant Purpose, 1945–1949*. Chicago: University of Chicago Press, 1986.

Greenberg, Clement. *The Collected Essays and Criticism*, edited by John O' Brian vol. 3, *Affirmations and Refusals, 1950–1956*. Chicago: University of Chicago Press, 1993.

Greenberg, Clement. *The Collected Essays and Criticism*, edited by John O' Brian vol. 4, *Modernism With a Vengeance, 1957–1969*. Chicago: University of Chicago Press, 1993.

Griffin, Jonathon. "Essay." In *Dianna Molzan*, 80–83. *Kaleidoscope* (2011): 80–3.

Hafif, Marcia. *Marcia Hafif, From the Inventory*. Wuppertal: Kunst- und Museumsverein Wuppertal, 1994.

Hainley, Bruce. "Interview by Bruce Hainley," in *Dianna Molzan*, 80–83. *Kaleidoscope* (2011): 95–8.

Hall, Stuart. "Museums of Modern Art and the End of History." In *Modernity and Difference*, edited by Stuart Hall and Sarat Maharaj, 8–23. London: Institute of International Visual Arts, 2001.

Halley, Peter. *Collected Essays 1981–87*. Zurich; New York: Brunobischofberger Gallery & Sonnabend Gallery, 1991.

Harrison, Charles and Paul Wood. *Art in Theory 1900–2000 An Anthology of Changing Ideas*, 2nd ed. Oxford: Blackwell, 2005.

Harrison, Charles. *Conceptual Art and Painting: Further Essays on Art & Language*. Cambridge, MA: MIT Press, 2001.

Helena Almeida. Gallacia: Centro Galego de Arte Contemporánea (cGac), 2000.

Herbert, Martin. "The Distance Between: The Political Peregrinations of Francis Alys." *Modern Painters* (March 2007): 84–9.

Herrera, Hayden. *Joan Snyder*. New York: Harry N. Abrams, Inc, 2005.

Herzog, Hans-Michael. *Jonathan Lasker: Gemälde/Paintings 1977–1997*. Ostfildern: Cantz Verlag 1997.

Hess, Thomas. "Review." *New York Magazine*, 8, no. 49 (8 December 1975): 114.

Hobbs, Robert. *Eleanore Mikus: Shadows of the Real*. Seattle: University of Washington Press, 1991.

Hoeber, Julian. "The Fan Club." *Frieze* 174 (October 2015): 202–8.

Hoptman, Laura. *The Forever Now: Contemporary Painting in an Atemporal World*. New York: MoMA, 2014.

Hulten, Pontus. *Niki de Saint Phalle*. Germany: Kunst und Ausstellungshalle der Bundesrepublik Deutschland GmbH, 1995.

Jameson, Frederic. *Postmodernism; Or the Cultural Logic of Late Capitalism*. Durham: Duke University Press, 1991.

Joachimides, Christos M. et al., *A New Spirit in Painting*. London: Royal Academy, 1981.

Joachimedes, Christos and Rosenthal, Norman (ed.) *Zeitgeist: International Art Exhibition*. London: Weidenfeld and Nicholson, 1983.

Jones, Amelia & Warr, Tracey. *The Artist's Body*. London: Phaidon, 2000.

Joselit, David. "Blanks and Noise On Cheyney Thompson." Texte Zur Kunst 75 (March 2010): unpaginated.

Joselit, David. *Mary Heilmann: A Survey*. Boston: ICA, 1990.

Joseph, Branden W. *Random Order: Robert Rauschenberg and the Neo-Avant-Garde*. Cambridge, MA: MIT Press, 2003.

Kakande, Angelo. Contemporary Art in Uganda: A Nexus between Art and Politics. PhD thesis 2008.

Kaprow, Allan. *Essays on the Blurring of Art and Life*, edited by Jeff Kelley, extended edition. Berkeley: University of California Press, 2003.

Kee, Joan. "Skin & Surface: What is Dansaekhwa and what is its legacy today?" *Frieze* 169. https://www.frieze.com/article/skin-surface.

Kitamura, Katie. "Dianna Molzan: Deconstructed canvases and layers of reference." *Frieze* 140 (2011). https://www.frieze.com/article/focus-dianna-molzan.

Krane, Susan. *Lynda Benglis: Dual Natures*. Seattle: University of Washington Press, 1991.

Krauss, Rosalind. "Notes on the Index: Seventies Art in America." *October* 3 (Spring 1977): 68–81.

Krauss, Rosalind. "Sculpture in the Expanded Field." *October* 8 (Spring1979): 30–44.

Krauss, Rosalind. "Sense and Sensibility: Reflections on Post '60s Sculpture." *Artforum* 12, no. 3 (November 1973): 45–53.

Krauss, Rosalind. *The Originality of the Avant-Garde and Other Modernist Myths*. Cambridge, MA: MIT, 1986.

Kushner, Robert (ed.) *Amy Goldin, Art in a Hairshirt: Art Criticism 1964–1978*. Stockbridge, Massachusetts: Hard Press Editions, 2011.

Kwon, Miwon. *One Place after Another: Site-Specific Art and Locational Identity*. Cambridge, MA: MIT Press, 2004.

Kyeyune, George. "Art in Uganda in the 20th Century." PhD thesis. School of Oriental and African Studies, University of London, London, 2003.

Kyeyune, George. "Artistic Entanglements: Elimo Njau, Theresa Musoke, Peter Mulindwa, and Jak Katarikawe." In Don Handa et al., *Mwili, Akili Na Roho: Ten Figurative Painters From East Africa*, 39–43. Nairobi: NCAI Publications, 2023.

Linder, Mark. *Nothing Less than Literal: Architecture after Minimalism*. Cambridge, MA: MIT, 2004.

Linville, Kasha. "Agnes Martin: An Appreciation." *Artforum* 9 (June 1971): 72–3.

Lippard, Lucy. "Sweeping Exchanges: The Contribution of Feminism to the Art of the Seventies." *Art Journal* 41, no. 1/2 (1980): 362–5.

Loock, Ulrich (ed.) *The 80s A Topology*. Portugal: Museu de Arte Contemporânea de Serralves, 2007.

Loock, Ulrich. *Katharina Grosse Atoms Outside Eggs*. Porto: Museu de Arte Contemporânea de Serralves, 2007.

Lowry, Glenn D. et al., *Drawing from the Modern 1975–2005*. New York: Museum of Modern Art, 2005.

Lucie-Smith, Edward. *Art in the Seventies*. Phaidon: Oxford, 1980.

Lucie-Smith, Edward. *Art in the Eighties*. Oxford: Phaidon, 1990.

Manovich, Lev. *The Language of New Media*. Cambridge, MA: MIT, 2001.

Marcoci, Roxanna. *Comic Abstraction: Image-Making, Image-Breaking*. New York: Museum of Modern Art, 2007.

Marriner, Robin "LA Law." *Contemporary Visual Arts* 32 (2000), 36–41.

Marshall, Richard. *New Image Painting*. New York: Whitney Museum of American Art, 1978.

McBride, Patrizia C. *The Chatter of the Visible: Montage and Narrative in Weimar Germany*. Ann Arbor: University of Michigan Press, 2016.

McEvilley, Thomas. "Absence Made Visible." *Artforum* 30 (Summer 1992): 92–6.

McEvilley, Thomas. *The Exile's Return: Toward a Redefinition of Painting for the Post-Modern Era*. Cambridge: Cambridge University Press, 1994.

Merewether, Charles (ed.). *Art Anti-Art Non-Art Experimentations in the Public Sphere in Postwar Japan 1950–1970*. Los Angeles: Getty Research Institute, 2007.

Merleau-Ponty, Maurice. "Cézanne's Doubt." In *Sense and Non-Sense*, 9–21. Evanston, IL: Northwestern University Press, 1964.

Meyer, James (ed.). *Minimalism*. London: Phaidon, 2002.

Miller, Dorothy C. (ed.) *Sixteen Americans*, New York: Museum of Modern Art, 1959.

Miller, M. H. "Tschabala Self." *New York Times Magazine*, New York April 24, 2022.

Min, Ines. "A conversation with Ha Chong-Hyun," *Ocula* July 13, 2017, https://ocula.com/magazine/conversations/ha-chong-hyun.

Moran, Joe. *Interdisiplinarity*. London: Routledge, 2002.

Morgan, Jessica. *John Baldessari: Pure Beauty*. Los Angeles, California: Los Angeles County Museum of Art, 2009.

Morley, Simon. "Dansaekhwa Korean Monochrome Painting." *Third Text* 27, no. 2 (April 2013): 189–207

Moszynska, Anna. "Jackson Pollock Revisited." *Contemporary Visual Arts* 22 (1999): 46–53.

Muller, Brian. *Real Art "A New Modernism": British Reflexive Painters in the 1990s*. Southampton: City Art Gallery, 1995.

Munroe, Alexandra, *Japanese Art After 1945: Scream Against the Sky*. New York: Solomon Guggenheim Museum, 1977.

Munster, Anna. *Materializing New Media: Embodiment in Information Aesthetics*. Lebanon: UPNE, 2006.

Myers, Terry R. (ed.), *Painting*, London; Cambridge, MA: Whitechapel Gallery; MIT Press, 2011.

Myers, Terry, "Polly Apfelbaum." *Artext* 70 (August–October 2000): 86.

Nesbitt, Judith. *Days Like These*. London: Tate Publishing, 2003.

Newman, Michael and Jon Bird (ed.) *Rewriting Conceptual Art*. London: Reaktion Books, 1999.

Njami, Simon. *Africa Remix: Contemporary Art of a Continent*. Johannesburg: Jacana Media (Pty) Ltd, 2007.

Nicodemus, Everlyn. "Inside. Outside." In *Seven Stories About Modern Art in Africa*, edited by Jane Havell, 29–36. London: Whitechapel, 1995.

O'Neill, John P. (ed.) *Barnett Newman, Selected Writings and Interviews*. Berkeley CA: University of California Press, 1992.

Okeke-Agulu, Chika. "The Challenge of the Modern: An Introduction." *African Arts* 39, no. 1 (2006): 14–91.

Ortner, Shelley B. "Is Female to Male as Nature is to Culture?" *Feminist Studies* 1, no. 2 (1972): 5–31.

Osaki, Shinchiro (ed.) *Traces: Body and Idea in Contemporary Art*. Kyoto: The National Museum of Modern Art, Kyoto, 2004.

Osborne, Peter. *Conceptual Art*. London: Phaidon, 2002.

Osborne, Peter (ed.) *From an Aesthetic Point of View: Philosophy, Art and the Senses*. London, Serpent's Tail, 2000.

Owens, Craig. *Beyond Recognition: Representation, Power, Culture*. Berkeley and Los Angeles, CA: University of California Press, 1994.

Pagel, David. "Monique Prieto." *Bomb* (Summer 2000): 76–82.

Papadakis, Andreas C. (ed.) *The Post-Avant Garde: Painting in the Eighties*. London: Academy Group, 1987.

Paparoni, Demetrio. *Jonathan Lasker Paintings 1977–2001*. Milan: Alberico Cetti Serbelloni Editoore, 2002.

Patterson-West, JaBrea. "Rest as Revolution: The Speculative Nature of Lynette Yiadom-Boakye's Figurations." *Flash Art* (Summer 2020) https://flash---art.com/article/lynette-yiadom-boakyes.

Pecoli, Vincent. "The American Action Printer," In *Wade Guyton 1 avril– 28 mai* 2006, 79–83. Le *Salle de Bains, 56, rue Saint-Jean, Lyon*, 2006.

Peters-Klaphake, Katrin. "Collecting Art at Makerere Institute of Heritage Conservation and Restoration, Kampala." *The International Journal of the Inclusive. Museum* 4, Issue 4 (2012): 1–14.

Peterson, Anne Ring (ed.) *Contemporary Painting in Context*. Denmark: Museum Tusculanum Press, 2010.

Potts, Alex. "Tactility: The Interrogation of Medium in Art of the 1960s." *Art History* Vol. 27, No. 2 (April 2004): 282–304.

Relyea, Lane. "Virtually Formal." *Artforum* 37, no. 1 (September 1998): 126–33; 173.

Robinson, Hilary (ed.) *Feminism-Art-Theory: An Anthology 1968–2000*. Oxford: Blackwell, 2001.

Rose A. R., Alias Kosuth, Joseph. "Four Interviews with Barry, Huebler, Kosuth, Weiner," *Arts Magazine* 43, no. 4 (February 1969), 43–5.

Rorimer, Anne. *New Art in the 60s and 70s: Redefining Reality*. London: Thames & Hudson, 2004.

Rose, Barbara. *American Painting: The Eighties: A Critical Interpretation*. New York: Vista Press, 1979.

Rose, Barbara (ed.) *Art-as-Art: The Selected Writings of Ad Reinhardt*. Berkeley: University of California Press, 1991.

Rose, Barbara. "Recommended," *New York Magazine*, 28 February 1972.

Roberts, Rebecca (ed.) *Robert Rauschenberg*. New York: MoMA, 2009.

Rosenberg, Harold. *The Tradition of the New*. New York: Horizon Press, 1959.

Rosenblum, Robert. *David Salle*. Zurich: Edition Gallery Bruno Bischofberger, 1986.

Rothkopf, Scott et al., *Wade Guyton: Color, Power and Style*. Cologne: Verlag der Buchhandlung Walther König, 2006.

Rugoff, Ralph. *Mixing It Up: Painting Today*. London: Hayward Gallery Publishing, 2021.

Rush, Michael. *New Media in Art*. London: Thames & Hudson, 2005.

Ryan, David. *Talking Painting: Dialogues with Twelve Contemporary Abstract Painters*. London: Routledge, 2002.

Sanyal, Sunanda K. "'Being Modern': Identity Debates and Makerere's Art School in the 1960s," in *A Companion to Modern African Art*, ed. Gitti Salami and Monica Blackmmun Visonà, 254–75. Oxford: Wiley, 2013.

Sardo, Delfim. "Helena Almeida," *Aperture* (Winter 2015), https://aperture.org/editorial/magazine-helena-almeida.

Sargent, Antwaun. "Lynette Yiadom-Boakye's Fictive Figures." *Interview*, May 15, 2017. https://www.interviewmagazine.com/art/lynette-yiadom-boakye-new-museum.

Sayre, Henry M. *The Object of Performance: The American Avant-Garde Since 1970*. Chicago: University of Chicago Press, 1992.

Scala, Mark W. (ed.) *Chaos and Awe: Painting for the 21st Century*. Cambridge, MA: MIT, 2018.

Schimmel, Paul (ed.). *Out of Actions: Between Performance and the Object, 1949–1979*. Los Angeles; London: The Museum of Contemporary Art: Thames & Hudson, 1998.

Schlieker, Andrea in Kelly Grovier, "Lynette Yiadom-Boakye's portraits that question history," BBC Culture, January 17th 2023. https://www.bbc.com/culture/article/20230116-lynette-yiadom-boakyes-portraits-that-question-history.

Schwabsky, Barry et al., *Jessica Stockholder*. London: Phaidon, 1995.

Schwabsky, Barry. *The Observer Effect On Contemporary Painting*. Berlin: Sternberg Press, 2019.

Schwabsky, Barry. *Vitamin P*. London: Phaidon: 2002.

Scott, Kitty. "Portrait Francis Alÿs." *Parkett* 69 (2003): 20–33.

Shabout, Nada. "Jewid Selim: On Abstraction and Symbolism." *Mathaf Encyclopedia of Modern Art and the Arab World*. Accessed October 20, 2023. https://www.encyclopedia.mathaf.org.qa/en/essays/Pages/Jewad-Selim,-On-Abstraction-and-Symbolism.aspx#3u.

Siegel, Jeanne (ed.) *Art Talk: The Early Eighties*. New York: De Capo Press, 1988.

Siegel, Katy (ed.) *High Times Hard Times New York Painting 1967–1975*. New York: Independent Curators International, 2007.

Slyce, John. "Alan Charlton: Vertical Integration." *Contemporary* 82 (2006): 32–5.

Smith, Roberta. "The Paintbrush in the Digital Era." *The New York Times*, December 11, 2014. https://www.nytimes.com/2014/12/12/arts/design/the-forever-now-a-survey-of-contemporary-painting-at-moma.html.

Sprague, Quentin. "Six False Starts For An Essay On Painting. More Painting," in *Painting. More Painting*, 12–15. Melbourne: Australian Centre for Contemporary Art, 2016.

Stella, Rachel. "Metamorphosis and Transmigration." *Rosemarie Castoro Working Out*, Thaddaeus Ropac London, 2022, https://ropac.net/usr/library/documents/main/rc_london_booklet_final.pdf

Stierli, Martino. *Montage and the Metropolis: Architecture, Modernity, and the Representation of Space*. New Haven, CT: Yale University Press, 2018.

Stiles, Kristine and Peter Selz. *Theories and Documents of Contemporary Art: A Sourcebook of Artist's Writings*. Berkeley & Los Angeles, California: University of California Press, 1996.

Stopa, Jason. "'I Don't Go to Crisis Just Yet': Four Painters Discuss the Rise of Figurative Painting." *MOMUS*, April 30, 2021. https://momus.ca/i-dont-go-to-crisis-just-yet-four-painters-on-the-rise-of-figurative-painting.

Storr, Robert. *Elizabeth Murray*. New York: Museum of Modern Art, 2005.

Streitberger, Alexander (ed.) *Situational Aesthetics: Selected Writings by Victor Burgin*. Leuven: Leuven University Press, 2009.

Suderberg, Erika (ed.) *Space Site Intervention: Situating Installation Art*. Minneapolis: University of Minnesota Press, 2000.

Swartz, Anne. (ed.). *Pattern and Decoration: An Ideal Vision in American Art, 1975–1985*. New York: Hudson River Museum, 2008.

Swenson, G. R. *The Other Tradition*. Philadelphia: Institute of Contemporary Art, University of Pennsylvania, 1966.

Taaffe, Philip. *Philip Taaffe*. Valencia: IVAM Institut Valencià d'Art Modern, 2000.

"*The Forever Now: Contemporary Painting in an Atemporal World*." Museum of Modern Art, New York. Accessed October 20, 2023. https://www.moma.org/calendar/exhibitions/1455.

Tobin, Amy. "Radical Figures: Painting in the New Millennium." *Art Monthly* 435 (2020): 33–4.

Tranberg, Dan. "Digital Artist Writes Own Code for Endlessly Changing Images." *The Plain Dealer*, February 2006, unpaginated.

Trembley, Nicholas. "Meet artist Christopher Wool, the master who creates tension between painting and erasing, gesture and removal." *Numéro* 12 (2012). https://numero.com/en/art-design/numero-art-en/meet-artist-christopher-wool-the-master-who-creates-tension-between-painting-and-erasing-gesture-and-removal-2.

"Tschabala Self with Natasha Becker." *The Brooklyn Rail*, March 2021. https://brooklynrail.org/2021/03/art/TSCHABALALA-SELF-with-Natasha-Becker.

Tuchman, Phyllis. "Interview with Robert Ryman." *Artforum* 9 (May 1971): 46–53.

Tufnell, Ben. "Colorado at a Distance," Dan Hays interviewed by Ben Tufnell, Spring 2006. http://danhays.org/coloradodistance.html

van Tuyl, Gijs et al., *Painting Pictures: Painting and Media in the Digital Age*. Kunst Museum: Kerber Verlag, 2003.

Wallis, Brian (ed.) *Art After Modernism: Rethinking* Representation. New York: Museum of Contemporary Art, 1984.

Warr, Tracey & Jones, Amelia, *The Artist's Body*. London: Phaidon, 2000.

Weyergraf, Claire. *Richard Serra, Interviews, etc., 1970–1980*. New York: The Hudson River Museum, 1980.

Weiner, Lawrence, Daniel Buren, Mel Bochner and Sol LeWitt. "Documentation Conceptual Art." *Arts* Magazine 44, no. 6 (1970): 42–4.

Wien, Iris, et al., *Pia Fries Paintings 1990–2007*. Dusseldorf: Richter Verlag, 2007.

Yau, John. "How Soutine Showed de Kooning a Way Out," *Hyperallergic*, July 24, 2021. https://hyperallergic.com/664044/how-soutine-showed-de-kooning-a-way-out.

Yau, John. *Young+Brash+Abstract*. Richmond, VA: Virginia Commonwealth University, School of the Arts, 2002.

Zelevansky, Lynn. *Beyond Geometry: Experiments in Form, 1940s–1970*. Cambridge, MA: MIT Press, 2002.

Zelevansky, Lynn. *Sense and Sensibility: Women Artists and Minimalism in the 1990s*. New York: MoMA, 2nd ed., 1995.

Zelizer, Barbie (ed.) *Visual Culture and the Holocaust*. London: The Athlone Press, 2001.

INDEX